Renaissance
Fantasies

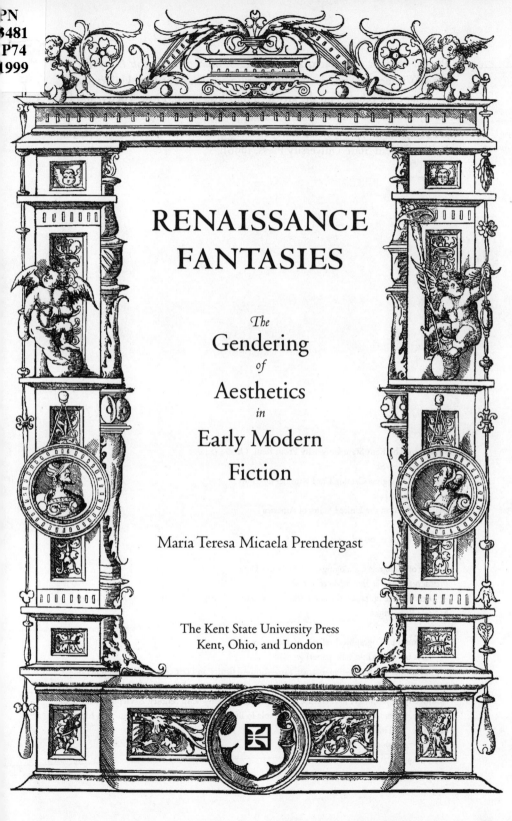

RENAISSANCE FANTASIES

The
Gendering
of
Aesthetics
in
Early Modern
Fiction

Maria Teresa Micaela Prendergast

The Kent State University Press
Kent, Ohio, and London

Part of chapter 3 appeared as an article in *Studies in English Literature, 1500–1900* (Winter 1995) and is reprinted with permission of Rice University.

Chapter 4 is based on the article "Philoclea Parsed: Prose, Poetry, and Femininity in Sidney's *Old Arcadia*," which appeared in *Framing Elizabethan Fictions: Contemporary Approaches to Early Modern Narrative Prose*, ed. Constance C. Relihan (Kent State University Press, 1996).

© 1999 by The Kent State University Press, Kent, Ohio 44242
All rights reserved
Library of Congress Catalog Card Number 99-21763
ISBN 0-87338-644-2
Manufactured in the United States of America

06 05 04 03 02 01 00 99   5 4 3 2 1

Library of Congress Cataloging-in-Publication Data
Prendergast, Maria Teresa Micaela, 1956–
     Renaissance fantasies: the gendering of aesthetics in early modern fiction / Maria Teresa Micaela Prendergast.
        p.   cm.
     Includes bibliographical references and index.
     ISBN 0-87338-644-2 (alk. paper) ∞
     1. European fiction—Renaissance, 1450–1600—History and criticism. 2. European fiction—Male authors—History and criticism. 3. Women and literature—Europe—History—16th century. 4. Androgeny (Psychology) in literature. 5. Aesthetics, Modern—16th century. 6. Gender identity in literature. 7. Femininity in literature. 8. Sex role in literature. 9. Fantasy in literature. 10. Men in literature.   I. Title.
PN3481.P74   1999
809.3'9359—dc21   99-21763

For Tom

Contents

Acknowledgments

As I was beginning to write chapter 5, I called Dan Kinney to ask him how I should acknowledge him as a source for the notion that Touchstone's dialogue with Audrey in *As You Like It* was influenced by Sidney's *A Defence of Poetry*. Dan told me that he had gotten the idea from Margaret Ferguson. A few months later I saw Margaret Ferguson at a conference, and asked her how I should acknowledge her; she told me that she had gotten the idea from Thomas Greene. These conversations remind me of the extent to which this project is a product of many conversations, acknowledged and unacknowledged, that I have shared with fellow scholars. Indeed, the inspiration for this project came from ongoing dialogue with Dan Kinney about Renaissance debates on *eikastiké* and *phantastiké*. My ensuing investigations of Renaissance aesthetic pamphlets led to my central argument that Renaissance polemicists and fiction writers seem unable to refer to poetry, drama, or fantasy without associating these genres with masculinity, femininity, or effeminacy.

Many friends and colleagues have helped me with this project. At the University of Virginia Gordon Braden and Dan Kinney tirelessly sent me back to classical and Renaissance sources, while Clare Kinney helped me think through the complexity of gender issues; her ongoing comments on the manuscript have been invaluable.

I am indebted, as well, to a number of other very supportive friends and colleagues, especially Lyell Asher, Jay Dobrutsky, Jim Nohrnberg, Alan Shepard, and Tricia Welsch. Much of this project was written while I taught at the University of Miami, where I am particularly grateful to Mihoko Suzuki and Tassie Gwilliam for their constant support and insightful comments on the gendered implications of my project; I am also grateful to Tom Dughi, whose valuable comments helped bring focus to chapter 4. At the University of South Alabama Steve Cohen's comments and Jim Swearingen's constant support as chairman helped bring this project to a finished form. Throughout this period, Constance Relihan's advice—particularly on chapter 4—added subtlety and nuance to my readings of Renaissance prose. Thanks also to fellow participants in the seminar on Sidney and Shakespeare at the Shakespeare Association conference in Albuquerque—particularly Ed Berry and Melinda Gough—for their helpful responses to early drafts of chapter five. Equally useful were Doug Peterson's careful comments on this final chapter. The very supportive remarks by the anonymous readers at The Kent State University Press also proved helpful for final revisions of the manuscript.

Two generous Orovitz Fellowships at the University of Miami allowed me to make use of the valuable resources at the Folger Shakespeare Library and the Beinecke and Sterling Libraries at Yale University. A leave from the University of South Alabama as well as a President's Travel Grant made it possible for me to complete revisions of this project. I am also grateful to *Studies in English Literature* for allowing me to reprint my article, "The Unauthorized Orpheus of *Astrophil and Stella*," as part of chapter 3 of this project.

But this project would never have gotten off the ground, much less been completed, had it not been for the constant encouragement and calming presence of Tom Prendergast. He has read every page of this project many times and is probably just as familiar with Sidney, Shakespeare, Pasquier, and Boccaccio as I am.

This project was conceived before the birth of Charles Arthur Roussel de Zaldo Prendergast and completed as he is pushing three years old; it is at once the older and younger sibling with whom Charles has constantly and quite good humoredly competed for attention. While progress on this project slowed down considerably when he was born, he, like his father, remains my constant muse.

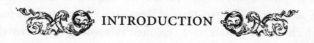

INTRODUCTION

Prodigality, Effeminacy, Fantasy

he Renaissance engenderment of fantasy as a feminine construct receives its clearest and perhaps most provocative articulation in 1653, when Margaret Cavendish writes that "*Poetry,* which is built upon *Fancy, Women* may claime, as a *worke* belonging most properly to themselves: for I have observ'd, that their *Braines* work usually in a *Fantasticall motion,* as in their *severall,* and *various* dresses, *in their many and singular* choices of *Cloaths,* and *Ribbons,* and the like."[1] This may seem like an odd way to defend writing by women: the statement calls attention to, even celebrates, common cultural conceptions of femininity as frivolous and "Fantasticall." Yet by claiming that she is not attempting to write serious literature, Cavendish protects herself from the anticipated charge (by hostile readers) that women cannot and should not write high-minded verse; at the same time she asserts that there is a certain kind of writing—frivolous fiction—that is inherently feminine. Thus, even as Cavendish shields herself from criticism by adopting a variant of the modesty topos, her strong association of poetry with feminine frivolity enables her to suggest that if history and philosophy are "masculine" forms of writing, fiction is a feminine prerogative.[2]

Cavendish's defense of poetry by women may be unusually colorful, but her stance is nonetheless fairly typical of Renaissance women who attempt to enter the public scene of writing: most anticipate and attempt to disable censorious comments by asserting that they are not tackling serious "masculine" topics.[3] In the process they imply that they are shaping, instead, an alternative "feminine" discourse. While scholars of Renaissance literature have focused on ways in which female writers have exploited this strategy, few have discussed why aspiring male authors would present themselves in the same way. William Shakespeare and Philip Sidney in England, as well as Etienne Pasquier and Giovanni Boccaccio on the Continent, are among Renaissance writers who associate their writings with frivolity and femininity; they do so not only to protect themselves from criticism by authoritative male writers but also to distinguish their writings from a traditional, patriarchal aesthetics.[4] Not surprisingly, their writings often celebrate other attributes associated with "feminine" writing, most notably deceit, seduction, and unruliness. This latter attribute was strongly associated with the subaltern position of women in patriarchal culture: denied a voice of their own through authoritative channels, women's voices were often linked with attempts to subvert cultural conventions.[5]

This identification with the feminine becomes entangled, as well, in a fantasy of social advancement, for the authors I study commonly direct their writings to a female audience at a time when women were becoming increasingly influential as patrons of the arts.[6] By locating themselves on the margins of patriarchy, these authors appeal to a group of readers which, while increasingly significant, remains largely disempowered within patriarchal culture. But if these writers wish to represent their works as "feminine" and original, they finally draw back from a radical identification with femininity and originality. For all their prodigal rebellion against patriarchal norms, these writers seem well aware of the cultural advantages that come with identifying one's self as a heterosexual male.[7]

The ultimate ambivalences inherent in this identification with femininity may be traced to close cultural and metaphorical associations between femininity (which has some constructive associations) and effeminacy (which is almost exclusively negative in conceptualization), for the boundaries between these two categories of gender are, ultimately, fluid. Indeed, the prodigal works I study slip easily from references to biological women to a metaphorics of femininity to discussions of effeminate men—a series of slippages that speaks to Renaissance biological theory. As Thomas Laqueur has argued, strict regulation of male versus female behavior within Renaissance patriarchal culture gestures to an underlying concern that biological differences between the sexes may be tenuous, even arbitrary. Indeed, Renaissance scholars often subscribed to a one-sex model in which woman's sexuality was viewed as an inverted or diminished version of man's.[8] Such ambivalences about gender boundaries describe the writers I study. While these authors often (and surprisingly) champion notions of the male authorial self as feminine, effeminate, even castrated, they are just as likely to attenuate or deny their playful interest in unconventional sexualities so as to affirm, eventually, the "masculine" authority of their writings. This ultimately conservative posture gestures to a common fear of becoming contaminated by the problematic gender categories with which these authors enjoyed experimenting.[9]

Yet for all their ambivalences about gender identification, these authors consistently depart from conventional categorizations of gender in order to celebrate an antipatriarchal aesthetics established on the unruly female body and the castrated male body. This focus on the cultural and aesthetic advantages that accompany an identification with feminized (or effeminized) fantasy opens up a more complex area of inquiry within Renaissance gender criticism. While scholars have long noted how some male Renaissance authors write from a profeminist perspective, they have done so largely to stress how this stance remains implicated in misogynistic and patriarchal structures.[10] Valuable as this stance is, it has left unarticulated the question of why—during an era that privileges the masculine position—these male authors would wish to present themselves (or their personas) not just as champions of women but, to a large extent, as "feminine." It is within these authors' common desire to constitute themselves as original—hence antipatriarchal—writers that I locate an aesthetics of "feminine" prodigality.

The close association, in the texts I study, between femininity and fantasy has for the most part been overlooked by twentieth-century scholars, particularly as the categories of femininity and fantasy have largely been examined from distinct scholarly perspectives.[11] Until recently scholars have read Renaissance debates on the nature of fantasy almost exclusively within the framework of aesthetic history, isolated from early modern cultural debates. Bernard Weinberg and Baxter Hathaway, for example, have pointed out how Renaissance controversies on fantasy represent fantasy as seductive and deceitful, yet these scholars overlook how seduction and deceit are just as strongly associated with femininity in treatises on the nature of women.[12] Conversely, treatises on the nature of women have been studied primarily as cultural documents—a focus that has led most scholars to neglect the aesthetic implications of these treatises. Although Linda Woodbridge and Constance Jordan have established how misogynistic treatises construct femininity as deceitful, seductive, and unruly, they have not noted how anti-poetry treatises project the same negative language onto fantasy.[13] By dwelling on how both fantasy and femininity were associated with seduction and deceit during the early modern period, this study discloses how closely interrelated the two categories conceptually were. More specifically, I study how the early modern identification of fantasy with femininity traces a common cultural desire to shape conceptual alternatives to "masculine" experience and authority.

As such, my project at once depends on and supplements an ongoing interest in unconventional gender constructions within early modern literature. Most scholars who have studied the category "woman" from this perspective have concentrated on one of two areas: they have either noted how unconventional categories of gender advanced (to an extent) the conceptual status of women by granting them a measure of "masculine" authority, or they have looked at the ways in which women are troped as monstrous and unnatural when they are associated with ambiguities of gender.[14] A somewhat different perspective has dominated scholarship concerned with unconventional desire in the Renaissance; the majority of such scholarship has focused on the diverse associations of the language of same-sex desire—whether it be associated with homosexual acts, with heterosexual male or female bonding, or with any inherent sexual preference.[15] Equally dominant has been the attempt to explore why references to sodomy in early modern texts were so strongly associated with notions of treason.[16] What these diverse perspectives share is a desire to identify and give voice to marginalized or effaced characters (most often women) and desires (most often homoerotic) of the early modern period.

While my project builds upon these significant cultural perspectives, I add to them the question of why it is that somewhat privileged, apparently heterosexual men would choose to give voice to—even speak from—the position of marginalized genders and desires. The writers of the prodigal fictions I study consistently present scenarios in which the male protagonist is identified with effeminate weakness, while women are associated with "masculine" empowerment. These writers do so, I suggest, to dramatize an aesthetic rebellion against patriarchal norms.[17] As such, texts like the *Decameron* and *The Old Arcadia* promote an inversion of the classic (Freudian) oedipal paradigm: rather than affirm patriarchal power by narrating the eventual submission of the son to the father, the prodigal texts I study promote the rights of the literary son over an established patriarchal text. It is, thus, in the interstices between cultural, aesthetic, and psychoanalytic perspectives that I locate these authors' critiques of the patriarchal literary machine.

PRECEDENTS

The marginalization of certain gender and sexual preferences during the early modern period does not, of course, emerge from a vacuum; it depends, among other things, on classical and medieval conceptualizations of gender and aesthetics, particularly on Platonic and Aristotelian thought. The earliest surviving writings about fantasy in Western tradition are found in Plato's *Republic* and *Sophist*, dialogues that associate fantasy with seduction and deceit. In the *Sophist* Plato distinguishes between two kinds of art—*eikastiké*, which he defines as "the making of likenesses" (235d, 236b), and *phantastiké*, which is the art of making something that "seems to be a likeness, but is not really so" (236b).[18] The difference, in other words, is between a mimetic rendering and an illusory or fabricated image—the latter of which Plato associates with distorting, sophistical rhetoric.[19] The distinctions between *eikastiké* and *phantastiké* were crucial to later poets and critics, for Plato characterized fantastical images and writings as deceitful, seductive, and hence, immoral (234c).

If Plato's works were the first (surviving) to associate fantasy with seduction and deceit, Aristotle's treatises are the main authority to which Renaissance writers turned in order to locate precedents for defining women as seductive, deceitful, and unruly.[20] This essentialist construction of women is perhaps most famously articulated in *The History of Animals*, 9.1, where Aristotle characterizes women as irrational, violent, shameless, and deceitful.[21] The notion is extended in the *Politics* and *Physics*, where Aristotle at once affirms woman's unruly nature and states that her threatening nature can only be controlled if, under the tutelage of male authority figures, she is trained to be passive, silent, and chaste—the very characteristics that formed the basis for Renaissance polemical treatises on the nature of women.[22]

The common cultural assumption that fantasy and femininity must be subordinated to the dominant order of didacticism (*eikastiké*) and patriarchy carries over into the Renaissance, determining the mirroring relationship between fantasy and femininity.[23] This common drive to affirm traditional authority leads Francesco Barbaro to assert that for a wife, "nothing should be more estimable than the will of her husband."[24] The analogous need to subordinate fantasy to didactic principles is expressed by Boccaccio in his didactic *Genealogia Deorum Gentilium*, where he defends fiction as an important vehicle for truth: "If, then, sense is revealed from under the veil of fiction, the composition of fiction is not idle nonsense."[25] Both Barbaro and Boccaccio, however, construe femininity and fantasy as deceitful, and hence threatening to male didactic authority, when these constructs are perceived to be independent of masculinity and didacticism. If Barbaro's almost obsessive characterization of the ideal wife as modest and obedient implies that far too many women subvert this cultural ideal, Boccaccio's repeated defense of poetry against its detractors indirectly calls attention to a common assumption that poetry is immoral and subversive.[26]

Inheriting this mode of thinking, sixteenth-century polemical writers often attack poetry by associating it with unruly femininity. Hence, in 1579, Stephen Gosson writes that "Virgil sweats in describing his gnatte; Ovid bestirreth him to paint out his flea: the one shewes his art in the lust of Dido; the other his cunning in the incest of Myrrha, and that trumpet of bawdrie, the Craft of Love."[27] By associating fantastical poetry and errant women with seduction and deceit, Gosson's diatribe illuminates distinctions between Renaissance and contemporary notions of "fantasy"—Gosson's favorite term for the seductive fictions that he attacks.[28]

BOCCACCIO AND THE PRODIGAL OEDIPUS

Paradigmatic of the fantastical works that Gosson condemns is Boccaccio's *Decameron*. Indeed, it is one of my arguments that the *Decameron*, while written significantly earlier than the sixteenth-century works I focus on, shaped a kind of template of prodigality upon which sixteenth-century French and English authors constructed their fictions. By looking at Boccaccio's complex responses to medieval constructions of fantasy we can come to understand how the gendering of fantasy, and by extension of prodigal fictions, as feminine or effeminate enables a series of rebellions against the dominant literary authority.

Sixteenth-century writers responded to the *Decameron* quite differently from the way that they responded to most influential Italian works. While French and English writers troped literature by Petrarch, Castiglione, and Tasso as authoritative and didactic, they often read the *Decameron* as a subversive, pleasurable text. Boccaccio indeed presents his text as unrepentantly pleasurable by shaping his own mutation of the classic oedipal paradigm: the stories of the *Decameron* interrogate the notion (expressed in Renaissance didactic treatises) that civilization depends on patriarchy as a system by which women are legitimately subordinated to fathers or father figures.[29] The narrative equivalent of this paradigm is a plot in which, as Robert Con Davis states, "the father is a 'no' that initiates narrative development by enfranchising one line of continuity over other possibilities; the son's desire is a 'yes' that leaves behind maternal demands, gets bound to the father's law and proceeds in a narrative advancement that plays out the father's meaning in time."[30] It is, by extension, through a growing acknowledgment of patriarchal authority—and the concomitant resignation of desire for the mother—that a classic text like *The Odyssey* (to use Davis's example) develops.[31]

Boccaccio inverts this classic paradigm from the first pages of his *Decameron*, where he purports to seduce female readers from their dominating "padri, . . . fratelli e . . . mariti" [fathers, . . . brothers . . . and husbands].[32] Rather than shape a narrative in which the youthful would-be seducer eventually acknowledges that the desired woman belongs to a father figure, Boccaccio claims that it is the young seducer who deserves the woman, because he acknowledges and satisfies her primal need for pleasure.³³ Boccaccio affirms this claim by representing the desired woman as a daughter (rather than mother). As such, any father figure who cleaves to the sexually ripe daughter is represented as repressive, even incestuous.³⁴ From this perspective, one might say that the *Decameron* is a version of *Oedipus Rex*, but one in which Jocasta turns out to be Laius's daughter rather than his wife, while the youthful Oedipus is only tangentially related to Laius. By extension, we may read Boccaccio's fiction as a series of plots which develop as "the son's desire" says "no" to "the father's law" by claiming the young woman from the father who unfairly possesses her.

This rewriting of the oedipal paradigm mutates the language of aggression that, classically, precedes the son's ultimate submission to patriarchy.³⁵ Rather than express any desire to kill or violently depose the father figure, Boccaccio's protagonists prefer to work indirectly—by secretly seducing the desired woman from the powerful man who owns her. This substitution of seduction for violence contains its own subversive implications, for as Marjorie Garber notes, "Eroticism is what escapes, what transgresses rules, breaks down categories, questions boundaries."³⁶ Boccaccio signals this fantasy of subversion at the threshold to the *Decameron*, where he subtitles his work the "Galeotto." The title shapes an analogy between the knight (Galeotto) who pandered between Lancelot and Guinevere, and the text of the *Decameron*—which panders between the seducing male narrator and his (he hopes) desiring female audience.³⁷ By invoking "Galeotto" in this way, Boccaccio displaces the literary tradition of chivalry (in which men are expected to save women by defending their chastity), and replaces it with his prodigal plots (in which the protagonist sexually liberates women from sterile husbands and repressive fathers). Simply by offering salacious stories to women readers, Boccaccio is challenging the dominant cultural notion that fiction, because of its problematic moral content, should be forbidden to women.³⁸ It is through the unleashing of female *jouissance* that this prodigal author knows he has told a good tale.³⁹

If Boccaccio claims to write in order to liberate women's imaginations from the oppressions of patriarchy, the prodigal fantasies inherent in the "Galeotto" frame also imply that Boccaccio has some quite self-interested reasons for offering narratives of pleasure to desiring women. Certainly this strategy allows him to tap into the growing influence of women as literary patrons. It is no coincidence that Boccaccio, like Pasquier, Sidney, and (to an extent) Shakespeare came from a literary culture in which women played an increasingly prominent role. Just as Boccaccio addressed his *Concerning Famous Women* to the sister of the seneschal of the Court of Naples, so Pasquier and Sidney identified their writings with courts in which women were important patrons of the arts.⁴⁰ At the same time, the projection of a desiring female audience enables these authors to represent themselves as innovative by laying claim to an unconventional poetics—

feminine, vernacular, and innovative—rather than masculine, Latinate, and conventional. For all their attempts to claim a disinterested celebration of femininity, these authors notably employ femininity, like fantasy and prose, as a way to call attention to their aesthetics of prodigality.

THE AESTHETICS OF CASTRATION

This, then, is one reason why prodigal fictions like the *Decameron, Monophile, Astrophil and Stella, The Old Arcadia,* and *As You Like It* project a female audience into their works: a sympathetic identification with the feminine position not only allows these authors to distinguish their works from the mass of serious writing directed to men, but also allows them to act out a fantasy of social advancement, of tapping into a neglected yet potentially influential female audience.[41] But if this prodigal paradigm allows authors to associate female characters and readers with a poetics of prodigality, it implicates prodigal tales in what might be termed a narrative of castration. Indeed a number of stories in the *Decameron* chart how an "adolescent" alliance with the desired female character against literary patriarchy invites castrating repercussions from powerful father figures, whether they be literal fathers who kill youthful aspirants or literary authorities who censor prodigal texts.[42]

This latter anxiety is openly expressed in the prologue to the Fourth Day; for if Boccaccio claims here that he writes "in istilo umilissimo" (275) [in . . . (a) . . . most unassuming style (325)] for a female audience in order to avoid criticism and censorship, he soon admits the failure of this defensive strategy: "Né per tutto ciò l'essere da cotal vento fieramente scrollato, anzi presso che diradicato, e tutto da' morsi della invidia esser lacerato" (275) [in spite of all this, I have been unable to avoid being violently shaken and almost uprooted by those very winds (of envy), and was nearly torn to pieces by envy (325)]. This passage is not only fraught with what Meredith Skura terms "oedipally suggestive scenes, images, and configurations," but also recalls the archetypal story of Orpheus—a writer torn to pieces, then beheaded (particularly in the notion of being "tutto da' morsi . . . lacerato").[43] Writing for women, it seems, leads to the fragmentation of one's text (if not literally of one's self) by powerful authority figures or even by the female audience itself.

This may in fact explain why it is the figure of Orpheus rather than Oedipus that is frequently invoked in Renaissance texts such as the *Decameron,* Castiglione's *The Courtier,* Nashe's *The Anatomie of Absurditie,* and Sidney's *Astrophil and Stella.* Orpheus—at least Ovid's version of Orpheus—is himself a youthful artist, whose errancy (literally, into the underworld, then sexually, into homosexuality) inspired his unconventional and unparalleled utterances; yet this errancy also led to his fragmentation and death.[44] In Ovid's version (as in the versions by Castiglione and Nashe) frustrated women fragment Orpheus; but in Boccaccio's version this role is assumed by authoritative critics and writers. In either case, Orpheus's eventual transfiguration into a kind of immortal singing head gestures at once to his fragmentation by more powerful forces and to the ultimate triumph of his poetry over the violent forces that would silence it.

The figure of Orpheus, then, emblematizes the dilemma that Boccaccio faces in this prologue—the problem of how to provide erotic narratives to the desired and desiring audience (in this case female), without awakening censorious repercussions from patriarchal literary authorities. Within the *Decameron* the solution often is to claim women secretly—to leave the authoritative male with the appearance of owning the desired woman while it is in fact the prodigal protagonist who secretly and potently enjoys her.[45] In the same way, Boccaccio implies that it is through such indirect means as seduction that he will avoid calling attention to his subversive aesthetics. Yet, in the prologue to the Fourth Day, Boccaccio admits that this strategy has failed: his attempt to "piani" (275) [quietly] claim the female audience has aroused the ire of "lo 'mpetuoso vento e ardente della 'nvidia" (275) [envy's fiery and impetuous blast (325)].[46] But I would argue that, by calling attention to his ultimate fragmentation by authority figures, Boccaccio is implying that there are some positive implications inherent in literary castration.

There are, I suggest, two reasons why Boccaccio repeatedly calls attention to his fragmentation by literary authority. The first is a variation on Cavendish's modesty *topos*. Cavendish, we have seen, anticipates and hence trumps critics who would condemn her writing as frivolous; she does so by openly asserting her intent to write frivolously. Similarly, Boccaccio hopes to stave off potential censorship by admitting his weakness, even impotence, against censors; in other words he castrates himself before authority figures may do so.[47] Boccaccio reinforces this process of self-castration—and, by extension, effeminacy—by allying himself with a female audience and against the traditional homosocial paradigm of male author writing for male readers; indeed it appears that his representation of himself as someone who (like his female readers) has been tormented by patriarchal authority, grants him the license to speak from the position of women.

While Boccaccio's tales focus on the father figure as the locus for the threat of castration, other writers—Nashe and Castiglione for instance—locate the threat of castration in the female body.[48] Certainly the association of the "feminized" prodigal author with castration, or lack, may be traced to a kind of contamination from woman's literal lack; the derivation is reinforced by the common cultural construction of woman as "nothing" within patriarchal culture: "woman . . . is *not*, because she is defined purely against the man . . . and because this very definition is designated a fantasy, a set which may well be empty."[49] This self-identification with feminine and fantastical "nothingness" may contain horrifying associations for men, but it has constructive aesthetic implications for the prodigal authors I study: to foreground the feminine is to turn from the "something" of patriarchal experience to the nothingness of fantasy; by extension, it enables the prodigal author to shape what Phyllis Rackin calls "an antiworld where object becomes subject and the feminine can be characterized as real."[50]

Yet if fantasy demarcates a conceptual space within which women may have a significant identity of their own, it may also sustain woman's continuing status as "nothing" within patriarchal experience. Certainly the male authors I study exploit woman's cultural position as "nothing" by speaking for women, rather than encouraging women to speak for themselves. Yet if these authors' celebration of feminine fantasy perpetuates, to a degree, the silencing of women within patriarchal experience, their prodigal fictions at least conceptualize articulate, even aggressive, female voices—voices that provided positive models for emerging Renaissance women writers and patrons. This, at least, is what Margaret Tyler claims as she defends writings by women: "And if men may and do bestow such of their travails upon gentlewomen, then may we women read such of their works as they dedicate unto us, and if we may read them, why not further wade in them to the search of a truth? And then much more, why not deal by translation in such arguments?"[51] For Tyler, the fact that books are written for and about women means that logically they should inspire women, in their turn, to write.

Certainly one can state that within these prodigal fictions women are strongly associated with the "something" of fertility, pregnancy, or creativity. This pattern is particularly marked in *As You Like It,* where Rosalind is radically disempowered in the patriarchal world of the court and just as radically generative in the Forest of Arden, a world strongly associated with fantasy.[52] Whether femininity is conceptualized as nothingness by patriarchy or as generative within fantasy, authors of prodigal fictions often foreground the feminine as a metonym for fiction—for a creative and perhaps illusory alternative to patriarchal experience. By extension, their own self-representations as castrated, or at least effeminate, allow them to construct an identity for themselves that lies outside of patriarchal authority while gesturing to the possibility of significant voicings by women.

This common distancing from patriarchal convention is, then, what enables strong associations between femininity (or effeminacy), fantasy, and originality. Indeed, originality shares with fantasy and femininity connotations of castration or at least nothingness. During a period when convention was associated with accepted cultural truths—including the truth of God—originality became associated with lies, with a departure from "masculine" authority, and, by extension, with "nothingness."[53] The resulting association of originality with the opposite of masculinity (femininity or effeminacy) confirms these problematic associations, implying that a movement away from patriarchal conventions may result in insignificant or meaningless work.[54] No wonder, then, that Renaissance fictions of prodigality seem to celebrate femininity, effeminacy, and originality while expressing ambivalence about this celebration: to promote these concepts is to associate one's authorial self at once with innovation and with absurdity, with a rich fantasy world and with literary impotence.

The Margins of Renaissance Culture

While my discussion of the *Decameron* has focused on psychoanalytical implications of femininity, effeminacy, and fantasy, this work's constructions of gender gesture as well to the cultural milieu from which writers of prodigal fictions emerged. As I mentioned above, this aesthetics is bound up with a fantasy of social advancement predicated on attracting patronage from an increasingly influential female audience. It is perhaps no coincidence that this interest in a previously (and still somewhat) marginalized audience is expressed by authors who themselves emerged from the margins of patriarchal culture. For if these authors later achieved more stable social positions, none of these men (in the period during which they wrote the works that I discuss) had yet attained any prestigious social or literary standing.[55] This experience of what Victor Turner terms being "betwixt and between" leads to a suspension of conventional boundaries between experience and fantasy, masculinity and femininity, authority and subordination, creating a space that licenses free exploration and transgression.[56] It may well be that these Renaissance authors' liminal situations led them to shape porous, transgressive, and femininely inflected fantasy worlds.

Perhaps the most notably liminal of these authors is Sir Philip Sidney, whom some scholars assume to be part of the aristocratic caste, but who in fact found himself on the margins of that culture. Sidney claimed aristocratic heritage from his mother but not his father; and his position as heir apparent to the Earl of Leicester was continually threatened by the possibility that the Earl might father a legitimate son. This position of in-betweenness would make Sidney particularly ambivalent about the patriarchal aristocratic structure that he simultaneously sought to join and rebelled against.[57]

In suggesting that Sidney represents himself as a poet whose "fall" into feminized fantasies enabled him to create a conceptual space outside of patriarchal culture, I draw my argument in part from Richard Helgerson's paradigm of literary prodigality.[58] Helgerson argues that during the mid to late sixteenth century a number of aspiring British writers found themselves frustrated in their attempts to employ their writings as a means for social and political advancement. Unable to follow in the footsteps of earlier, successful courtier-writers, Sidney, among others, structured his fictions on a dilated fantasy of irresponsibility that gave a *raison d'etre* for his life of forced idleness.[59] What I add to this now classic paradigm is a study of the gendered metaphorics of prodigal rebellion, particularly its association with fantasy and femininity, an association that inspired emerging writers to rewrite any oedipal subordination to patriarchy.[60] At the same time I widen Helgerson's English perspective by looking at French and Italian, as well as English writers; this larger perspective allows me to examine nationalist (or anti-nationalist) stances in terms of their expressions within the popular genres of this period—notably polemical treatises (chapter 1), dialogue (chapter 2), lyric poetry (chapter 3), prose fiction (chapter 4), and drama (chapter 5). By exploring a multiplicity of cultural, gendered, and generic perspectives, I hope to illuminate the ways in which the rebellious attitudes of these authors are inscribed in their resistance to narratives that affirm the authority of nation or conventions of genre, even as these authors shape their narratives in response to specific cultural and generic structures.[61]

If, then, I focus to an extent on English writers—Nashe, Jane Anger, Sidney, and Shakespeare—I supplement this focus with Continental writers such as Boccaccio, Castiglione, and Pasquier. And while an ongoing concern with gender identity informs the literary texts that I study, I explore how this enabling structure is expressed in a variety of Renaissance genres.[62] Etienne Pasquier's stress on the chastity of his female protagonist, Charilée, both marks his dialogue's divergence from Boccaccio's fabliau structure and reflects a cultural awareness that the aristocratic French woman could best authorize her discourses by affirming her chastity.[63] And if the more aggressive virgins that are associated with Sidney's and Shakespeare's fictions reveal these authors' relative ease with a female sovereign, Sidney's continued emphasis on the court world contrasts with the more open and heterogenous culture suggested both by the forest of Arden and the English theater. Equally distinct are representations of literary fathers in these works. While Pasquier's rather playful relationship with *The Courtier* is, I suggest, enabled by France's partial conquest of Italy, Boccaccio's much stronger insistence on displacing literary authority has been traced in part to his disappointment with male, aristocratic patrons.[64] Within these distinct cultures and genres one common desire remains: to shape an alternative to patriarchal truths by celebrating fantasy, femininity, even effeminacy. If the authors I study are never quite able to break away from the patriarchal patterns that their culture takes for granted, their problematic works shape a conceptual space within which cultural authority yields, for a time, to alternative conceptualizations of gender, nation, and morality. As such they pleasurably encourage readers to interrogate inherited notions of class, gender, and aesthetics.

I begin my exploration of Renaissance perspectives on fantasy as feminine and the feminine as fantastical by focusing on three Renaissance polemical treatises that discursively condemn fantasy and femininity (or effeminacy), while indirectly betraying a marked proclivity for these states—Sidney's *A Defence of Poetry*, Jane Anger's *Jane Anger, Her Protection for Women,* and Thomas Nashe's *The Anatomie of Absurditie.* I argue that this language of indirection is picked up by writers of prodigal fiction like Sidney and Shakespeare to displace defenses of patriarchy by means of a rhetoric of feminized fantasy. This pattern of reading authoritative texts against themselves structures the chapters that follow, each of which focuses on an authoritative Italian or Italianate text— such as *The Courtier,* the *Rime Sparse,* or *A Defence of Poetry*—whose language and metaphors are imitated by prodigal writers in order to empty them of their cultural authority and replace them with an aesthetics of feminized fantasy.[65]

Chapter 2 looks at Etienne Pasquier's *Monophile* (1555), which takes on the most celebrated, authoritative, and (from Pasquier's point of view) patriarchal of Italian debate treatises, Castiglione's *Book of the Courtier* (1518). Pasquier challenges Castiglione's representation of men as active and women as passive, as he grants dominant powers of articulation to the amazonian Charilée; this strategy enables Pasquier to represent himself as a hermaphroditic champion of unruly women. By deconstructing the paradigms of masculinity upon which his powerful literary father depends, the French Pasquier is able to represent Italianate tradition as outdatedly and rigidly patriarchal.

In my third chapter I examine how a similar agon with authoritative Italian tradition characterizes *Astrophil and Stella,* a sonnet sequence in which Sidney disrupts the monolithic male voice of Petrarchism by granting his heroine her own (limited) voice in the work. By representing Stella as the voice of Petrarchan authority while identifying Astrophil with effeminate fantasy, Sidney questions the traditional conventions of gender representation upon which Renaissance literary and gender theorists depend, even those of his own *A Defence of Poetry* (which includes a defense of a "masculine" poetics). Ultimately, Sidney's almost exclusive attention to Astrophil's effeminate thoughts and motives suggests that his profeminist stance is a means by which he, like Pasquier before him, may identify his poetry with "effeminate" originality. As such Sidney's sequence exists in contrast to Spenser's *Amoretti,* a sonnet sequence that enacts the poet's constant desire to reclaim and absorb the voice of the beloved.

My fourth chapter provides a somewhat different perspective on Italianate tradition, as I look at the ways in which Sidney in his earlier *Arcadia* enters into a close identification with Boccaccio's the *Decameron,* an Italian work whose strong and salacious interest in a framing female audience kept this work within the margins of literary authority. By framing their prose fictions with a flirtatious female audience, these authors lay claim to an unconventional poetics—feminine, prosaic, and new—rather than masculine, poetic, and conventional. Curiously, this defense of "feminine" prose depends on constructing patriarchy as homosexual—as unproductive and sterile—and opposing it to a generative commingling of masculinity with femininity.

I conclude my project by focusing on how Shakespeare, writing almost a generation after Sidney, constructs Sidney as an Italianate literary father, deeply attached to conventional notions of gender and fiction. Not surprisingly, Shakespeare reads Sidney almost exclusively in terms of the somewhat didactic and conservative *A Defence of Poetry,* in which Sidney condemns drama as the weakest and most effeminate of literary genres. Shakespeare invokes *A Defence* in order to suggest the opposite—that drama, because it is effeminate, is the preeminent vanguard literary genre. He does so by celebrating the unruly, effeminate, and fantastical body of Rosalind/Ganymede. If Shakespeare ends his drama by characterizing Rosalind's powers as a fantastical illusion, the boy actor's final conjurations of pleasure to both the male and female members of the audience remind us that drama's powers of effeminate seduction may quietly seep into the realm of experience.

While these prodigal fictions celebrate the feminine by interrogating patriarchal conventions, their invocations of conventional structures (in order to interrogate them) gesture to an inadvertent collusion with the very patriarchal authorities that they question. For this reason, these works often indirectly reinforce cultural constructions of fantasy and femininity as "nothing," even as they affirm their primacy over patriarchy. Cultural pressures also reveal themselves in the conclusions to these works, which often seem to negate an affirmation of fantasy and femininity by reaffirming patriarchal conventions of nationalism (*Monophile*), marriage (*As You Like It*), or even submission to father figures (the *Decameron*). While these problems undermine any consistent and unproblematic celebration of fantasy, femininity, and effeminacy, the marginal status of these authors within their aristocratic courts does enable them to distance themselves from the patriarchal conventions that they inherit. It is this distance that allows them to create a conceptual space within which the feminine and the effeminate may have aesthetic significance of their own. However prejudiced and partial these authors' fantasies of femininity and effeminacy may be, their fictions generate a number of assertive, articulate, and independently minded female characters and readers, figurations that provoke debate with the dominant cultural ideal of women as silent and of femininity as "nothing." The concomitant identification of the male narrator or protagonist with effeminacy opens up a field of inquiry about the nature of gender identity that is never fully absorbed into traditional hierarchies of male authority and female subordination.

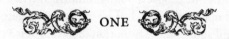

ONE

Sidney, Nashe, Anger,
and the Renaissance Aesthetics
of Effeminacy

In a characteristic passage from *On the Beauty of Women*, Agnolo Firenzuola represents the ideal woman's breasts as "two hills filled with snow and roses, with two little crowns of fine spouts at the top, like drinking straws for that beautiful and useful vessel. . . . The breasts have a certain splendor, with such a novel charm, that we are forced to rest our eyes upon them in spite of ourselves."[1] Firenzuola seems less intent on representing a recognizable breast than in artistically transforming a woman's breasts into landscape and drinking vessel. The resulting displacement of the reader's attention from breasts to the "splendor" and "novel charm" of Firenzuola's figurative language is clearly intended to privilege the writer's elegant rhetoric over the female body part it describes.

This transformation of discrete female body parts into artistic prose is, Firenzuola tells us, inspired by the legendary Greek painter Zeuxis, who "chose the five most elegant girls of Croton and, taking from each her most exquisite feature, painted such a beautiful picture of Helen of Troy that in all of Greece one spoke of nothing else" (13). This ideal of representing female beauty expresses a male fantasy of mastering women by fragmenting them, then transforming these fragments into a celebration of male dominance and artifice.

Such a fantasy appealed to a number of Renaissance artists and writers, who came to see "the portrayal of a beautiful woman . . . [as standing] for the descriptive power of words."[2] So powerful is this ideal that it spills over onto cultural contexts as well; in *Directions for Love and Marriage* Francesco Barbaro asserts that it is better to choose a young, unformed wife, "for we can eaſily make impreſsions upon ſoft Wax, but we can scarce deface thoſe which are impreſs'd upon hard and ſolid."[3] The notion that woman is a piece of wax to be shaped by an authoritative male maker is perhaps most famously articulated by Shakespeare's Theseus, who tells Hermia

> To you your father should be as a god;
> One that compos'd your beauties; yea, and one
> To whom you are but as a form in wax,
> By him imprinted.[4]

Without employing the Zeuxian terms of fragmentation here, Barbaro and Theseus share with Firenzuola a tendency to view woman as malleable raw material which exists to be shaped by men into an ideal, artificial form.

Yet while Barbaro and Firenzuola proclaim a common ideal of mastering women, their writings simultaneously imply that this ideal is unattainable. As *Directions for Love and Marriage* progresses, Barbaro narrows down the arena within which his ideal marriage can take place. He first eliminates older women, then widows, because both are not malleable enough; then he excludes poor women, because they cannot bring their husbands a good dowry; finally he suggests that the ideal, malleable wife is a product of the past. The difficulty of mastering woman's independent nature also threatens Firenzuola's artistic ideal. Just as Celso (the narrator of the treatise) is congratulating himself for creating a woman who is "more beautiful . . . than that famous 'Helen' Zeuxis created," Verdespina (a member of the female audience) dryly notes that he has forgotten to give his ideal woman hands or arms (66). Verdespina's riposte foregrounds two problems that preoccupy Renaissance writers like Firenzuola. On the one hand this response discloses the disjunction between the artificial, silenced woman of Zeuxis and actual unruly women, like Verdespina, who are more likely to point out weaknesses in the male artist's rhetoric than allow themselves to be transformed into art objects. At the same time, Verdespina's remarks point to the ultimate absurdity of trying to piece together an ideal woman out of diverse fragments: the discrete parts are more likely to yield something patched up and ephemeral (much like Victor Frankenstein's monster) than a harmonious ideal. In either case the "manliness" of the artist is called into question, as he is ultimately unable to follow through on the patriarchal ideal of mastering the female object of desire.

The ideals and problems underlying the paradigm of Zeuxis became something of a cultural commonplace in sixteenth-century discourse. Three English treatises of the 1580s and 1590s—Philip Sidney's *A Defence of Poetry*, Thomas Nashe's *The Anatomie of Absurditie*, and Jane Anger's *Jane Anger, Her Protection for Women*—are paradigmatic of this ongoing preoccupation with a Zeuxian poetics. I have chosen these treatises in part because they emerge from distinct, even contradictory, polemical stances: Sidney writes a defense of poetry; Nashe condemns poetry and women; Anger attacks poetry and defends women. Yet, like a number of other early modern writers on poetry and women, these authors share a tendency to affirm, discursively, the paradigm of Zeuxis even while metaphorically subverting it.[5] Each writer expresses this splitting of the authorial consciousness somewhat differently: Sidney invokes Zeuxis as a version of the platonic, disembodied *Idea,* but his *peroratio* gestures to his own art as effeminate and unruly. Nashe compares himself openly to the manly Zeuxis yet figuratively identifies his writings with a metaphorics of castration. Anger affirms the importance of male artistic and cultural dominance, yet her self-representation as an assertive woman ultimately undermines this discursive stance.

There are, I suggest, two quite different reasons why the paradigm of Zeuxis is discursively affirmed yet metaphorically problematized in these treatises. On the one hand, as we have seen, this aesthetics is ultimately unrealizable. Perhaps more curious is the way that these authors seem somewhat ambivalent about even wanting to sustain such an ideal. I argue that the strong association of Zeuxis with a conventional aesthetics of mastery may be somewhat stultifying for emerging writers.[6] Perhaps then, even as Sidney, Anger, and Nashe laid claim to a masculine aesthetics of mastery, they were experimenting with an alternative aesthetics grounded in femininity or effeminacy.[7] By looking at the complex and contradictory voices within these pamphlets, I illuminate a common inability on the part of these authors to conceptualize fiction as anything other than fantastical and effeminate, even as they discursively affirm the conventional ideal of fiction as masculine didactic art.[8]

This repression of and fascination with effeminacy emerges from a complex field of cultural, historical and aesthetic contexts. The fact that England was governed by a gender solecism—a didactic, masculine queen who ruled over a subordinated, fantastical, and, by analogy, effeminate younger generation of (male) literary producers—would reinforce this confusion about gender and literary production.[9] As I will go on to argue, Sidney and Nashe cannot write about aesthetics without writing about Queen Elizabeth. But, as we have seen, this tendency to associate fiction with unruly femininity also results from common conceptualizations of fantasy and femininity as threatening to authoritative cultural truths.[10] I have suggested (and will focus on) a third reason for this ambivalent rendering of fiction as feminine, even effeminate: because fiction and femininity are deeply implicated in subverting authority, they come to be associated, as well, with originality—with a rebellion against established literary authority.

Originality, we have seen, was regarded with suspicion during the Renaissance. Stephen Gosson articulates this perception, as he condemns writers for despising "the good rules of their ancient masters" by "defacing olde stampes, forging newe printes, and coining strange precepts."[11] His attitude explains why Sidney, Nashe, and Anger, audacious as they are in their writings, always seem to be anticipating and attempting to elude possible negative criticism or censorship.[12] Focusing on the triple threat of fantasy as subversive of Renaissance cultural, aesthetic, and gender conventions, I trace how pamphleteers of the period align themselves with a didactic masculine authority while betraying proclivities for feminine, even effeminate, and fantastical originality.

SIDNEY'S ZEUXIS

Prototypical of this ambivalent inscription of originality is Sidney's *A Defence of Poetry.* Sidney's heroic and untimely death in 1586 along with the ensuing publication of his manuscripts (*A Defence of Poetry* was published in 1595) led to an almost universal interest in England in Sidney's aesthetic theories.[13] It is, then, not surprising that during the late 1580s and the 1590s we should find an increasing number of treatises on the nature of poetry. It may be no coincidence that these treatises fall into what might be termed a metaphorics of gender, for *A Defence* depends heavily on conceptualizing poetry as masculine, feminine, or effeminate.[14] If Sidney is not the first writer to associate fantasy with femininity, his ongoing dependance on this association most likely caught the attention of writers like Nashe, Puttenham, and others whose treatises were heavily influenced by *A Defence of Poetry.*[15]

Throughout *A Defence* Sidney adumbrates either a masculine poetics free of seduction and deceit or a virtuous feminized poetics that is subordinated to masculinity. Yet, towards the end of his treatise, Sidney gestures to an effeminate poetics that he characterizes as seductive, deceitful, and unruly. What exactly is implied by this heterogenous gendering of fiction is not at first apparent. Sidney's *Defence* is, after all, known for its many slippages and inconsistencies. This reputation arises from Sidney's curious refusal to follow the model of most works in the polemical tradition; such works either present a single narrator with one point of view (as do Nashe's and Anger's treatises) or ascribe contrasting opinions to different characters. Giuseppe Malatesta, for example, in his *Della Nuova Poesia, Overo della Difese del "Furioso,"* has one character—

Scipione—defend Ariostean multiplicity, while he has another character—the Archbishop—speak for Aristotelian unities. In contrast, Sidney ascribes contradictory aesthetic positions to the work's single narrator, a narrator who seems to be closely identified with Sidney himself. In the first part of the work this narrator associates poetical making with freedom and autonomy, while in the second half he attempts to ground it in restrictive Aristotelian rules.[16]

Not surprisingly, Sidney's narratorial inconsistencies have made him an attractive example for critics who argue that Renaissance writers are haunted by a "fragmentary" worldview, a perspective that marks them as "ontologically anxious."[17] If this fairly common perspective illuminates the ways in which Sidney's works proceed via problematic gaps and narrative uncertainties, it often overlooks the ways in which Sidney himself calls attention to self-contradiction throughout the work.[18] Rather than claim that Sidney failed to impose discursive and structural unity on the work, I will look instead at how and why Sidney's *Defence* is built on self-contradictory theories about poetry, contradictions that are reinforced by shifting figurations of gender throughout the work. What one *can* say about this treatise is that it reflects and refracts cultural uncertainties about the gendered status of fiction, uncertainties which yield at once an anxious desire to affirm a masculine didactic poetics and a fascination with poetry as a feminine or effeminate construct.

This tendency to think of fiction in terms of gender yields a logic of development that Sidney's treatise shares with those by Nashe and Anger. Sidney, like these contemporaries, moves from a consideration of "natural" women to ideas about women as Zeuxian art objects, to notions about effeminate fantasy. Unlike Nashe and Anger, however, Sidney dissociates gender from seduction until the end of his treatise, thus strategically deferring notions of femininity and effeminacy as threatening to the male Zeuxian ideal. It is only towards the end, then, that he gives voice to the problems of gender that emerge when femininity becomes associated with fantasy and sexuality.

Certainly the early sections of *A Defence* are dedicated to positive conceptualizations of fiction. Sidney begins by discussing the golden age of poetry, when poetry was a "nurse" to mankind and poets were our "fathers in learning" (18, 19).[19] This genealogy places the origins of poetry in a maternal site that nourishes and enables masculine poets and poetry. Sidney here identifies the feminine as an inspiring and enabling muse who supports, but is subordinate to, masculine poets. Indeed, from this point on, poetry is almost exclusively referred to as masculine.

Sidney then presents a kind of etiology for this hierarchy of inspiring femininity and masculine artistry, as he asserts, famously, that "only the poet, disdaining to be tied to any such subjection [to nature], lifted up with the vigour of his own invention, doth grow in effect another nature, in making things either better than nature bringeth forth, or, quite anew, forms such as never were in nature, as the Heroes, Demigods, Cyclops, Chimeras, Furies, and such like" (23). The narrator establishes here how the creations of maternal nature, though significant, are nonetheless inferior to those by male poets.[20] Indeed if Sidney's references to "Heroes, Demigods, Cyclops" clearly allude to the kinds of imaginings that Plato condemned as fantastical, Sidney nonetheless represents fantasy here as an idealizing, perfecting force, superior to the *mimesis* of Nature.[21] It appears that in separating poetry from its origins in "natural" femininity, the poet is able to conceptualize what Plato could not: *phantastiké* without seduction.[22]

This, in effect, is the logic of *A Defence,* a work that constantly reaffirms the notion that masculine poetry arises from, but outdoes, maternal, desexualized inspiration. As the treatise proceeds, poetical inspiration is no longer associated with nurse-like figures, but it is linked with "feminine" philosophical concepts—whether it be the "Muses" (20), the "mistress-knowledge" (29), "*Ius* . . . the daughter of Justice" (31), or "mistress Philosophy" (41).[23] Sidney's characterization of the feminine here (which is later echoed by Anger's assertion that virtue is feminine) is consistent with the classic defenses of women by Edmund Gosynhill, Sir Thomas Elyot, and Edward More, defenses which construct woman as a supportive helpmate to man; following this template, *A Defence of Poetry* represents the ways in which feminine virtue inspires great poetry.[24] Sidney clearly invokes conventional abstractions of femininity to support his decarnalized, and hence unthreatening, notions of women and poetry.

Interwoven with these references to virtue, justice, and philosophy are a number of instances in which the paradigm of Zeuxis is indirectly invoked, as women are transformed from flesh and blood creatures into idealized artifice. One of these instances occurs as Sidney compares what he calls "right poets" to excellent painters, "who having no law but wit, bestow that in colours upon you which is fittest for the eye to see: as the constant though lamenting look of Lucretia, when she punished in herself another's fault, wherein he painteth not Lucretia whom he never saw, but painteth the outward beauty of such a virtue" (26). Sidney seems to be following Castelvetro here, who comments that "Zeuxis portrayed men and women as more beautiful than they are or can naturally be, for as he painted he contemplated not the sitter so as to portray him as he was, but the model of perfect beauty which he kept at home or in his mind."[25] In much the same way, Sidney makes manifest the poet's superiority over the feminine object of inspiration, when he characterizes the poet as an artist who recreates woman in his own image of her ("in his mind"). From this perspective, Sidney's vision of Lucretia follows Firenzuola's ideal of artistry, as the narrator invites us to look not at Lucretia herself, but rather at the way that she figures forth the beauties of poetry—Sidney's aesthetically pleasing sentences, his parallel phrasings, and his ornamental metaphors.[26]

Significantly, these diverse representations of the feminine become associated with a process of mediation, as the desexualized, feminine art object enables a kind of homosocial bonding between male poet and male reader, a triangular structure markedly different from the highly sexualized relationship that Boccaccio posits between male writer and female reader.[27] This notion is pursued as the narrator notes how Plato and Boethius "made mistress Philosophy very often borrow the masking raiment of poesy," adding how "those hard-hearted evil men . . . will be content to be delighted . . . and so steal to see the form of goodness . . . as if they took a medicine of cherries" (41). This notion of desexualized seduction is, in fact, how most writers in the tradition envisioned fantasy at its best—as a force that, like a beautiful woman, could (if well managed) seduce the male spectator into a love of virtue.[28]

SIDNEY'S POETICS OF EFFEMINACY

Sidney's ongoing attempts to sever poetry from its associations with sexually charged fantasies involves, we have seen, three related associations of poetry with desexualized femininity: poetry's origins in maternal nature; its expression of virtuous women as a trope for the aesthetic process; and its figurations of feminine art as a way to move the audience to virtue. It is no wonder that British authors so often drew upon Sidney's treatise on poetry: his metaphorics of masculine poetry and virtuous feminine inspiration presented the most eloquent and stirring idealization of poetical language in Renaissance England.

Not surprisingly, what puzzles most readers of *A Defence of Poetry* is Sidney's ensuing tendency to undermine the highly idealized figurations of poetry that otherwise dominate his treatise. A radical shift in tone, language, and imagery emerges as the narrator digresses from magisterial pronouncements about the aureate literature of Greece, Rome, and Italy to problematic assertions about contemporary writing in England. The shift is signalled by the narrator's move from a celebratory affirmation of aesthetics to a strongly defensive stance about poetry, as he declares that poetry is "not . . . an art of lies, but of true doctrine; not of effeminateness, but of notable stirring of courage" (61). Yet soon after this passage the narrator goes on to charge poets with all that golden poetry is "not of." His language here shows increasing sensitivity to the many charges against poets summarized by Boccaccio in his *Genealogia Deorum Gentilium:* "They say . . . that poets are tale-mongers, or, in lower terms, liars; . . . . They say, besides, that their poems are false, obscure, lewd, and replete with absurd and silly tales . . . . Again and again they cry out that poets are seducers of the mind, prompters of crime."[29] This notion of fiction as seductive and deceitful is picked up by numerous Renaissance writers. George Puttenham, for example, states that, "For as well Poets as Poeſie are deſpiſed, . . . for commonly who ſo is ſtudious in th'Arte or ſhewes himſelfe excellent in it, they call him in diſdayne a *phantaſticall*".[30] Sidney adds a strong inflection of gender to such charges as he contends that English poetry has become feminine (if not quite effeminate), that its father tongue (Latin) has given way to the "mother tongue," that it is a school of lies, and that it is a craft of idleness (69, 70, 63). As Sidney's language begins to slip into an abuse of poetry, the narrator implies that this fall into bad English poetry is the fault of one particular woman—Queen Elizabeth.

Sidney is not about to criticize his queen openly; in fact, he never mentions her name in this treatise. This very absence is itself potentially suspicious, given the ways that Nashe (as we will see), Puttenham, Spenser, and other contemporaries openly address and invoke Queen Elizabeth as their great inspiration. Where Puttenham refers to Elizabeth's "learned, delicate, noble Muse," Sidney sets up a subtle critique of his queen as an anti-inspirational force by representing her as displacing Mother Nature—a natural, enabling, and subordinate female—with England (the metonym for Elizabeth) as an unnatural, forbidding, and dominating stepmother to English poets:[31]

> methinks, before I give my pen a full stop, it shall be but a little more lost time to inquire why England, the mother of excellent minds, should be grown so hard a stepmother to poets. . . . Sweet poesy, that hath anciently had kings, emperors, senators, great captains, such as, besides a thousand others, David, Adrian, Sophocles, Germanicus, not only to favour poets, but to be poets; and of our nearer times can present for her patrons a Robert, king of Sicily, the great King Francis of France, King James of Scotland; . . . that poesy, thus embraced in all other places, should only find in our time a hard welcome in England. (61–62)

Queen Elizabeth's marked absence from this list of generous patrons suggests that she is among those giving a "hard welcome" to poetry in England. As a metonym for England, Elizabeth is, then, the "stepmother" who will not support England's poets.[32] Indeed, by listing male kings, cardinals, preachers, teachers, philosophers, orators, and wits who have been great patrons to poetry, Sidney implies that men are more responsible nurturers of poetry than are unnatural women like Queen Elizabeth. Finally, Sidney pointedly notes that

England (the country that Elizabeth rules) is the place where poetry is least valued.[33] If Sidney begins his treatise by representing women as inspiring and enabling, here one unnurturing woman has left poets without creative or material support.

Queen Elizabeth remains unnamed in the enigmatic passage that follows this one, but its mixture of politics with creativity gestures to problems that emerge when a woman neglects her subordinate position as inspirer of men:

> And now that an overfaint quietness should seem to strew the house for poets, they are almost in as good reputation as the mountebanks at Venice. Truly even that, as of the one side it giveth great praise to poesy, which like Venus (but to better purpose) had rather be troubled in the net with Mars than enjoy the homely quiet of Vulcan: so serves it for a piece of a reason why they are less grateful to idle England, which now can scarce endure the pain of a pen. (62)

This dense passage, once untangled, reiterates the essential contrast between the aureate classical poetry of the past and the degraded English poetry of the present.[34] Poetical inspiration ("poesy"), here associated with Venus, has abandoned "idle England" (associated with Vulcan) for nations that support martial, epic poetry ("Mars"). She has done so because England, like Vulcan, has become associated with "homely quiet." From this perspective Vulcan may be read as a version of the androgynous Queen Elizabeth, known for her dovelike policies. By extension, the passage suggests that Elizabeth's famous avoidance of armed conflict has led to the rather humdrum verse that, the narrator claims, characterizes English poetry written under her rule.[35]

By stating (in a convoluted manner) that England's literature flourished most in times of war, Sidney indirectly blames his peace-loving queen for what he claims is the sad state of his nation's literature, particularly as he had earlier asserted that poetry ought to be "the companion of camps" (56).[36] Without actually using the term "effeminate," the passage suggests that English poetry, under the rule of a Vulcan-like monarch, has become weak and effeminate; for, as we saw above, Sidney associates femininity here with idleness, weakness, and effeminacy. This point of view is echoed by Sidney's friend, Hubert Languet, who writes to Sidney about the Elizabethan court that "the habits of your court seemed to me somewhat less manly than I could have wished. . . . I was sorry therefore, and so were other friends of yours, to see you wasting the flower of your life."[37] Languet expresses here what Sidney's *Defence* suggests— that English courtiers and poets, made effeminate under a peace-mongering female monarch, are no longer capable of raising their pens (62).

If Sidney's metaphorics affirms the common association, in antipoetry treatises, between poets, idleness, and effeminacy, his governing trope is not that of
castration or even of cuckoldry; instead it is that of arranged marriages: the
association of poetical inspiration (Venus) with domestic effeminacy (Vulcan)
is the product of an arranged marriage that prevents the ideal union between
poetry and war (Venus and Mars).[38] It would, of course, be tempting to read
this passage as a veiled allegory for Sidney's well known criticism of the Queen's
flirtation with marrying the Duke of Anjou, for political reasons, rather than
marrying her longtime favorite (Sidney's uncle) the Earl of Leicester. If we
follow the accepted dates of 1579–81 for the composition of this work, then *A
Defence* was written at about the time that Sidney wrote to Queen Elizabeth
urging her not to marry the Duke. Certainly most biographers of Sidney agree
that Sidney's retirement to his sister's estate from 1579–80 resulted at least partially
from the queen's negative reaction to this letter.[39] In Sidney's case, it appears that
a queen on the throne led to his temporary existence as an idle, and hence
conceptually effeminate, writer.

What is curious about Sidney's poetical self-representation here is that it
departs from the common stance of treatise writers like Gosson, Nashe, and
Philip Stubbs, who dwell on the degraded nature of poetry in order to distance
themselves from their fellow "mountebank" poets. Sidney instead identifies his
own output with bad Elizabethan poetry by insisting that he has found himself
"sick among the rest" (72). I would argue that Sidney here is setting up a curious paradigm that he revisits in *Astrophil and Stella, The Old Arcadia,* and *The
New Arcadia*—the concept that creative innovation inheres in the experience
of a fall from authority, truth, and masculine *eikastiké* into unruliness, deceit,
and effeminate *phantastiké*.[40] By negating the authoritative Italianate and classical
forces of poetry, by associating his output with *phantastiké* (which "doth . . .
infect the fancy with unworthy objects" [54]), Sidney is creating the idea that
England is in a state of poetical decay; this state at once allows him to dissociate
English poetry from its conventional Italian and Greek sources and to promote
himself indirectly as a candidate for the renewal of English poetry.[41]

Thomas Greene has articulated the notion that Renaissance writers, in order
to call attention to their dynamic renewal of classical literature, "needed a death
and burial to justify itself"—the death of what they "called the Dark Ages."[42]
Sidney, I argue, is doing something similar: in order to establish the dynamic and
innovative quality of his writings, he needs to represent English literature as
moribund. Thus, England is represented both as the threatening competitor whose
literary legacy must be declared dead, and, simultaneously, as the site out of
which a new poetry will arise—as Sidney leaves behind the paternal language of
Latin and turns instead to his maternal tongue for renewing literature.

Sidney, of course, does not discursively articulate the idea that he may renew English literature by associating himself with the fantastical and effeminate poets of his time, but this notion can be gleaned from his use of double entendres and subordination. One passage in the *digressio* illustrates this rhetorical tendency: "I think this digression will make my meaning receive the fuller understanding: which is not to take upon me to teach poets how they should do, but only, finding myself sick among the rest, to show some one or two spots of the common infection grown among the most part of writers, that, acknowledging ourselves somewhat awry, we may bend to the right use both of matter and manner" (72). The passage appears to be a straightforward confession of the narrator's unworthiness as a poet: where poets are supposed to espouse a virtuous *phantastiké*, he, like all other English poets under the rule of the queen, has fallen into a poetics of deceitful and seductive fantasy. This "illness" (as Nashe suggests later) seems to come from men who contaminate themselves with effeminacy by subordinating themselves to powerful women. But this mask of self-deprecation hides a naked desire to usurp the position of poetic authority—a position, Sidney tells us, left empty when Elizabeth abandoned her patronage of English poetry. By "*showing* some one or two spots," Sidney is in fact taking on the role of teacher that he claims he will not assume; in doing so he is granting himself authority over his fellow writers, despite his claims to the contrary (emphasis added).

It is in this sense that Sidney's *Defence* most resembles—perhaps even provides a template for—the tracts by Anger and Nashe. (*A Defence* was written about six years before *The Anatomie of Absurditie* and *Anger, Her Protection*.) Like Anger and Nashe, Sidney shapes a narrative voice that strongly condemns the writings of his contemporaries by characterizing them as fantastical and effeminate; yet the narrator's own implications in an ornamental, seductive, and, hence, fantastical style suggests a collusion with, or at the very least sympathy for, the very writings he condemns. Sidney accentuates this association by stating that it is very much an English problem: in Europe, according to him, poets can write fantastical, virtuous, femininely inflected works, while in England (under a female monarch) fantasy is always associated with seduction, deceit and effeminacy. And while it is difficult to pinpoint the extent to which Sidney is conscious of his participation in the very writings that he condemns, the highly self-conscious inflections of his language suggest that he is well aware of his dependence on a fantastical, effeminate style. It would seem that, while Sidney prefers to align himself, discursively, with conventional, authoritative literature, he is tempted by the implications of originality suggested by fantasy and seduction—implications that are more clearly foregrounded in the abusive rhetoric of Nashe and Anger.

Nashe, Zeuxis, and Unruly Women

The Anatomie of Absurditie and *Jane Anger, Her Protection for Women* come so close on the heels of each other in 1589 that it is tempting (even probable) to assume that one treatise was written in response to the other.[43] At the very least it is clear that both writers enthusiastically participate in the genre of abuse literature, and that their treatises—with their repeated references to anger, their near-obsession with gender boundaries, and their vituperative style—seem to be in some sort of passionate no-holds-barred argument with each other. While we cannot assume that one pamphlet specifically influenced (and inflamed) the other, it is clear that the texts' energies emerge from a cultural tendency, shared with Sidney, to associate fantasy and femininity (or effeminacy) with threats to both masculine authority and traditional literary forms. What distinguishes Nashe's piece most clearly from Anger's and Sidney's is his open conflation of gender with aesthetics. While Sidney claims to write exclusively about poets and Anger purports to write solely about women, Nashe lets us know early on that the title to his treatise refers both to absurd women and absurd writers. Of the three treatises, then, his most openly affirms and problematizes the Zeuxian ideal of artistic mastery over women.

This structuring of the treatise on the Zeuxian paradigm belies current critical consensus that *The Anatomie* lacks any coherent organization or focus.[44] It is true that Nashe shifts abruptly and apparently arbitrarily from associations of women with unnaturalness to associations of women with art, then ignores women to discuss male poets. Structurally, however, this pattern follows the same kind of Zeuxian logic that organized *A Defence of Poetry.* By discussing first the "natural" state of women, then dwelling on woman as art object, Nashe traces the Zeuxian ideal of transforming biological woman into a carefully crafted artifice. And by moving from a discussion of woman as art to a diatribe against his fellow practitioners, Nashe is able to foreground his superiority over his contemporaries, who, he claims, have fallen from the Zeuxian ideal by allowing themselves to be mastered by women.

Yet, much like Sidney, Nashe eventually associates himself with these effeminized authors by implying that he has been "castrated" by the piercing gaze of his sovereign, Queen Elizabeth. I will argue that Nashe ultimately betrays a certain proclivity for literary castration, a concept that enables him to trope his poetical self as innovative and unconventional (outside of the phallic order). This is in fact where Nashe most violently marks his departure from Sidney's perspective. Where Sidney tropes an aesthetics of effeminacy without in the process discussing its implications of castration, the violence of castration becomes an ongoing, even obsessive, metaphorical and aesthetic concern throughout *The Anatomie of Absurditie*. Indeed, one might say that Nashe's treatise is generated out of the

Freudian notion that "The text, any text, is always a tissue that, for fear of castration, disguises a terrible and most tempting [maternal] nudity."[45]

Nashe's preoccupation with the dangerous, unruly, and castrating powers of sexualized women is made evident from the first paragraphs of the treatise:

> Howe euer the Syren change her shape, yet is she inseperable from deceit, and how euer the deuill alter his shaddowe, yet will he be found in the end to be a she Saint. . . . Onely this shall my arguments inferre, and my anger auerre, that constancie will sooner inhabite the body of a Camelion, a Tyger or a Wolfe, then the hart of a woman; who predestinated by the father of eternitie, even in the nonage of nature, to be the Iliads of euils to all Nations have neuer inuerted their creation in any Countrey but ours.[46]

There is no mention of Sidney's nurturing, subordinate Mother Nature here. Rather, Nashe generates a series of anxiety-inducing tropes about women; in the process he distinguishes his treatise from others that focus on the nature of poetry itself as sirenic. Sidney, for instance, cites the "siren's sweetness" as one of the main charges against poetry (51), perhaps referring to Gosson's own association of poetry with a "Syrens songue."[47] In both cases male poets are problematically associated with the seductive and destructive voices of sirens. For Nashe, however, women themselves literally are sirens. As such, his pamphlet figures forth an anxiety about the power of unruly women to usurp the poet's prerogatives of speech. Nashe's list of demonic women in this passage ends with the infamous Helen of Troy ("the *Iliad* of all euils")—a *figura* for woman as the most seductive, inconstant, and unruly of all creatures. This Helen is clearly not Zeuxis's idealized art object; rather she is the imperfect raw material which Zeuxis later reshaped into perfected art.

Nashe's purpose, it seems, is to make women seem as threatening as possible in order to represent himself as a Zeuxian savior who, through his powers of making, can control women by transforming them into art. But his is a Zeuxis with a difference. After rehearsing Zeuxis's ability to fragment, anatomize, then transform diverse women into an integrated art object, Nashe adds, "euen so it fareth with mee, who beeing about to anatomize Absurditie, am vrged to take a view of sundry mens vanitie, a suruey of their follie, . . . to runne through Authors of the absurder sort, . . . sucking and selecting out of these vpstart antiquaries, somewhat of their vnsauery duncerie, meaning to note it with a *Nigrum theta,* that each one at the first sight may eschew it as infectious" (9). Identifying his writing with Zeuxis's anatomizing tendencies, Nashe asserts that his enterprise is not to assemble an idealized and mastered version of Helen (as Zeuxis did) but rather to piece together a portrait of absurdity and misogyny out of bits and pieces of foolishness concocted by diverse male writers.[48] Hence he inks out a *Nigrum theta*. Much as this black mark of Thanatos branded all houses infected by the plague, so Nashe's treatise marks all those writers who have become infected by bad writing. Distinct as his project may seem to be from that of Zeuxis, it sets up Nashe's own fantasy of artistic mastery, one that is based on associating his male contemporaries with unruly women; he asserts that he will bring these bad versifiers and unruly women under his aesthetic control by anatomizing them. In this way, Nashe creates a conceptual universe in which only he has Zeuxian powers of mastery over his subjects.

Nashe is able to claim sole Zeuxian authority because, as he asserts, most of his contemporaries have fallen into an "effeminate" worship of "*Venus* Court" (7, 11). The result, Nashe claims, is that English writers are now churning out the kind of "licence of lying" and "fantasticall dreames" that Renaissance theorists long associated with deceitful and seductive femininity (11).[49] This loss of masculinity is emphasized by Nashe's reference to writers' "idle pens" (11). His easy slippage here from descriptions of biological women to representations of femininely contaminated male writers, is, we have seen, typical of sixteenth-century writers: this slippage dramatizes how, for Nashe, proximity to women contaminates men with feminine deceit and seduction.[50]

For Nashe, then, the most egregious effect of this "infectious" "duncerie" (9) is that it reverses traditional gender hierarchies.[51] This unnatural inversion leads not only to effeminate male artistry but also to woman's usurpation of the artistic process, one that makes art seductive, deceitful, and—like women—ornamental. Since woman's artistry traditionally inheres in her choice of clothing and makeup, Nashe asserts that "women decke themselues so gorgiously and lace themselues so nicely, because foule deformed things seeke to sette out themselues sooner, then those creatures that are for beauty far more amiable" (13).[52]

The close conceptual association between femininity, ornamental language, and deceitful dress is similarly expressed in the anonymous *Schoolhouse of Women,* whose author tells us that

A fool of late contrived a book
And all in praise of the femin[ine];
Whoso taketh labor it to overlook
Shall prove all is but flattery.
Paean he calleth it: it may well be
The Peacock is proudest of his fair tail
And so be all women of their apparel.[53]

Buried in this doggerel is the association of woman with fantasy, as this focus on overdressed women is closely associated with the "flattery," or fantasy, of those who write books "in praise of the feminine." Here, as in Nashe's treatise, women usurp the male Zeuxian paradigm and employ it to hide behind ornamental masks of beauty so as to deceive, seduce, and entrap men.

The problematic association between female and rhetorical ornamentation is exemplified in the face painting controversy of the early modern period, a controversy that arose, according to Frances Dolan, from the notion that such ornamentation is a type of creativity.[54] As such, it discloses woman's attempt to reshape herself artificially, rather than allow a male artist (like Zeuxis) to recreate her. This kind of thinking is articulated in the anonymous *Proude Wyves Pater Noster,* whose female protagonist tells her well dressed friend that she, too, wishes to "be accepted with euery man / Which me beholdeth bothe ferre and nere."[55] To achieve this goal, she asks her friend to tell her how "Lusty fresshe gere . . . I may gete, / And to go trym in lusty wede," heedless of her husband's urgings that she economize.[56] Woman's desire to reshape herself ornamentally is presented here as a scheme concocted between two women to subvert the husband's mastery of his wife. This desire undermines the patriarchal convention that husbands should be all-controlling artists who form wives in their own images of them.[57] These women, instead, usurp their husbands' creative powers by artistically re-forming themselves via expensive clothing and elaborate makeup. They employ these artistic devices, according to Nashe, for seductive, deceitful, and disruptive ends.

WOMAN AS MEDUSA

For Nashe, we have seen, natural woman, like fantastical art, is conceptually Aristotelian—unruly and deceitful. It is only a great artist like Zeuxis (and apparently Nashe) who can tame unruly women by conceptualizing them as mastered art objects, much as the authoritative male artist subordinates fantastical rhetoric to didactic truths. This attempt to master women, however, is threatened by unruly women who usurp the prerogative of artistry by ornamenting themselves. Equally dangerous for Nashe is the way that women have seduced male writers into writing fantastically. The implication is that women have subverted male Zeuxian creativity by, metaphorically, castrating it: "But what should I spend my yncke, waste my paper, stub my penne, in painting forth theyr [women's] vgly imperfections, and peruerse peeuishnesse, when as howe many hayres they haue on their heads, so many snares they will find for a neede to snarle men in; how many voices all of them haue, so many vices each one of them hath; how many tongues, so many tales; how many eyes, so many allurements" (16). What holds together Nashe's fertile and heterogenous references to women here is the anxiety that women are supplanting man's cultural and aesthetic dominance, as Nashe takes on the part of a perverse Zeuxis ("painting forth theyr vgly imperfections"), whose artistry is threatened by competing tales told by women ("how many tongues, so many tales"). Fittingly, the underlying image of this passage is that of the Medusa, whose snake-like head stands for woman's appropriation of male potency.[58] The image, converging as it does with the multiplication of Medusa's murderous eyes ("how many eyes"), represents a nightmare of female ingratitude that, according to Nashe, threatens to overwhelm his writings. In the process the passage anticipates Freud's assertion that "The terror of Medusa is . . . a terror of castration that is linked to the sight of something."[59] In Nashe's *Anatomie,* the narrator focuses on the ways that unruly women (with snakelike hair) have usurped the phallus; as a result, the work concentrates on the anxieties inherent in losing control of the writer's phallus—the pen.

This anxiety is perpetuated as Nashe fixes on how the gaze of Medusa-like women ("how many eyes, so many allurements") is enhanced by woman's ability to obscure herself.[60] The work's initial representation of woman as chameleonlike ("Howe euer the Syren change her shape") centers on woman's ability to elude the potent male gaze by disguising her essential self with deceitful masks. This same figuration underlies Nashe's discussion of female cosmetics and ornamentation, which, as he complains, may be employed to hide an ugly face. As Nashe goes on to discuss the Zeuxian powers of the artist, he again associates artistic empowerment with the ability to control the Other through the medium of sight—or to avoid this form of control by putting on deceitful masks. If, then, Nashe initially affirms how Zeuxis first "viewed" the women that he selected as his models and then defines his own enterprise as based on taking "a view" of absurdity, this project of mastery via the gaze is problematized by woman's usurpation of male sight and speech (9).

Here again we see how Nashe's focus on sexually powerful women precludes the kind of positive conceptualizations of women that Sidney's more desexualized representations of Mother Nature and Virtue admit. This difference is made evident in the way that the two authors employ the imagery of sight. Where for Nashe such imagery often implies the need to control unruly women, Sidney associates this imagery with the need to influence and hence control the (male) audience by discussing how a good artist creates portraits of women that are "fittest for the eye to see" (26). Woman (or the representation of a woman) from this perspective is a mediatress between artist and audience rather than a usurper of the male artistic process.[61]

Because Nashe asserts that women have usurped the gaze, his treatise, unlike Sidney's, turns into a battle between the sexes over control of artistry. Nashe's narrator attempts to reassert the male gaze by disclosing women's veiled attempts to subvert the male prerogative of writing. He does so by taking up his phallic pen. His reference to the way that he will "spende my yncke" is, after all, a common metaphor for the spilling of sperm. This symbolical gesture would imply that artists recover their male potency when they ink out truths about unruly and usurping women on paper. In the same way, writing, for Nashe, is a defense against the castrating effects of woman's gaze. But this spillage of ink is also associated with a loss of male potency, recalling as it does the common Renaissance notion that each emission of sperm diminishes a man's life and powers. By analogy, each spillage of ink signals a loss of creative potency, particularly as Nashe represents his attempt to control women as overwhelmed by women's "many tongues," "many tales," and "many eyes."

Given the tenor of this paragraph, it is not surprising that we should soon come across a reference to "*Orpheus* the excellentest Musition in any memory, torne in peeces by Women," who are "prone unto carnall cōcupiscence" (16). Anticipating Lacan's statement that images of castration and dismemberment indicate the traumatic effects of aggressivity by the Other, Nashe's imagery crystallizes how sexual and creative potency are symbiotically associated with each other, as the figuring forth of sexual deception by a woman is closely linked to woman's usurpation of man's creative (Orphic) powers.[62] Fantasy, sexuality, and femininity converge here to threaten the creative potency of the icastic male writer.

That woman's usurpation of man's authority should be troped with the language of castration anxiety is something that we have been prepared for early on in the work. Beginning as it does with a reference to Nashe's deception by a woman, *The Anatomie* locates Nashe's very impulse to write in an effort to redress the imbalance caused by his symbolic castration. Sexual frustration, it appears, may be compensated for by creativity in writing.[63] Yet, throughout the work Nashe represents his Zeuxian ideal of mastering women (by writing about them) as a futile enterprise, in part because the cause of unruly women has been taken up by fantastical male writers who have entered into collusion with them (24). Indeed his own reference to the "spillage" of his pen implies that he himself has lost phallic authority to female writers, readers, and patrons.[64]

The imagined usurpation of the icastic poet's authority by deceitful women and fantastical writers is heightened by Nashe's assumption that articulate and aggressive women are reading and critiquing his work, women who, as he puts it, "seeke to stop my mouth by most voices" (11). In a culture in which women are increasingly influential as readers and patrons, if not writers, the notion that women are usurping man's privilege of speech takes on strong cultural resonances as Nashe indirectly demonstrates how his literary output depends on the very female readers whose authority he condemns. Nashe is of course but one of many writers who vividly and vituperatively represent female speech as a direct threat to writing by men. Richard Brathwait writes in much the same vein when he comments, "Truth is, their [women's] tongues are held their defensive armour: but in no particular detract they more from their honour than by giving too free scope to that glibbery member. . . . What restraint is required in respect of the tongue may appear by that ivory guard or garrison with which it is impaled. See how it is double-warded, that it may with more reservancy and better security be restrained!"[65] With words like "impaled" and "double-warded" Brathwait represents the mouth and teeth as a kind of scold's bridle, the brutal form of punishment employed by men to keep women silent. Indeed the details by which Brathwait catalogs the mouth's "natural" defense against speech speaks to the extreme danger that he associates with woman's freedom of expression.

The woman who may well have given rise to many of these fears is the one upon whom Nashe and Brathwait most depended—Queen Elizabeth—yet Nashe wisely excludes this powerful woman from his discursive abuse of womankind. Instead, Nashe represents her as a notable exception to the general run of womankind:

> Whose heauenborne *Elizabeth,* hath made maiestie herselfe mazed, and the worlds eye sight astonied. . . . Peace, sing *io paean,* for that in despight of dissention, she . . . patroniz'd thee vnder her wings. Felicitie saw her invested with royaltie, ... Why seekes my penne to breake into the buildings of Fame, and Eccho my amazed thoughts to her brasen Towres, when as my tongue is too to base a *Tryton* to eternise her praise, that thus vpholdeth our happy daies? (6)

Framing his discourse in the language of praise employed by Boccaccio, Castiglione, Spenser and other defenders of women, Nashe represents Elizabeth as a quasi-celestial being who oversees a golden age of peace and prosperity.

Yet the language that Nashe employs to praise Elizabeth remains disturbingly close to his descriptions of unruly women. Although Elizabeth may be the object of her people's gaze, she controls their sight, turning them into "astonied," or stony, objects of her visage—a Medusa-like power that emanates from her usurpation of male prerogatives of patronage and "royaltie" (not to mention her phallic "Towres").[66] Astonished by her powers, Nashe can do no more than "Eccho" his thoughts; in the process he identifies himself with the female nymph Echo, whose ability to speak is controlled here by an overpowering masculine woman.[67] Immediately juxtaposing Elizabeth with his condemnation of women as sirens and she-devils, Nashe only partially obfuscates a vision of Elizabeth as an unruly woman who, by usurping the privileged position of men, has turned men into emasculated, silenced, and subordinate creatures. If, then, Nashe and Sidney differ in their metaphorical language, both come to associate poets under Queen Elizabeth with idleness, effeminacy, and lies. What further allies Sidney's representation of Elizabeth with Nashe's treatise is their common insistence on the degraded nature of English poetry under their queen.

NASHE'S AESTHETICS OF LACK

If the leitmotif of *The Anatomie* is that femininity and fantasy have usurped the privileged position of male, icastic writers, the text simultaneously gestures to its dependence on the very figurations of femininity and fantasy that it so strongly condemns; for if Nashe succeeds in properly subordinating fantasy and femininity to didacticism and masculinity, he will have no reason to keep on writing. This may be why Nashe's writings, in their infamous tendency towards ornamentation and excess, come to resemble the seductive and deceptive attributes associated with fantasy and femininity.[68]

Given the playful and self-conscious nature of Nashe's writing, it is perhaps not surprising that he should admit to having been contaminated by the very forces that he criticizes; as the work progresses, he not only employs fantastical ornamentation but audaciously equates writers of abuse literature (like himself) with *phantastiké*. He does so most notably when he condemns writers who "anatomize abuses and stubbe vp sin by the rootes, whē as there waste paper beeing wel viewed, seemes fraught with nought els saue dogge daies effects" (20). Although this statement may seem to be a way for Nashe to separate himself from irresponsible anatomizers by satirizing them, his own reputation for expressing himself excrementally would suggest that he is indeed one of these "waste paper" writers whom he condemns.[69] Such inconsistencies may indicate the strain that results from the attempt to assimilate a number of complex and self-contradictory notions about fantasy and femininity; but it is equally true that Nashe often celebrates, even calls attention to, the contradictions inherent in his writings.

What can be affirmed is that *The Anatomie of Absurditie* lends itself to two complementary approaches. For if—on the discursive level—Nashe thoroughly abuses fantasy and femininity, his style, narrative structure, and metaphors all implicate him in the very processes that he inveighs against.[70] Indeed, by implying that the threatening, even castrating aspects of fantasy and femininity are the sources of his inspiration, Nashe is indirectly (perhaps not quite consciously) setting forth a potentially enabling aesthetics of symbolic castration, or Lack. In contrast to current assertions that "phallocentrism . . . depends on the image of the castrated women to give order and meaning to its world," the metaphorics of Nashe's text depends on projecting a world of phallic women and castrated male authors; for the sense of Lack caused by the threat of authorial castration is what inspires this author to fill his writings with a Rabelaisian profusion of words.[71]

The very overdetermination of these images of castration reinforces my contention that they project a playful alternative to orthodox notions of inspiration. By covertly identifying his writings with the threatening forces of fantasy and femininity, even effeminacy, Nashe implicates his writings in what is marginal, provocative, and potentially original. On the discursive level he may associate his writings with masculine, icastic authority, while structurally and metaphorically he shapes his work as a playful, unauthorized feminine (or effeminate) mode of writing. He is, it seems, less interested in making sense of this inherent contradiction than in celebrating himself as generating both modes of writing. His icastic, discursive, and misogynistic statements place him firmly in the didactic and conventional mode of debate treatises of the period, while his fantastical, rhetorical, and castrating metaphorics implicate him in a paradoxically enabling aesthetics of effeminacy—enabling because it allows him to distance himself from convention and, by extension, to imply that he is an original writer. In the process, this gendered association with effeminacy enables him to suggest that he is among a new generation of feminized writers who are renewing English literature by displacing the traditional, masculine hegemony over writing.

JANE ANGER AND EFFEMINATE *PHANTASTIKÉ*

It would be tempting to argue that Nashe's treatise was a vituperative response to writings by women, writings like Jane Anger's *Jane Anger, Her Protection for Women,* since both treatises were published in the same year. Equally inviting is the notion that Nashe's invective inspired Anger to retaliate with her heated defense of women. While we cannot ascertain whether either scenario is correct, it certainly seems true that Anger's treatise threatens to fulfill the anxieties about womankind that define Nashe's treatises. Anger seems determined to "stop . . . [Nashe's] mouth" by arguing vehemently against his claim that women are seductive and deceitful creatures. And she does so—perhaps coincidentally—by echoing, while problematizing, the structure of Nashe's treatise. Nashe, we have seen, moves from a discussion of woman's essential unruliness to a description of women as art objects, to a diatribe against men who have allowed themselves to be metaphorically castrated by "masculine" women. Anger parallels (while mutating) this structure by, first, affirming male (rather than female) unruliness, then condemning men for scapegoating women via their artistic fantasies, and, finally, suggesting that it is men who have castrated themselves by wallowing in effeminate fantasies about women. Yet while Anger's outline inverts Nashe's argument, she ends up tracing the same conceptual ground as does Nashe. For when Anger associates men with fantasy, she (like Nashe and Sidney) characterizes them as effeminate. Fantasy and effeminacy, then, remain strongly associated with each other, except that, in Anger's construction, it is exclusively effeminate men—not women as well—who represent seductive and deceitful fantasy.

Anger first sets forth her analogy between fantasy and effeminacy by condemning men's deceptive ways: "Fie on the falsehood of men, whose minds go oft a-madding and whose tongues cannot so soon be wagging, but straight they fall a-tattling!"[72] Already she has charged men with lying and garrulousness, two attributes that Nashe consistently associates with unruly women. By thus inverting misogynistic abuses like Nashe's, Anger suggests that men, having misused their privilege of speech, have lost their right to employ it exclusively, or even to employ it at all.[73] As such, she is able to shape a defense of woman's "many tongues" and "many tales." This is why Anger adds that male writers "run so into rhetoric as oftentimes they overrun the bounds of their own wits, and go they know not whither. . . there remains but one help, which is, to write of us women" (32). Where, for Nashe, fantastical writings are the product of men who have been effeminized by seductive women, Anger claims that these writings result from male writers who have simply run out of ideas to write about. By extension, works like Nashe's, which abuse womankind, are "dogge daies effects," since they contain nothing of truth or significance.[74]

The urgency of Anger's voice here seems to emerge from her desire to dissociate women from a particularly abusive series of associations between women, fantasy, and prostitution. The easy linkage between these three concepts is articulated in Sidney's *A Defence of Poetry,* as he condemns English eloquence for its "courtesan-like painted affectation: one time, with so far-fet words that may seem monsters but must seem strangers to any poor Englishman; another time, with coursing of a letter, as if they were bound to follow the method of a dictionary; another time, with figures and flowers, extremely winter-starved" (70). Both Anger and Sidney condemn writers who privilege rhetoric over matter, thus creating fantastical, sophistical, and, hence, insignificant writings; but Anger's language lacks the misogynistic rendering of rhetoric as a "courtesan-like painted affectation"—a simile that Nashe comes close to echoing in his portrayal of female artistry as seductive, deceitful, and heavily ornamental. Anger attempts to undo this problematic association by linking male, rather than female, artistry with fantasy, with a love of rhetorical ornamentation for its own sake and with a fantastical stretching of invention. Men, she asserts, are fantastical, sophistical poets in search of a scapegoat to victimize through their writings, and that scapegoat is almost inevitably woman.

I pause at this passage because it illuminates how Anger unmasks a tendency among Renaissance writers to slip from discussions of fantasy, to femininity, to prostitution. This slippage is most famously expressed and exposed throughout *Hamlet*, notably in Hamlet's famous projection onto Ophelia of all the deceits and seductions associated with womankind—his "nunnery" speech. Yet if Hamlet sounds like Sidney's narrator when he links women with prostitution, Shakespeare seems to have been thinking more like Anger; for Claudius, it turns out, is the actual "courtesan" of this play. Spying on the scene between Ophelia and Hamlet, Claudius confesses to himself that

> The harlot's cheek, beautied with plast'ring art,
> Is not more ugly to the thing that helps it
> Than is my deed to my most painted word.[75]

Claudius's association of his dark deeds with prostitution, makeup, and deceitful rhetoric illuminates Anger's contention that conceptualizations of women as seductive and deceitful are simply male projections of their own problematic practices. As she puts it, "we being well formed are by them foully deformed" (35).

Anger's project, then, is to undo misogynistic models of femininity, such as those articulated by Nashe and by Sidney in his *digressio*. Thus, if for Nashe woman is inherently an unruly, deceitful, and seductive creature who can only be tamed by the Zeuxian artist, woman is for Anger naturally obedient. She is, in fact, a creature of "honest bashfulness" (33) who has been slandered by the misogynistic fantasies of male artists.[76] To bolster her defense of womankind, Anger depends heavily on one positive cultural association with women (ignored by Nashe)—the tendency to express virtue as feminine (35). This common expression leads her to affirm that a woman "loveth good things and hateth that which is evil; she loveth justice and hateth iniquity; she loveth truth and true dealing and hateth lies and falsehood" (35–36). Each of these statements defuses the concept of woman as aggressive and castrating, without, in the process, affirming woman as art object.

ANGER'S UNRULINESS

Yet if Anger's purpose is to overturn negative constructions of women, the effect of her project is less radical than it might seem. Like most participants in defenses of women—like Boccaccio (in *Concerning Famous Women*), like Edward More, and like Gosynhill (in *Mulierum Paean*), Anger does not claim that woman is superior to or even necessarily socially equal to man; rather she demands respect for woman within her appropriately subordinated position as "the greatest help that men have" (36). By extension, Anger claims that her purpose is to berate men so as to return them to their traditional position of authority and truth; for this reason she stresses how easily men have allowed themselves to lose their position of superiority: "Wealth makes them lavish, wit knavish, beauty effeminate, poverty deceitful" (37). Anger, in other words, argues that it is only by reaffirming and reestablishing the traditional hierarchy of authoritative, virtuous men and subordinate passive women that men will cease projecting onto women such vices as deceit and seduction.

Anger's articulated desire to return society to its traditional hierarchy at once enables and problematizes her defense of womankind. Much as Nashe's emotional and elaborate invective against fantasy implicates him in the very processes that he purports to condemn, so Anger's energetic defense of women belies her contention that woman is the weaker, more modest sex. This may, in fact, explain why mention of Queen Elizabeth—an obvious *exemplum* of virtuous womankind—is omitted from the treatise. Elizabeth, we have seen, may be read as an aggressive usurper of masculine prerogatives. The tension between Anger's representation of women as essentially modest and her self-representation as aggressive is made apparent in her occasional tendency to contradict her assertions that women should be subordinated to men (so long as men remain virtuous); in fact she remarks that "God making woman of man's flesh— that she might be purer than he—doth evidently show how far we women are more excellent than men" (39).[77]

Where Nashe never quite attempts to get himself out of the contradictions inherent in his treatise (in fact he seems to take great pleasure in them), Anger employs discursive argumentation to affirm a solution to the conflict between her argument in favor of passive women and her self-representation as a strong, aggressive woman. Much as Shakespeare, in his comedies, represents aggressive women as arising from a culture in which men are incapable of governing well, so Anger, in her treatise, states that "in this year of '88 men are grown so fantastical" that only a woman can redress the order of society (40). Despite this rationale, Anger's tendency to dwell on the effeminate character of men and to represent herself as aggressive, even castrating, makes her treatise resemble Nashe's in a number of ways. Like Nashe, Anger creates a sense of urgency to her mission, and, like his argument, hers depends on scapegoating the opposite sex: just as Nashe blames the downfall of English writing on men's effeminacy (brought on by seductive women), so Anger blames effeminate men for their fantastical writings (about women). And if both authors condemn fantasy for its association with lies, subversion, and lust, their very preoccupation with these terms, as well as their own inventive modes of representation, indicate that fantasy is at once the kind of writing they condemn and the kind of writing they employ to get their readers' attention. Anger and Nashe are not, finally, as opposed in ideology as they at first appear; for both come to associate effeminacy, lies, and subversion with fantastical male poets.

Anger's pamphlet most recalls Nashe's in a tendency to employ rhetoric which undermines her discursive statements. Anger's delight in proliferating abusive language, ornamental rhetoric, and elaborate metaphors suggests an ultimate dependance on the very seductive, fantastical, and ornamental phrasings that she associates with deceptive, effeminate male writers. This splitting of the narratorial ego points in several directions at once. Most notably, it demonstrates how impossible, conceptually, it is for a sixteenth-century woman to conceive of a female authoritative voice: she may only speak authoritatively by identifying with masculinity. Hence her discursive speech—aggressive, authoritative, and didactic—is often indistinguishable from that of male writers of abuse literature like Gabriel Harvey, Nashe, and Gosson.[78] Yet by employing fantastical rhetoric that she has characterized as effeminate, Anger has, on some level, castrated her authoritative voice, hence returning her to a feminine (lacking the phallus), subordinate position. And indeed part of her ongoing project in this treatise is to make the conceptually difficult distinction between effeminate fantasy and feminine virtue. This distinction is made all the more difficult because Anger can only articulate a virtuous female voice by silencing both her authoritative male and ornamental effeminate voices—by becoming silent, chaste, and subordinate to patriarchal authority.

While, then, this confusion of narrative identity results from cultural conceptualizations that an authoritative voice can only be masculine, it also seems to result from Anger's ultimate fascination with the very fantastical and effeminate rhetoric that she is so busy condemning. Indeed, by the end of the work Anger seems more intent on calling attention to the extravagance of her writing than on attending to her discursive defense of woman's virtue. Unlike, for instance, Shakespeare's comic heroines (with whom she shares characteristics of aggressivity and masculinity) she does not, in the end, re-feminize herself by subordinating herself to a man; rather her peroration recasts the different arguments throughout her tract in such a way as to open up the possibility for continued female dominance:

At the end of men's fair promises there is a labyrinth, and therefore ever hereafter stop your ears when they protest friendship lest they come to an end before you are aware—whereby you fall without redemption. The path which leadeth thereunto is man's wit, and the miles' ends are marked with these trees: Folly, Vice, Mischief, Lust, Deceit and Pride. These, to deceive you, shall be clothed in the raiments of Fancy, Virtue, Modesty, Love, True-meaning and Handsomeness. (44)

Anger once more projects upon men the characteristics of fantasy, deceit, and seduction normally associated with women. As if responding to Nashe's early reference to women as sirens, this passage attributes the seductive and fatal call of the sirens to men. She then goes on to blame Adam (rather than Eve) for the fall of mankind, and to associate men's deceitful wit with the metaphor of clothing, a metaphor that, we have seen, Nashe employs to associate women with lies and seduction.[79]

Yet if this brilliant inversion of misogynistic metaphors draws attention to Anger's skill at undermining arguments such as Nashe's, it also undermines Anger's own stated purpose. For one thing, it shows no hope that Anger will succeed in transforming men from effeminate, seductive creatures into masculine, virtuous heroes—as it ends with no vision of a return to conventional gendered hierarchy. For another, Anger's rhetoric consistently resonates with the very attributes that she rails against. Her narrative structure can only be described as labyrinthine; her language is as seductive and witty as that of the male pamphleteers whom she condemns; and her rhetoric is as ornamental as the "clothed" writings of these men. Different as they are in content, the methods that Anger employs to convert her male readers are, ultimately, as dependent on seduction and deceit as are those by Nashe. Like Nashe she appears to concede, on some level, that deceit, seduction, and fantasy are crucial to the experience of writing.

If, then, Nashe's discursive condemnation of effeminate men is contradicted by his metaphorics of castration, Anger's abuse of effeminacy and fantasy cloaks her self-representation both as a castrating woman and an effeminate male. The result is a narrative self-representation that fits in neither with traditional defenses of women nor with misogynistic pamphlets (both usually scripted by men). It is true that Anger's treatise, to a large extent, recalls a defense like More's—which defends women by focusing on the ways in which men slander women, or like Gosynhill's *Mulierum Paean*—which emphasizes woman's essential chastity. Yet Anger complements such traditional defenses with a narrative metaphorics of woman as articulate and aggressive—as a kind of white knight who defends her own sex's reputation. In the process she establishes a model of womankind as aggressive, garrulous, and unruly, yet free of the vices of deception and seduction which Nashe and even Sidney associate with unruly women. Anger, in other words, makes it possible for a biological woman to speak in a "masculine" authoritative voice. In the process she demystifies the fantasy of Zeuxis, the notion that the ideal woman can only be a fantastical artifice shaped by the poet.[80]

This project of representing woman's voice constructively is, of course, attenuated by Anger's second voice—effeminate, fantastical, and deceitful. Without foregrounding this problem as consciously as does Nashe, Anger seems to identify her metaphorics with a language of ornamentation, Lack, and frivolity. She appears to do so in order to lay claim to one positive aspect of misogynistic writing—the tendency, inadvertently, to associate a feminine or effeminate style with originality, with an alternative to patriarchal, conventional writing. Of course, simply by being a woman, Anger is already disrupting the conventional voice of Renaissance debate pamphlets. But it seems that, like Nashe and Sidney, the almost automatic association between effeminacy (or femininity) and disruption of masculine convention leads Anger to affirm, indirectly, the very fantastical style that she claims to be silencing throughout her tract.

If Anger's treatise serves as an interesting complement to Nashe's invective—sharing the same language and metaphors as Nashe but employing them to different ends—her work is nonetheless something of an anomaly in this project, which is almost exclusively devoted to male writers. I have discussed Anger's defense here because the areas in which she differs from male writers like Nashe illuminate, by contrast, certain fairly constant preoccupations among male—and often female—writers of the period. Most marked is the tendency to associate authority, truth, and convention with masculinity, while expressing fantasy as the opposite of masculinity—as effeminate. Equally interesting is the way that both pamphleteers indirectly affirm a poetics of effeminacy, even castration, a poetics that betrays an ultimate proclivity for the fantastical, deceitful styles that they are so busy abusing. The difference between Nashe and Anger, then, inheres primarily in the gender to which they attribute fantasy—and even that is not always so different: Anger associates fantasy with effeminacy; Nashe associates it with both effeminacy and femininity. Echoing consciously or inadvertently Sidney's ambivalent gendering of poetry, Nashe and Anger epitomize how a splitting of discursive statement and metaphorical rhetoric gestures to a cultural fascination with and concern about the seductive, deceitful and effeminate style of fantasy. Sidney's eventual identification with the effeminate poets whom he at first condemns allows him to identify with an emerging and innovative English poetics separate from the dominant, masculine, and Italianate tradition of the past. On the other hand, Nashe's tendency to employ the very ornamental and effeminate rhetoric that he condemns implies that, on some level, he celebrates an alternative to a conventional Zeuxian aesthetics of artistic mastery. So, too, then, Anger's aggressively masculine voice along with her effeminately ornamental rhetoric problematize her discursive affirmation of subordinated and silenced women.

This veiled but consistent interest in effeminate fantasy is why, I suggest, all three treatises conclude with the very fantastical flourishes that they so actively condemn. Within this feminine or effeminate ornamental language lies the possibility for shaping a poetical identity that is distinct from the dominant, didactic and patriarchal tradition of Renaissance prose treatises like Castelvetro's

Poetica d'Aristotele and the anonymous *Proude Wyves Pater Noster*—whether these treatises be about poetry, women, or both. Yet Sidney, Nashe, and Anger never fully articulate this alternative and emerging tradition of writing. Indeed it may well be that the very strictures of the genre of polemical writing keep them from doing so. Certainly a number of writers openly celebrate a fantastical and feminine (or effeminate) style only when they move from didactic treatise to fiction—hence Boccaccio's strong defense of didactic poetry in his treatise, *Genealogia Deorum Gentilium* and his celebration of fantasy in his *Decameron*. Sidney is perhaps the most salient example of this pattern, as his *Old Arcadia* and *Astrophil and Stella* (written contemporaneously with *A Defence of Poetry*) express far more openly a poetics of feminine or effeminate fantasy than do the indirect, metaphorical references to such a poetics in *A Defence*. The chapters that follow trace how prodigal fictions foreground the very feminine or effeminate poetics that are only adumbrated in treatises. Whether it be Pasquier's dialogue (itself liminally poised between fiction and nonfiction), Sidney's lyrics, Boccaccio's prose fiction, or Shakespeare's drama, the fictional status of these varied genres seems to liberate their authors from any experiential obligations to the cultural conventions of patriarchy. It is to these fictional genres that I turn, in the following chapters, to trace how and why authors of prodigal fictions celebrate a poetics of feminine or effeminate fantasy that didactic treatises by Sidney, Nashe, and Anger discursively condemn.

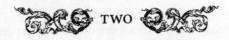

TWO

Exchanges of Women and Words: Etienne Pasquier's Rewriting of *The Courtier*

Monophile speaks, above all, to the gaps between sixteenth-century tastes and our own. While the text was popular enough to gain Etienne Pasquier entry into the French court, neither this early piece nor, for that matter, any of Pasquier's writings, have acquired and retained the canonical status that writings by Pasquier's friends Montaigne, Ronsard, and du Bellay hold.[1] Indeed those few scholars who mention *Monophile* dismiss it as a "light diversion" or as "all but unreadable today."[2] Given the text's interest in the trade in women, in figurations of women as silenced objects, and in the commodification of gender construction, one would expect this dialogue to claim the attention of contemporary literary scholars; yet critics read the work almost exclusively from an aesthetic perspective, generally representing it as a less engaging version of *The Courtier.* Hence critics note that the characters in *Monophile* lack the kind of lively personalities that Castiglione gives to his characters in *The Courtier;* or that Pasquier's speakers tend to utter long monologues that contrast strongly with the short, witty repartee of Castiglione's speakers.

But these perceived weaknesses tell us more about twentieth-century aesthetic expectations than they do about early modern responses to dialogues like *Monophile;* for sixteenth-century readers were quite accustomed to the conventions of dialogue, a genre which has as much to do with essay writing and philosophy as it does with fiction.[3] These readers would have known that most dialogues lack the kind of careful attention to character and pacing that is conventional to much of narrative fiction.[4] And they would have been attentive to pleasing cultural encodings in the work, such as Pasquier's strong nationalistic perspective—which led him to interrogate the Italo-centric (specifically Urbino-centric) leanings of *The Courtier.*[5] At a time when France was achieving military dominance over Italy without having acquired literary dominance over it, Pasquier's text (like texts by many of his French contemporaries) purports to displace Italian with French literature by foregrounding a prophecy in *The Courtier* that France will be the next important center of aesthetic production.[6]

Pasquier displaces *The Courtier* by consistently demystifing its profeminist utterances. In doing so he essentially follows the advice of the Count in *The Courtier,* who asserts that, "se Virgilio avesse in tutto imitato Esiodo, non gli serìa passato inanzi; né Cicerone a Crasso, né Ennio ai suoi antecessori" [if Virgil had slavishly imitated Hesiod he would not have surpassed him; neither would Cicero have surpassed Crassus, nor Ennius those who preceded him].[7] At a time when France was surpassing Italy politically, Pasquier competes with *The Courtier* by representing this earlier classic as pathologically dependent on the silencing of women. Pasquier replaces this homosocial paradigm with a heterosocial dialogue based on exchanges of words rather than women.

The means by which Pasquier displaces *The Courtier* are inscribed within *The Courtier* itself. Early in the dialogue Castiglione represents Federico da Montefeltro (the former Duke of Urbino) as an unparalleled poet-soldier whose generous patronage of arts and letters made Urbino the cynosure of Renaissance courts.[8] It is, according to Castiglione's courtiers, the lack of such a figure that explains why the French have yet to experience the kind of cultural Renaissance that made Urbino famous. But one character, the Magnifico, notes that France may soon gain such a ruler, if, as he comments,

> la bona sorte vole che monsignor d'Angolem, come si spera, succeda alla corona, estimo che sì come la gloria dell'arme fiorisce e risplende in Francia, così vi debba ancor con supremo ornamento fiorir quella delle lettere. (158)

> good fortune has it that Monseigneur d'Angoulême, as it is hoped, succeeds to the throne, then I believe that just as the glory of arms flourishes and shines in France, so also with the greatest brilliance must that of letters. (88)

Lodovico goes on to praise Monseigneur d'Angoulême—the future Francis I—for his good looks, graciousness, valor, and learning, implying that he will soon become the French Federico da Montefeltro.[9]

Writing under the aegis of Francis I, Pasquier is able to confirm this prophecy by calling attention to the growing hegemony of France over Italy during the reign of Francis I. He does so, first, by claiming that the events of *Monophile* took place

> Peu de têps apres le voyage d'Almaigne, & la glorieuse entreprise du Roy, tant pour l'illustration de ce siecle que de la posterité, les ennemis ayans levé le siege de Mets, avec leur grande honte & confusion.

shortly after the invasion of Germany, and the glorious undertaking of the king, when as much for the glory of the era as for posterity, the enemy raised the siege of Metz, to their great shame and confusion.[10]

Pasquier refers here to Francis I's victory over Charles V at Metz, a victory so overwhelming that it led Charles V to abdicate his position as Emperor of the Holy Roman Empire. This triumphant victory—which secured France a great deal of influence over Italy as well as Germany—contrasts strongly with the minor military victory around which *The Courtier* is structured. As Castiglione himself reminds us, Urbino, under its current ruler Guidobaldo, is no longer the great nation that it was under Federico da Montefeltro.

For Pasquier and Castiglione, then, military prowess depends on a strong patriarchal figure, a common preoccupation that gives rise to an ongoing concern about gender in both works. Scholars have noted how fears about the loss of masculine military power are expressed in *The Courtier* via anxieties about the effeminization of the court, dominated as it is by a woman—the Duchess of Urbino. In *Monophile,* on the other hand, such anxieties are transformed into celebratory experiments with gender roles. It is as if, secure of its masculine prowess, France becomes a space within which its citizens may safely play with gender conventions. Perhaps for this reason characters in *Monophile* tend to envision the courtly world as a constructive feminine complement to its warrior identity—rather than as a weak, effeminizing enclosure.[11]

By openly engaging and critiquing issues of power and gender expressed in *The Courtier, Monophile* enters into a complex oedipal relationship with its influential Italian predecessor. Up to a point this relationship fits the classic pattern of the return of the repressed: Pasquier displaces Federico da Montefeltro with Francis I, only to have Francis I identify with the same military and cultural characteristics that defined Montefeltro. Yet the discussions about gender that take place within *Monophile* never fully return to those broached in *The Courtier,* as the characters in *Monophile* are more likely to affirm unconventional notions of gender—such as amazonian women or hermaphrodites.

Anticipating later works within the tradition of the "querelle des femmes" (anticipating, indeed, recent theories by feminist scholars), Pasquier has his characters unveil the ways in which *The Courtier,* despite (or because of) its profeminist statements, depends on a homosocial paradigm which perpetuates the conventional ideal of woman as chaste, silent and obedient. In strong contrast Pasquier shapes a community that privileges heterosocial dialogues, dialogues dependent on mediations of words rather than women. Pasquier is thus able to accommodate female debaters within his courtly circle; in the process he suggests that this newer paradigm is more vital and, perhaps, more French, than the somewhat conservative, conventional, and Italianate structure of *The Courtier.*[12] Looking, first, at the ways that Castiglione and Pasquier gender their courts as feminine or effeminate, I will go on to examine how Pasquier interrogates the three major structures by which patriarchal culture has, traditionally, established its authority over women (all three of which are encoded in *The Courtier*): mediations by women; the Zeuxian objectification of women; and the patriarchal system of dowries. These structures are most radically interrogated by Pasquier's own interruption of his dialogue towards its end, an interruption which he associates with hermaphroditic voicings.

Pasquier has, it turns out, a somewhat self-interested reason for promoting innovative constructions of gender—a reason that is associated with his background as a commoner. Where Castiglione, born into the Italian court, reveals an ongoing desire to maintain the patriarchal conventions by which Italian nobility defined itself, Pasquier, as an outsider to the French court, would be more interested in interrogating such conventions so as to make room for nontraditional aspirants, like himself, within the court.[13] He does so by displacing issues of class onto those of gender; for it is by defending the access of women to courtly debates that he opens up the possibility of allowing other outsiders—such as commoners—into this coterie.[14] Equally self-interested are Pasquier's associations of unconventional femininity with originality: by defending amazonian women Pasquier is able to represent his own voice as unconventional and innovative. Yet these self-interested positions do not, finally, vitiate the work's powerful defense of aggressive and articulate women. Pasquier's novel conceptualization of the French court may well have been a fiction, but it proved powerful enough to attract the patronage of Marguerite de Navarre and the Dames des Roches—women whose own precarious positions of power would have drawn them to Pasquier's rendering of women as constructively active and articulate.[15]

FICTION AND FEMININE ENCLOSURES

Pasquier is, of course, no radical; his intent is to open up the aristocratic coterie, not to dismantle it. In much the same way, he defends articulate women, but draws the line at including women within such traditionally masculine roles as military service. Indeed Pasquier's unquestioned association of military aggression with masculinity explains why his dialogue, like Castiglione's, is framed by references to military skirmishes—actions that set up a decided contrast to the construction of the courtly space as feminine. In much the same way *The Courtier* takes place as the Prefect returns from a successful military engagement; however, the celebration that follows this victory calls attention to the larger failure of military activity in Italy—its scattering and fragmentation by the French, symbolized by the impotent body of Guidobaldo, the current Duke of Urbino.[16] Against this larger framework of the impotent male warrior, Castiglione crafts a compensating model of cultured aristocrat, whose successes lie in entertaining his prince and the court ladies by engaging in verbal skirmishes with fellow courtiers.

But this model of courtly dialogue becomes inescapably associated with notions of femininity as passive, idle, and ornamental (notions articulated later by Nashe).[17] These problematic associations lead Ottaviano to contend that

> queste attillature, imprese, motti ed altre tai cose che appartengono ad intertenimenti di donne e d'amori, . . . spesso non fanno altro che effeminar gli animi . . .; onde nascono poi questi effeti che'l nome italiano è ridutto in obbrobrio. (450)

> these elegances of dress, devices, mottoes and other such things that belong to the world of women and romance often, . . . serve simply to make men effeminate. . . . And the consequences are that the name of Italy is brought into disgrace. (284)[18]

The familiar associations between femininity, effeminacy, and ornamentation are articulated here in order to affirm distinctions between the ways that men and women ornament themselves. The implication is (as Ottaviano goes on to note) that male ornamentation is somehow more useful and experiential than its female counterpart, promoting as it does significant artistry and important diplomatic victories. Count Lodovico attempts to make the same distinction when he asserts, famously, that

> voglio io che sia lo aspetto del nostro cortegiano, non così molle e feminile come si sforzano d'aver molti, che non solamente si crespano i capegli e

spelano le ciglia, ma si strisciano con tutti que' modi che si faccian le più lascive e disoneste femine del mondo; e pare che nello andare, nello stare ed in ogni altro lor atto siano tanto teneri e languidi, che le membra siano per staccarsi loro l'uno dall'altro. . . . Questi, poichè la natura, come essi mostrano desiderare di parere ed essere, no gli ha fatti femine, dovrebbono non come bone femine esser estimati, ma, come publiche meretrici, non solamente delle corti de' gran signori, ma del consorzio degli omini nobili esser cacciati. (114)

I don't want him (the courtier) to appear soft and feminine as so many try to do, when they not only curl their hair and pluck their eyebrows but also preen themselves like the most wanton and dissolute creatures imaginable. Indeed, they appear so effeminate and languid in the way they walk, or stand, or do anything at all, that their limbs look as if they are about to fall apart. . . . Since Nature has not in fact made them the ladies they want to seem and be, they should be treated not as honest women but as common whores and be driven out from all gentlemanly society, let alone the Courts of great lords. (61)

The very details into which the Count enters suggests how difficult it is for the male courtier to distinguish his courtly dress from idle, effeminate ornamentation.[19] Indeed the Count not only characterizes the ornamental courtier as effeminate but reaffirms an early modern tendency to associate femininity and effeminacy with whorish eloquence—an association, we have seen, that would later be employed by Nashe, Sidney, and Shakespeare. Behind the aureate description of the cultured and sophisticated courtier lies the anxiety that such courtiers are courtesan-like creatures who employ their ornamental dress and elegant ways not to improve the court but to prostitute themselves before the prince.

In order to distinguish the ideal male courtier from his whorish and effeminate double, Lodovico attempts to reinscribe conventional distinctions between men and women; hence he affirms that men are active performers, while women make up a passive audience. But, as Lodovico's comments make clear, the courtiers in Urbino are painfully aware that most of them can at best fulfill the latter half of the fundamental definition of the courtier as a man active in arms and letters (90). If their failures as soldiers inspire them to speak and perform eloquently, their constant need to reaffirm traditional distinctions between men and women calls attention to how difficult it is, ultimately, to separate masculine from feminine ornamentation.[20] The fact that the debates take place in the inner recesses of the Duchess's private rooms only reinforces the close symbiotic relationship between the courtly model of masculinity and the traditional construction of the courtly lady; for the locus of the dialogues implies that the feminine space overpowers and thus symbolically castrates the ambitious courtier (as Nashe and Sidney would later imply that Queen Elizabeth does). It suggests, by implication, that the courtly world is a kind of ornamental fiction, isolated as it is from the external workings of the male political realm. Yet it is within the feminized enclosure of the Duchess's chambers that these courtiers shape a compensatory fiction for their failure as a warrior class. This is why, I would argue, the courtiers at once celebrate femininity and attempt to distance themselves from it: their self-articulation as successful male courtiers depends on nonchalantly concealing their complicity in a fictionalized world of ornamental effeminacy.[21]

Pasquier's speakers, in contrast, seem far less concerned with the possible effeminization of the French court. Indeed, in *Monophile*, the movement from an exterior, public, masculine space into an interior, feminized fiction is represented as a deserved and welcome retreat from the experience of war—a necessary complement to the courtier's practice in arms, rather than a debased substitute for it:

> Celuy qui festoyoit les autres, estoit contraint et obligé convier à leur festin les plus honestes e mieux disantes Damoyselles qui se trouuvassent celle part: à fin que chacun d'eux peut prendre avec elles contentement en tout honneur: esperans, par ce moyen se payer en partie des arrerages du bon temps, que Fortune leur avoit tenu en espargne depuis le commencement des guerres. (1v)

> Whoever entertained the others was constrained and obligated to invite to his celebrations the most chaste and well-spoken ladies who might be found there: so that each young man might partake in honorable pleasure with them, hoping, by this means, to find partial repayment for the arrears of pleasure which fortune had held in deposit for them since the beginning of the wars.

Like Castiglione, Pasquier associates the courtly space with femininity; yet, for Pasquier, this identification leads not to male effeminacy but rather to an affirmation of traditional male and female roles: women grant pleasure to men in return for their military protection.

It is perhaps because Pasquier's work lacks anxieties of effeminacy that this early passage unthreateningly disrupts convention by representing women as not only conventionally chaste but also "well-spoken"—an attribute that, in *The Courtier*, is almost exclusively a male prerogative. As Peter Stallybrass and Margaret Ferguson have noted, the pairing of chastity with speech was a problematic and precarious association for an aristocratic woman, as it disrupted the almost automatic association, during the Renaissance, between chastity and silence, sexual license and speech.[22] Yet the chaste, articulate lady is clearly, for Pasquier, the ideal court lady, who alone can aid the courtier to "partake in honorable pleasure." A discourse that substitutes verbal for sexual intercourse is, it appears, the ideal exchange between men and women in Pasquier's vision of the French court.[23] This representation at once enables women to participate in courtly circulations of speech and prevents them from becoming silenced, sexualized objects. By extension, Pasquier's dialogue shows far less concern with demarcating the boundaries between serious, masculine speech and ornamental, feminine fiction; both are celebrated in the work as proper for male and female speakers.

It is within the pleasurable context of this respite from battle that we encounter four of Pasquier's five main characters: Monophile, the conventional Petrarchan lover; Philopole, the promiscuous courtier (whose acerbic wit recalls that of Castiglione's Gaspare Pallavicino); Glaphire, a man who loves many women honorably; and, later in the dialogue, Pasquier himself, who, unlike Castiglione, claims to have been a witness to and participant in the proceedings he writes about. Pasquier's tendency to move freely in and out of his own text as author, narrator, and participant is paralleled by his representation of Charilée as a court lady who navigates fluidly between conventions of femininity and the processes of masculine debate. Although she does not participate in the debate between older and younger courtiers on the duties of a military commander, she judges it by noting that "tels discours ne se rapportent assez mal à vostre aage" [such discourse has little to do with the interests of young people] (4), thus inspiring Glaphire and Philopole to retreat from the older crowd into an isolated garden. They have already been preceded by the melancholy Monophile, who enters the garden in order to meditate on his passion for his unnamed beloved.

This conscious movement from the conventionally masculine experience of war, to a debate about war in the court, to a retreat into a lush garden is represented as a movement from experience to fiction. Much as Urbino is associated with "infinità di statue antiche di marmo e di bronzo, pitture singularissime" (17) [countless antique statues of marble and bronze, with rare pictures (41)], so the court garden of Francis I, with its "petit tapis d'herbe verte" [small tapestry of green grasses] and its trees which resemble a "temple umbrageux" [shady temple] (6v) is as much a locus of art as it is of nature.[24] For both Castiglione and Pasquier, then, the enclosures of court and fiction are equally feminine; the difference is that Castiglione's characters often attempt to shore up and reconstruct a world of masculine privilege within the feminized space of the court, while Pasquier's characters more often employ this space to interrogate such patriarchal conventions as the trade in women, the objectification of women, and the patriarchal system of marriage.

Women and Mediation

We have seen that in Castiglione's work the ambiguous gendering of the ideal courtier gestures to anxieties of courtly effeminacy; in contrast, Pasquier's much stronger foregrounding of femininity expresses a greater ease with feminine influences on the courtier. This is why characters in *Monophile* often foreground the ways in which homosocial culture depends on mediations by women, while characters in *The Courtier* more often elide this issue. Castiglione avoids the issue by representing his courtly women as actively and voluntarily excluding themselves from the courtly processes of debate.[25] By extension, his work implies that mediations by women are simply not relevant to the structure of the debate; instead, woman's role is simply to act as witness to male courtly exchanges. Yet in his dedication to Ariosto Castiglione describes the Duchess in such a way as to suggest that the court of Urbino in fact depends on mediations by women:

> ché, . . . a tutti nascea nell'animo una summa contentezza ogni volta che al conspetto della signora Duchessa ci riducevamo; e parea che questa fosse una catena che tutti in amor tenesse uniti, talmente che mai non fu concordia di voluntà o amore cordiale tra fratelli maggior di quello, che quivi tra tutti era. (85–86)

> For, we all felt supremely happy whenever we came into the presence of the Duchess; and this sense of contentment formed between us a bond of affection so strong that even between brothers there could never have been such harmonious agreement and heartfelt love as there was among us all. (43)

Homosocial bondings between courtiers are described here as dependent on the Duchess's mediatory presence. From this perspective the role of women in *The Courtier* is to foster "discussion, without themselves . . . exercising the power of speech that is rightly theirs."[26] *The Courtier* as a result projects two distinct representations of the courtly coterie: its internal circle consists of men whose debates (frequently involving definitions of femininity) reinforce this circle's status as the center of social power; the external circle of this group consists of a predominantly silent audience of women which mediates and judges the mens' linguistic exchanges.[27] It is because this external circle is crucial to the exchanges within it that Cesare Gonzaga affirms

> come corte alcuna, per grande che ella sia, non po aver ornamento o splendore in sé, né allegria senza donne, né cortegiano alcun essere aggraziato,

piacevole o ardito, né far mai opera leggiadra di cavalleria, se non mosso dalla pratica e dall'amore e piacer di donne. (340)

There is no Court, however great, that can possess adornment or splendour or gaiety without the presence of women, and no courtier, no matter how graceful, pleasing or bold, who can ever perform gallant deeds of chivalry unless inspired by the loving and delightful company of women. (210)

Gonzaga's statement clarifies why there are such ambiguities about the status of women among the courtiers of Urbino. While women are silenced and effaced by exchanges between men, this silence gestures to their powerful and mysterious role as final arbiters of the male aristocrats' words. Indeed it might be said that by assuming the role of passive audience to active, performing courtiers, these women appropriate the male gaze, an action that we have seen is associated with castration in many English Renaissance treatises. The distinction between voluntarily passive (female) audience and active (male) speakers does not, in other words, vitiate the dependence of the courtly system on the exchange of women; rather it redefines it as a Girardian triangle in which the exchanges of language between men emerge out of a competition for the attention of women, a competition that threatens male hegemony.

Pasquier critiques this repressed dependance on mediations of women in two overt ways. First, he dismantles the conventional paradigm of active male speaker and passive female audience by representing a woman (Charilée) as an active member of the courtly exchanges. Even more audaciously he gives voice to the ways in which the role of mediatress often objectifies women. Both critiques are articulated as Charilée argues that the trade in women is a middle-class institution, and, hence, irrelevant to constructions of the French court.[28]

Charilée's comments are in direct response to Philopole's argument in favor of the trade in women. He initiates his argument by attacking Monophile's idealization of monogamous, extramarital love—the kind of love associated with Tristan and Isolde. Philopole's point is that

beaucoup plus est pernicieux en une Republicque, celuy qui prend son adresse à une Dame mariée . . . pour en faire son propre & particulier, . . . que l'autre qui sans arrest prend son vol en tous lieux, ou le vent luy donne en queue (16).[29]

in a nation, he who courts a married woman . . . to make her his own and particular object of affection is far more pernicious . . . than he who ceaselessly flies into all places, wherever the wind may blow him.

For Philopole, Monophile's affirmation of an ideal passion between man and woman outside of social institutions undermines the system of patriarchy, which depends on conceptualizing women as valuable objects to be exchanged between men.

As he develops his defense of male promiscuity Philopole begins to sound like a sixteenth-century version of Claude Lévi-Strauss, for he represents women as valuable property to be exchanged between men. After discussing the idea that men might share in a "communauté des biens"(16v) [community of goods], Philopole adds, "Donques descendons maintenant des biens aux femmes (qui semblent avoir quelque simbolisation de l'un à l'autre)" (16v) [Now let us descend from the subject of goods to that of women (since they seem to have some sort of symbolic association, one with the other)]. This casual transition from goods to women is, in fact, central to the dialogue—much of which is dedicated to the question of whether women should be construed as objects of exchange or as autonomous subjects unto themselves. Philopole affirms traditional analogies between women and property in order to declare that Monophile's adulterous desire for a married woman is tantamount to coveting another man's property.

Philopole's notion that heterosexual promiscuity is crucial for establishing and maintaining homosocial relations leads him to proclaim that

> Ainsi furent en toutes Republicques introduytes les venditions, emptions, locations, & d'abondant les prestz, empruntz, & precaires, sus lesquelz sans plus ie pretend me fonder. Et . . . en recognoissance du bien que ie reçoy, les maris d'un autre part, reçoyvent mile courtoysies & gratieusetez de moy, . . . i'emprunte sus eux pour un temps, aussi . . . en recognoissance d'un tel bien, ie leur en sache bon gré. (18v)

> in all nations were introduced sales, purchases, leases, and, in abundance, loans, borrowings, and negotiable documents, on which, without further ado, I base my argument. And . . . in recognition of the good that I receive, the husbands, on their side, receive from me many courtesies and gifts, . . . I borrow from them for a while . . . and so . . . in recognition of this good, I pay them back with good interest.

Where Monophile rejects married love because it has been sullied by the financial system of dowries, Philopole strongly associates love with finance, as he argues that the ideal commerce consists of men trading women and goods with each other.

This slippage from conquest of women to the trade in women is too much for Charilée, who retorts that

Lesquelles [prouesses] neantmoins abastardissez en partie par le fait de march-
andise, que sus la fin de voz propos vous vantez exercer parmy voz braves
entreprises. Et crains qu'elles ne vous soient non plus honorables, qu'à celuy
qui de noble devient marchand. (19)

you partially bastardize these deeds by the analogy to merchandizing, which,
as part of your argument, you boast to be among your heroic enterprises.
And I fear that they will do you no more honor than it does to any man
who, though an aristocrat, becomes a merchant.

Picking up on the hint that Philopole pays husbands back for the temporary
loss of their wives with the "good interest" of bastard children, Charilée implies that it is Philopole who is illegitimate, for he bastardizes his noble blood
when he indulges in petty commerce. By allowing Philopole his self-definition
as a merchant, Charilée implies that he debases himself by trading in women.
The debate, then, takes a more complex turn as notions of gender become
intermingled with those of class; for Charilée suggests, by her statement, that
the trade in women is a bourgeois system, one with which aristocrats like Monophile, Philopole, and herself should not allow themselves to be tainted. By
extension, she implies that it is Philopole, not herself, who is the illegitimate
speaker in this courtly circle.

Charilée, of course, overlooks the fact that early modern aristocrats also
based their culture on exchanges of goods and women—via the system of dowries; but since none of her interlocutors challenges her perspective, it appears
that Pasquier himself supports Charilée's contention that the aristocratic patriarchy is unsullied by such trading practices.[30] Yet if we look back to the beginning of the work, we find that Pasquier indirectly affirms something like
Philopole's trade in women. We have seen that the celebrations which follow
the siege of Metz involve a social contract between men, based on the premise
that men who have access to "chaste and well-spoken" ladies are "constrained
and obligated" to bring these ladies to the celebrations, so that "each young
man might partake in honorable pleasure with them." The courtly system is,
hence, based on friendly exchanges of women between men. But where Philopole (like Lévi-Strauss) would have the system depend on one man granting
the sexualized and silenced body of a woman to another man, Pasquier bases
the system of courtly exchange on men lending chaste, articulate women to
other men. This alternative model grants women a larger measure of autonomy
and greater powers of articulation than does Philopole's, or for that matter,
Castiglione's system.

Pasquier's variation on the trade in women at once affirms and complicates
Irigaray's contention that woman "exists only as the possibility of mediation,

transaction, transition, transference—between man and . . . himself."[31] Irigaray's language suggests that woman, unable to engage in any transactions other than sexual ones, is perceived as "unfit for the seriousness of symbolic rules": she is considered to be incapable of entering into capitalist trade, ritual exchanges of gifts, or even the exchanges of language which, in *The Courtier* and *Monophile,* define the aristocratic coterie.[32] But Pasquier's presentation of Charilée as an active speaker problematizes such a theory. Charilée cannily evades Philopole's notion that women should be mere objects of exchange; she does so by claiming that his notion is middle class and therefore irrelevant to courtly exchanges. By presenting a model of articulate exchanges that competes with Philopole's system, Charilée illustrates how a courtly debate which includes women disrupts the kind of homosocial exchanges upon which *The Courtier* depends. Because the characters feel free to speak and disagree among themselves, Charilée's outspokenness is associated not with anxieties of courtly effeminization but rather with an affirmation of heterogeneity that allows for the articulation of any number of competing constructs of gender—Charilée's or Philopole's.

SPEAKING FOR WOMEN: MONOPHILE AND THE MAGNIFICO

One might say, then, that the construction of the court in *The Courtier* and *Monophile* depends on the issue of speech—specifically the issue of whether speech should be exclusively a male prerogative or whether it should be ungendered and hence open equally to men and women. To argue for the former notion is to affirm a homosocial system structured on the objectification of women; to argue for the latter is to articulate a system of debates between empowered men and women. Metonymically related to this issue is that of woman's relationship to art. In the previous chapter I argued that notions of male artistry, during the Renaissance, depend on objectified images of women. Pasquier takes on this issue by critiquing the way that his central character, Monophile—like Magnifico in *The Courtier*—objectifies women even as he purports to defend them. As such, Monophile and the Magnifico are particularly interesting for their ambiguous roles as defenders and exploiters of women.

If Philopole and Gaspare Pallavicino (in *The Courtier*) are characters who frankly affirm misogyny, Monophile and the Magnifico critique such abuses of women even as they tend to appropriate images of women to enable their own creative and erotic fantasies. The Magnifico indulges in a personal act of Zeuxian artistry, of creating a personal ideal out of bits and pieces of court ladies he has known. As he puts it, "e, formatta ch'io l'averò a modo mio, non potendo poi averne altra, terrolla come mia" (341) [when I have fashioned her (the Court lady) to my own liking, since I may have no other I shall . . . take her for my own (211)]. The language of possession in this passage, the frequent allusions to the Court lady as a woman of the Magnifico's fashioning, and the reluctance to share this lady with other members of the courtly debate affirm an ideal of artistry that is based on the silencing and objectification of the women whom the Magnifico purports to defend.[33] Indeed the language of fragmentation and refashioning in the Magnifico's discourse gestures to the threat of castration that threads throughout the work: as if to efface woman's castrating power over men, Magnifico symbolically castrates women by fragmenting and reassembling them to his "own liking."[34]

Monophile, like Pasquier's other characters, is less preoccupied with threats of castration and effeminacy. His description of women is, hence, free of the language of fragmentation; yet Monophile shares with the Magnifico a strong desire to control women by idealizing them. Up to a point this idealization is constructive: Monophile strongly critiques Philopole's affirmation of homosocial exchanges by pronouncing that the ideal bonding occurs not between men, but between a man and a woman outside the patriarchal institution of marriage.[35] While this alternative paradigm grants greater voice and equality to women, it nonetheless remains controlling: it promotes Monophile's ideal of contemplating his beloved in isolation without allowing articulate, independent women a constructive identity within courtly culture.[36]

Yet if both the Magnifico and Monophile attempt to control and possess the beloved by means of their shaping fantasies, they are also the speakers who most eloquently articulate the ways in which women are mistreated by possessive men. Hence, Monophile asks,

> Et puis esmervieillez-vous . . . si une Dame, froissant la porte de voz loix, outre son acoustumé mary, trouuve bien souuvent un amy. . . . Car si . . . un chacun s'adressoit à celle ou reposeroit son entiere devotion, osterions toutes les peines & travaux, que voyons ce iourd'huy regner entre tous les humains. (25)

> And then are you amazed . . . if a lady, brushing the threshold of your laws, often finds, beyond her established husband, a friend. . . . For if . . . each one could address himself to the woman in whom his entire devotion lies, we would free ourselves of all the pain and travails which we see now-a-days reigning between men.

Monophile counters Philopole's affirmation of the trade in women by proposing that women have as much right to commit adultery as do men. In much the same way, Magnifico's fashioning of the Court Lady includes within it some of the most eloquent defenses of women in *The Courtier*. It seems, then, that the protoromantic desire to brood upon and recreate the absent beloved betrays at once an impulse to shape fantasies about the beloved and a strong sympathy for the plight of women in patriarchal culture.

The ambiguous and complex constructions of gender and power expressed by these characters, the curious symbiotic relationship between their sensitivity to the plight of women and their narcissistic broodings suggest that, at least during the Renaissance, the defense of women and the tendency to transform women into art objects were not irreconcilable. As critics have long reminded us, chivalric fantasies of women present us with some of the more constructive images of empowered women during this period.[37] It would seem that Monophile and the Magnifico accommodate these apparently contradictory visions of womankind by virtue of the chivalric notion that woman's freedom of action is enabled by an empowered male protector. This notion is particularly evident in *The Courtier*, in which the Magnifico does not so much enable the women to speak as he speaks for them, simultaneously championing them and shaping his own fantasy about them. Ultimately, however, this notion is interrogated in *Monophile*, in which the dominance of Charilée as a speaker suggests that Pasquier is more willing to give women a voice than is their purported defender, Monophile.

CHARILÉE AND EARLY MODERN NOTIONS OF MARRIAGE

What makes a character like Charilée potentially threatening, then, is her partial usurpation of the male prerogative of speech. Instead of having male courtiers speak for her, Pasquier has her speak in her own defense.[38] In a place like Urbino—in which the active role of the male courtier is circumscribed by his loss of military prestige—this further diminishment of a male prerogative would indeed be problematic. For this reason, chaste, articulate, and active women have often been characterized as amazons, women who symbolically castrate men by silencing them.[39]

No woman is called an amazon in *The Courtier*, but there are women like Emilia Pia and the Duchess of Urbino who are associated with certain amazonian traits. This notion is made evident by Castiglione when he suggests that it is the Duchess, rather than her husband Guidobaldo, who most resembles Guidobaldo's father, the previous Duke of Urbino; for it is in the Duchess that "possono stare la prudenzia e la fortezza d'animo e tutti quelle virtù che ancor ne' severi omini sono rarissime" (86) [dwell prudence and a courageous spirit and all those virtues very rarely found even in the staunchest of men] (44). These virtues are closely linked with a kind of amazonian chastity, for, according to Cesare, the Duchess "essendo vivuta quindeci anni in compagnia del marito come vidua" (407) [has lived with her husband for fifteen years like a widow (253)].

While the Magnifico presents constructive examples of women warriors, the representation of the Duchess Elisabetta as an influential woman married to an impotent man serves as a paradigm for veiled fears of castration that result from a woman usurping traditionally male positions of power.[40] These fears are gestured to in the first pages of the work, where Castiglione refers to an analogously threatening woman, Vittoria Colonna, who usurped Castiglione's authority over his writings by passing his manuscript of *The Courtier* on to other men who "tentassero di farla imprimere" (69) [would try to have it printed (31)]. Colonna, a chaste, articulate, independent woman, exploits the conventional position of woman as mediator to transform Castiglione's private memoirs into an exchange between men that wrests control of the work from its originator. As such, she demonstrates how woman's secondary position as mediatress can be turned into a position of power. Under Colonna's influence, Castiglione purportedly takes on a somewhat passive role in the dissemination of his own work, as a woman not only enables but also controls its representation.[41]

The concomitant praise and fear of chaste, powerful women in *The Courtier* highlights the doubled meaning of this virtue. While chastity ensures husbands that they possess a pure (perhaps even rare)—and hence valuable—object, the association of chastity with amazonian independence makes it the occasional subject of extreme, even hysterical, views among courtiers who feel threatened by female autonomy. This latter reaction is made playfully evident early in the work, when the Unico Aretino describes the Duchess as a woman who has "occhi d'angelo e cor di serpente" (94) [the eyes of an angel and the heart of a serpent (48)]. He adds that she is like a Siren "che tanto di sangue umano sia vago" (94) [who is avid for human blood (48)]. These vampiric attributes result from the Duchess's very chastity—her apparent refusal to be seduced by Aretino. Aretino's revenge is to displace the archetypal ideal of woman as generous mother and replace it with that of woman as an amazonian vampire whose usurpation of male privileges is symbolically equivalent to drinking her courtiers' blood. This curious association of chastity with unnatural femininity explains why it is that, in *The Courtier*, and, to an extent, in *Monophile*, men constantly seek to define, regulate, protect, and control female chastity. If such amazonian threats to male courtiers are more often hinted at than expressed in *The Courtier*, they are foregrounded in *Monophile*, where Pasquier openly calls Charilée an amazon (Aiij). We have seen that this open expression reflects the characters' relative ease with unconventional gender roles. But Pasquier does present us with one character—Philopole—who consistently attempts to devalue and objectify chaste, articulate women. His contentious responses to Charilée's defense of women make evident his discomfort with her amazonian identity. While Philopole's stance is eventually deflated by Monophile and Glaphire, his remarks nonetheless reveal how vulnerable Charilée's position is within the courtly coterie.

That Philopole is somewhat disturbed by Charilée's association of female chastity with (male) speech becomes dramatically apparent on the second day of the debate, when the protagonists reunite after having paused for sleep and sustenance:

> Mais ne fusmes si tost arrivez que Philopole selon son acoustumée liberté, ne se voulust ingerer d'accaresser Charilée, non de propos accompagnez de quelque honneste entretien, comme possible est l'usance de tout homme faisant estat d'honneur, ains par atouchemens trop hardis: Voire à mettre la main au poinct que toute femme doit avoir en plus grande recommendation. (97v)

> But no sooner had we arrived than Philopole, making use of his usual free ways, was not satisfied with simply greeting Charilée affectionately, but, not accompanied with remarks of honest intention, as is the custom with men of honor, he went on to touch Charilée brazenly: for he placed his hand at that place which all women should consider as most carefully to be protected.

Philopole's aggressively sexual gesture threatens to rupture the social fellowship between the men and Charilée, a fellowship which had grown out of exchanges of words as a substitute for the sexualized exchange of women. By turning Charilée into a sexual object Philopole effaces her symbolical position as intellectually masculine—a position made possible by her identity as a chaste, amazonian woman.

In attempting to efface Charilée's masculine authority, Philopole is essentially engaging in the kind of class warfare that caused Charilée, earlier, to characterize Philopole as middle class. According to Margaret Ferguson, concern about women's wantonness applied particularly to women of nobility, for their transgressions of sexual mores could endanger the integrity of primogeniture—a system based on the handing down of "untainted" aristocratic blood from one generation to the next. For this reason, Ferguson argues, articulate aristocratic women—women like Charilée—were particularly vulnerable to being defined as promiscuous. Thus it is that the aristocratic writers Christine de Pisan and Vittoria Colonna were careful to call attention to their chastity, while commoners like Veronica Franco, Gaspara Stampa, and Louise Labé were less concerned with representing themselves as chaste.[42]

To regain her status as an articulate yet chaste woman Charilée must follow the examples of Colonna and de Pisan, who carefully separate speech from sexuality. For this reason Charilée responds to Philopole's sexual gesture with strong, but chaste, speech:

> Ie ne doute poinct, seigneur Philopole, que la grande priuauté dont i'ay usé envers vous, me commettant en ce lieu si solitaire & indeu, es mains de vous quatre ieunes Gentilz-hommes ne soit, peut estre, cause de celle que voulez exercer en mon endroit: toutesfois si ainsi est, i'espere trouver bon sauf conduit en vostre foy, & celle du seigneur Glaphire, souz l'asseurance desquelles i'apris hier le chemin. (97v–98)

> I have no doubt, Lord Philopole, that the great familiarity which I have shown to you, by walking with you to this solitary and private garden, and placing myself in the hands of you four gentlemen, may be, perhaps, the reason for that gesture which you would make in my direction; however, if that is the case, I should hope that I might find safe conduct in your honor, and that of Lord Glaphire, under whose assurances I took this road yesterday.

Charilée's retort reminds us that the private garden which the main characters enter—the garden of fiction—may also be interpreted as the *hortus conclusus,* the garden of love. If Philopole succeeds in moving the dynamics of the group from sublimated words about love to the sexual act itself, he will transform Charilée from independent speaker into an object of male pleasure. Charilée, well aware of her vulnerability, protects herself by reminding her fellow debaters that an aristocrat is honorable and chivalrous—as both Monophile and Glaphire have maintained. If Charilée cannot physically defend herself, she can, at least, employ language to remind the other men that, as aristocrats, their role is to protect her chastity. As a result of her remarks, Glaphire and Monophile form a symbolically protective ring around Charilée.

Fascinating as this section of *Monophile* is in its own right, it appears even more interesting when we read it in terms of *The Courtier;* for this transgressive moment displays a chiasmic relationship to that moment in *The Courtier* when, after Pallavicino makes one too many misogynistic remarks, the ladies take their revenge:

> Allora una gran parte di quelle donne, ben per averle la signora Duchessa fatto così cenno, si levarono in piedi e ridendo tutte corsero verso il signor Gasparo, come per dargli delle busse, e farne come le Baccanti d'Orfeo, tuttavia dicendo: —Ora vedrete, se ci curiamo che di noi si dica male. (328)

At this, seeing the Duchess making a sign, a large number of the ladies present rose to their feet and, laughing, they all ran towards signor Gaspare as if to rain blows on him and treat him as the Bacchantes treated Orpheus, saying at the same time: "Now you shall see whether we care whether evil things are said about us." (200)

As in *Monophile,* this problematic passage takes place almost at the exact center of the work; but where, in *Monophile,* it is Charilée who is physically threatened by the transgressive actions of Philopole, here it is the normally passive women who threaten to silence men.

If this histrionic rebellion is treated as a joke, its paradigmatic relation to the myth of Orpheus is nonetheless relevant to the sexual tensions underlying *The Courtier.* The myth, after all, is about a poet who is martyred by anarchic and passionate women. Given that the dominant paradigm of *The Courtier* is of men performing before an audience of women, this section gestures to the ways in which women agree to be passive and silent only if the performances before them are to their liking. Much as Nashe later employs the figure of Orpheus to express how writers are silenced, fragmented, and effeminized by usurping women, so here the women's attack underscores the underlying threat of castration that courtly women represent, particularly as their rebellion is initiated by the wife of the impotent Guidobaldo.[43] The suggestion seems to be that Guidobaldo's impotence arises not just from an unfortunate illness, but also from his wife's usurpation of the phallus, a concept that would appear to contaminate the court as well.[44]

The two bodies of Charilée and Orpheus dramatically express the problematics involved in conceptualizing women as chaste yet autonomous and articulate. Simply by being articulate Charilée places herself in danger of being read by Philopole as a sexualized object to be shared between men. The text of *Monophile* ultimately affirms a belief that an articulate woman like Charilée can participate constructively in the male coterie; in contrast, in *The Courtier,* order is restored only when women return to their accepted roles as (somewhat) passive mediators. This situation implies that Castiglione is less optimistic than Pasquier about the possibilities of a woman entering the male coterie without threatening its structures.

It is perhaps because Pasquier's court is not defined by a strong and powerful female leader that his characters are less likely to perceive chaste and articulate women as threatening to male privileges. It is true that, during the period when the events of *Monophile* took place, Marguerite de Navarre's writings and patronage made her a significant presence in the French court; yet her position, unlike that of Elisabetta Gonzaga, was more than compensated for by her more active, aggressive and quite powerful brother, Francis I. Less concerned than are

Castiglione's courtiers with the ideal of silenced, subordinated women, Pasquier is more interested in exploring the creative implications that result from the dynamic interminglings of aggressive female with male voices in the aristocratic coterie.

CHARILÉE AND THE SYSTEM OF DOWRIES

The threatening associations of courtly women with bacchantes and amazons gesture to a problem of boundaries inscribed in *The Courtier:* so long as the feminized space of the court is envisioned only as a fiction, the passive yet influential power of women is easily contained within a courtly game; but insofar as this game suggests that women are secretly exploiting their mediatory powers to manipulate men, then women are presented as transforming the aristocratic warrior into an effeminate, ornamental courtier. *Monophile* reveals fewer authorial concerns about such contaminations, for Pasquier represents this threat only in the words and actions of one character, Philopole, rather than in the larger symbolic structure of his text. Perhaps the best evidence for Pasquier's more generous position towards women is his creation of a female character who (unlike the Duchess or Emilia Pia) articulates her own constructions of masculinity and femininity, constructions that compete with those expressed by Philopole, Monophile, and even Pasquier (when he eventually appears as a character in the debate).

Given Charilée's vulnerability to attacks by the likes of Philopole, it is perhaps not surprising to discover that Pasquier would have this articulate, independent, and young woman espouse some rather conservative views on love and marriage—views that would represent her as unthreatening to patriarchal conventions. Early in the debate Charilée reveals her conservative stance as she opposes both Philopole's praise of promiscuity and Monophile's ideal of adulterous love. Thus she affirms the ideal of married chastity by asserting that the ideal wife must not imagine anything better than what her husband has to offer (20). Anticipating Jane Anger's ultimately conservative stance, Charilée's discourse implies that even within Pasquier's more generous vision of female articulation, woman's ability to speak remains limited.

But if Charilée perhaps represses a more radical perspective on love—one that would be consistent with her independent personality—it is also true that her defense of marriage grants her a voice of her own, as she challenges both Monophile's condemnation of dowries and Philopole's affirmation of dowries as a system which objectifies women.[45] To make her point, Charilée, like Philopole, employs the language of commerce, although to a different purpose:

Et si, entre marchans est permis pour entretenir leur trafique, que l'un parfournisse aux frais, en contre-eschange de l'autre qui preste son industrie, que devons nous estimer en ceste association d'homme à femme, en laquelle . . . tout le fait de ceste humaine pratique depend du cerveux de l'homme? En bonne foy, seigneur Monophile, il seroit tresmal seant & convenable (encores que ie parle au desavantage de mon sexe) que ce double fais et fardeau regorgeast dessus vous autres . . . et qu'à la seule femme fust deslaissé le contentement & plaisir. (22–22v)

And if merchants, in order to maintain their commerce, may have one person invest the principal in exchange for another who invests his labor, what are we to think of this association between man and woman, in which . . . all the human labor depends on the brains of the man? In all good faith, Lord Monophile, it would be very unseemly and improper (even if I say this to the disadvantage of my sex) that the double obligation and labor should fall upon you . . . and that to the women would only be left contentment and pleasure.

This complex and witty argument moves in two contradictory directions at once. On the one hand Charilée appears to be conceding the conventional wisdom that marriage has everything to do with the intellectual superiority of men and very little to do with the gray matter of women; while on the other hand she states that the system of dowries transforms wives from being objects of pleasure to becoming active investors in their marriages. The latter stance undermines Philopole's declaration that women are akin to goods. In this way Charilée conceptually transforms the system of dowries from being part of homosocial exchanges to becoming a private transaction that binds a husband to his wife. By extension, Charilée implies that the focus of social relationships is not (as Philopole would have it) between men; rather it inheres in domestic interactions between husband and wife. At the same time, Charilée's argument allows her to maintain a position independent from the definitions of love and marriage proposed by Monophile: where Monophile believes that equal exchanges between men and women can only take place in isolation from cultural institutions (a notion that leads him to condemn marriage altogether), Charilée affirms that marriage—the interaction between man and woman—is the central exchange that underlies all cultures.

Given Charilée's forceful defense of marriage, it may seem surprising that she is represented as unmarried. Her continued virginity indeed implies that her defense of marriage is more ideal than real. Certainly the system of dowries rarely empowered wives; instead, dowries were perceived to be an exchange between the woman's father and her future husband—an exchange in which the wife-to-be had very little say.[46] Charilée's unmarried state suggests that she is wary of falling into the kind of marriage against which Federico Fregoso so strongly inveighs in *The Courtier,* when he states that

> perché molte se ne trovano, alle quali i mariti senza causa portano grandissimo odio e le offendono gravemente, . . . alcune sono dai padri maritate per forza a vecchi, infermi, schifi e stomacosi, che le fan vivere in continua miseria. (267)

> there are many [married women] to be found whose husbands hate them for no reason at all and do them great injury, . . . and then again, some women are forced by their fathers to marry old men, who are in poor health and filthy and disgusting, and who make their lives one long misery. (260)

Fathers and husbands, Federico reminds us here, often do not have the best interests of their daughters and wives in mind when they contract marriages for them.

But if Charilée seems somewhat unrealistic in suggesting that the system of dowries empowers married women, her stance is no more fantastical than are the versions of love and marriage proffered by Philopole or Monophile. All three, speaking within the garden of fiction, seem more interested in asserting ideal notions of love (notions that befit their personalities) than in puzzling out the problems and complexities inherent in their divergent models of love and marriage. Monophile's desire for platonic love outside of marriage is in keeping with his own penchant for privacy; Philopole's contention that women are objects which affirm fellowship between men befits his gregarious, homosocial inclinations; while Charilée's proposal that marriage consists of face-to-face exchanges between husbands and wives reveals her preference for interacting equally with men.[47] By articulating three distinct fantasties of gender, Pasquier suggests that any shared "truths" about gender are fictions imposed on the court by the dominant powers. What Pasquier adds to this equation is a perspective that takes into account both the plight of women within a patriarchal culture and a woman's fantasy of how to turn her victimization by this system into a narrative of self-empowerment.

PASQUIER'S ANDROGYNE

Pasquier further disrupts the courtly debates when, halfway through the work, he transforms himself from an omniscient (Castiglione-like) narrator into an active participant in the debates: he suddenly reveals his presence to the characters and confesses that he has been hiding in the shrubbery, eaves-dropping on their debates. Suddenly the configurations of the debate change, as the characters realize that they have been directing their debates to an external audience all along. That this audience should also be the author of the work disrupts distinctions between historical author and fictionalized characters. This interruption, it turns out, further complicates notions of class and gender expressed throughout the work, as it allows for a commoner (Pasquier) to enter the debates. Perhaps for this reason Pasquier's intrusion into the coterie debate—in order, he claims, to defend Monophile's affirmation of monoga-mous adultery—dismays the speakers almost as much as did Philopole's sexu-ally aggressive gesture towards Charilée; indeed Charilée reacts with similar alarm (56).

Pasquier never articulates why he chooses to disrupt his own work in this way, but his decision makes sense if we read it as one more attempt to compete with *The Courtier* by making this earlier work appear conventional by contrast. As open-ended as *The Courtier* is, the omniscient view of the narrator is never in question. When Pasquier presents himself both as objective narrator and subjective character he opens the work up even more radically to a number of diverse interpretations. Indeed, even if we continue to accept Pasquier's point of view as authoritative, we make little progress in discovering which charac-ter's argument he deems to be the most valid. For if Pasquier claims that he has joined the debate in order to defend Monophile's position, it soon becomes clear that he is creating a paradigm which would validate all of the characters' perspectives at once. He first affirms Monophile's Neoplatonic affirmation of Plato's androgyne, then extends this interpretation to include the perspectives of Philopole, Charilée, and Glaphire as well:

> A laquelle opinion vous mesmes [Monophile] volontiers fussiez condescendu . . . quand nous avez confessé, l'Androgine estre l'apetence de reunir les deux moitiez esgarées: Et si peut estre voulez venir à celle que Dieu des le commencement de ce monde nous proposa . . . ne nous fut en icelle, par termes beaucoup plus expres ordonné, que fussions deux espritz en un corps & une chair, qu'un esprit dedans deux corps? (61–61v)

> You yourself [Monophile] willingly partook of this idea . . . when you told us that the Androgyne symbolized the desire to reunite two separated halves: And if perhaps you wish to come to the idea that God, from the beginning of the world proposed this to us [the union of man and woman], . . . did not He, in terms far clearer, order us expressly that we should become two spirits in one body, and one flesh, rather than a spirit in two bodies?

Pasquier supplements Monophile's Neoplatonic reading of the myth with the notion that passion consists of a physical, as well as spiritual, union of two bodies. As such he incorporates Philopole's and Glaphire's defenses of carnality into his paradigm for idealized passion. Pasquier then adds that the end of such unions should be the procreation of children; in this way he absorbs Charilée's defense of marriage into his paradigm of the androgyne.[48]

It would seem, then, that Pasquier's all-embracing reading of the myth of the androgyne functions as a crucial trope for the work as a whole. Not only does it allow for the speakers' different perspectives on the nature of passion but it describes, as well, the fundamental conceptualization of this coterie— made up as it is of different bodies which are joined neither physically nor spiritually, but rather intellectually—through the medium of words. It is this more flexible conceptualization of the body which vitiates images of fragmentation or objectification associated with Charilée's physical body; it allows, as well, for the entrance of outsiders (women or commoners) into these courtly exchanges.[49]

Given Pasquier's tendency to compete with Castiglione, it is no coincidence that he takes the figure of the androgyne from Plato's *Symposium,* the same work from which Castiglione derives his concluding paradigm of platonic love—articulated by Pietro Bembo. Pasquier's shift from Socrates's oration on love to Aristophanes' fable of the androgyne indicates a movement from an ethereal, transcendent and idealized vision of the court to a more comic, earthy, and provocative conceptualization. And much as Aristophanes's fable is far more frank about issues of gender and sexuality than is Plato's discourse, so characters in *Monophile* are far more likely to foreground issues that are repressed or sublimated in *The Courtier.* There are, it is true, characters in *The Courtier* (like Gaspare, and even Emilia Pia) who represent a more Aristophanic viewpoint; nonetheless the difference in the authors' choices of final archetypes highlights how Pasquier's strategy is to make his work look innovative by contrasting it with the more conventional, idealized, and patriarchal narratives of *The Courtier.*

In shaping this debate with Castiglione's work, Pasquier foregrounds the ways in which *The Courtier* is grounded in traditional affirmations of patriarchy— most notably mediations by women, a Zeuxian mastery of women, the system of dowries, and, finally, a platonic desire to transcend male dependance on women. By articulating and debating issues which are more often sublimated in *The Courtier,* the characters in *Monophile* (even to an extent Philopole) seem to free themselves from anxieties of effeminacy implied in *The Courtier;* hence characters in *Monophile* more often celebrate archetypal images that problematize patriarchal prerogatives, images like those of amazons and androgynes. More to the point, *Monophile* moves from metaphorical articulations of women to the inclusion of an articulate and aggressive female participant in the debates. Ironically the very strength of his nation's patriarchy (its identification with the military, absolutist power of Francis I) enables Pasquier to conceptualize a court that allows room for certain commoners and women. At the same time, such characters remain empowered solely within the fictionalized space of the courtly garden. Like *The Courtier, Monophile* ultimately speaks to the ways that the feminized enclosures of the court enable unconventional speech while delimiting it within these enclosures. What *Monophile* adds to *The Courtier* is the concept that a woman's articulated presence within this enclosure may strengthen rather than weaken the identity of the courtly coterie. Metonymically associated with the feminine, Pasquier implies that women, as well as commoners like himself, may initially disrupt the debates, but will, in the long run, strengthen and invigorate them.

THREE

Effeminacy and
the Anxiety of Originality:
Astrophil and Stella and
the *Rime Sparse*

When, in *The Anxiety of Influence*, Harold Bloom claimed that "Shakespeare belongs to the giant age before the flood, before the anxiety of influence became central to poetic consciousness," he set forth a kind of challenge to Renaissance critics, inviting them to investigate for themselves whether Renaissance writers were concerned with the anxiety of influence.[1] I have mentioned that critics who have taken up this challenge tend to construe the Renaissance as a liminal period during which authors attempted at once to find room for an autonomous poetics and to ground their works in the authority of convention.[2] The continued invocation of one's *auctor* during this period suggests that Renaissance writers, if anything, suffered from an anxiety of originality, an anxiety which, according to David Quint, derives from the concept that an original artist sets himself apart "from an absolutely prior, authorizing origin. The imprint of his own individuality and historicity upon his creations reveals the counterfeit nature of their meaning, a man-made significance that stands in place of divine truths."[3] If originality allows writers to call attention to an autonomous craftsmanship, its alienation from convention is also associated with the severance of one's words from authority, truth, and the originating Word of God. As Quint goes on to add, originality comes to be aligned with such problematic concepts as subversion, deceit, and narcissism.

The contrast between originality as subversive and self-indulgent on the one hand and convention as authoritative and didactic on the other is crucial to understanding the aesthetic underpinnings of *Astrophil and Stella;* for I propose that Sidney represents Stella as a *figura* for a conventional icastic poetics, much as Astrophil emblematizes an aesthetics of fantastical originality. By viewing Sidney's protagonists from this perspective, I differ from most critics of the sequence, who (focusing on the work's autobiographical roots) tend to read Astrophil and Stella almost exclusively as complex psychological characters that dramatize certain aspects of Philip Sidney's and Penelope Devereux's personalities.[4] But if we look at Astrophil's and Stella's personality traits as embodying certain aesthetic concepts that are distinct from Astrophil and Stella as characters, then the work may be read not only as a psychological drama between a lover and his beloved but also as a dramatic enactment of Renaissance debates on femininity and fantasy (debates articulated in treatises like *The Anatomie of Absurditie* and *Jane Anger, Her Protection for Women*). Just as sixteenth-century debates on the *Divine Comedy* and on Tasso's and Ariosto's works grow out of the tension between an authoritative didactic literature and a subversive literature of pleasure, so the conflicts between Astrophil and Stella dramatize the tension between Stella's conventional, didactic voice and Astrophil's more problematic, seductive utterances. At the same time, these aesthetically based conflicts speak to debates on the nature of women. Rather than represent woman as seductive, deceitful, and unruly—as do Gosson, Nashe and Castiglione's Gaspare—Sidney associates these traits instead with the fantastical Astrophil.[5] By shaping his sequence as a kind of *psychomachia* of Renaissance poetical theory—as a debate between a conventional masculine authority (embodied in Stella) and an autonomous feminized poetics (expressed as Astrophil)—Sidney discloses the Renaissance writer's dilemma of choosing between the masculine truths of literary tradition and the feminine, or effeminate, fantasies of originality.[6]

In examining Astrophil as a *figura* for originality, I will focus on how this character's agonistic relationship with his beloved rehearses a concomitant quarrel with Petrarch's *Rime Sparse*—the originating template for Renaissance sonnet sequences.[7] Much as Astrophil's self-definition as unruly and unconventional depends on his opposition to Stella's position of authority, so his (and, to an extent, Sidney's) claims to originality inhere in his ongoing rebellion against Petrarch. Yet if the opposition between Stella's authority and Astrophil's unruliness remains fairly consistent throughout the sequence, Astrophil's scene of rebellion against Petrarch masks an ultimate reliance on the poetics of his literary progenitor.[8] This tendency to shape an alternative poetics that covertly depends on the practices of the authorizing poet discloses Astrophil's underlying concern that, by identifying himself with a radical poetics of originality, he may drift progressively into a solipsistic space which ultimately alienates him from any coherent, unified conception of self. The paradoxical loss of selfhood that results from the search for poetic autonomy reveals how, during the Renaissance, conceptualizations of the self remain too deeply invested in larger familial and cultural conventions to allow for any clear sense of identity outside of social circulations.[9] In much the same way Sidney discloses how Astrophil is finally unable to shape a distinctive sonnet sequence without depending on the very authority against which he rebels. This simultaneous affirmation and interrogation of the processes of originality finds its ultimate expression in the archetypal myth of poetical origins and originality—the story of Orpheus. It is by tracing palimpsestic versions of Ovid's, Virgil's, Horace's, and, especially, Petrarch's Orpheus that I explore the anxieties of originality that inform this originating English sonnet sequence.

Allusions to Virgil's and Ovid's Orpheus in *Astrophil and Stella* betray the ambivalences inherent in elemental fantasies of poetic origin and autonomy. For if both classical authors present Orpheus as a tragic artist whose unparalleled poetry is inspired by the loss of his beloved, they gesture as well to a narcissistic, even idolatrous impulse underlying this poetics of loss. As Quint has noted, after Eurydice's death Orpheus comes to worship not so much the memory of his beloved as his own autonomous transformation of Eurydice into art.[10] The analogies between an autonomous poetry, narcissism, and originality are particularly telling in the Ovidian version of the tale, which deviates from Virgil's source in ways that draw attention to Orpheus's rhetorical powers, his self-love, and his immorality. Ovid's Orpheus wins over his underworld audience by depending on flashy, sophistical rhetoric—not by employing icastic, moral arguments.[11] And just as Orpheus's flamboyant rhetoric calls attention more to itself than to any external, didactic significance, so his movement from a heterosexual love for Eurydice to a homosexual love for young men suggests that the origin of his passions inheres not so much in any one young woman or man, as in the poet's own self-perpetuating desires. Indeed, throughout *The Metamorphoses,* Ovid associates homosexuality (like incest and idolatry) with narcissism—with desiring one's mirror image.[12]

By looking back to the influential works of Virgil and Ovid, Renaissance authors appear to have inherited a Janus-like notion of Orpheus as a figure who represents at once a conventional didactic poetics and an originary sophistical poetry. This dual identity is dramatized in *Astrophil and Stella,* where Stella comes to be associated with the conventional Orphic poet (didactic, virtuous, and authoritative), while Astrophil identifies himself increasingly with Ovid's problematic Orpheus (seductive, deceitful, and subversive). Rather than assume that Sidney identifies himself narrowly with Astrophil, I argue that this antipodal portrayal of the poet represents a dialectical testing ground that pits a conventional and authoritative poetics of truth against an unconventional and subversive poetics of seduction. If Sidney seems finally to sympathize more with his protagonist's position, he clearly distances himself from Astrophil by, unconventionally, giving him a distinct name; this strategy allows him to disassociate himself from some of the problematic implications of indulging in originality.

SIDNEY'S ORPHEUS

When Sidney invokes Orpheus as a symbol for a conventional, magisterial poetics, he employs not the Virgilian or Ovidian version, but a third, less problematic Orphic tradition. In *A Defence of Poetry* Sidney makes use of Horace's Orpheus, a figure whose unparalleled didactic and rhetorical gifts endow him with power over the elusive beloved, over death, and, most of all, over barbaric, chaotic nature. Because Orpheus can "draw with . . . charming sweetness the wild untamed wits to an admiration of knowledge," he is said "to be listened to by beasts—indeed stony and beastly people" (19).[13] This representation of Orpheus expresses every poet's deepest fantasy, that of entrancing and controlling one's audience by means of aureate rhetoric. As Elizabeth Sewell puts it, "This story seems to say that poetry has power not merely over words and hence over thoughts, but . . . to some extent, in conjunction with love, power over life and death."[14]

Curiously, though, Sidney's affirmation of the poet's almost superhuman ability to charm and civilize his auditors follows closely upon a passage in which we are told that poetry is "fallen to be the laughing-stock of children" (18). This conscious appropriation of poetical power within a larger context that subtly questions such power is, in fact, common to *A Defence of Poetry, Astrophil and Stella,* and *The Old Arcadia*—the latter a work in which Sidney refers to the Orphic ability to inspire "Trees [to] dance" within a poem about the speaker's inability to attract his beloved's attention.[15] This problematic and contradictory invocation of the Orphic paradigm appears to be part of a sixteenth-century literary pattern; for, in Shakespeare's *Merchant of Venice,* Lorenzo tells Jessica that,

> the poet
> Did feign that Orpheus drew trees, stones, and floods;
> Since nought so stockish, hard, and full of rage,
> But music for the time doth change his nature.[16]

Incantatory and powerful as Lorenzo's utterance is, it is weakened by its language of fantasy ("feign") and contingency ("for the time"): his version of the myth suggests that the poet can only affect his audience within the provisional and illusory space of his fiction. Such examples suggest that the myth of Orpheus symbolically embodies a collective fantasy that the poet can dominate his culture with magisterial rhetoric, while covertly acknowledging that such power is ultimately ephemeral.[17]

Although Sidney does not refer explicitly to Orpheus until later in the sequence, the tension between the two modes of creativity associated with Orpheus (Horace's conventional and magisterial Orpheus, and Ovid's unconventional and seductive Orpheus) is already invoked in the first lines of the first sonnet:

> Loving in truth, and faine in verse my love to show,
> That she, dear She, might take some pleasure of my paine;
> Pleasure might cause her reade, reading might make her know,
> Knowledge might pitie winne, and pitie grace obtaine. (ll. 1–4)[18]

In this oft-quoted quatrain the apparent meanings of "faine" and "in verse" express how love for a woman (faining) inspires the speaker to write poetry (verse). This initial assertion is supported by the ensuing Neoplatonic *gradatio,* which gestures to Stella's idealized progression from earthly "pleasure" to heavenly "grace."[19] But the punning implications of "faine" and "in verse" ("feign" and "inverse") suggest the opposite—they encode a desire to invert conventional meaning by validating the feigning, sophistical poetics to which both Ovid's Orpheus and Sidney's Astrophil adhere. In fact, the *gradatio* that follows may also be interpreted as containing a series of sexual puns on the words "pleasure," "reading," "knowledge," "pitie," and "grace"—puns that direct the reader (and Stella) away from spiritual love and towards carnal desire. If, then, Astrophil purports to win Stella by employing language that would encourage her to transcend physical preoccupations (and thus embrace a spiritualized love), his language reveals a covert fixation on Stella's body and on a poetics of feigning that would alienate him from didactic, Neoplatonic sonnet conventions.[20]

As the sonnet develops, apparent (Neoplatonic) meanings and sexual allusions continue to multiply until both implications come to a crescendo in the last line: "'Foole,' said my Muse to me, 'looke in thy heart and write.'" As critics have told us, the conventional meaning of "heart" is Stella, the Neoplatonic love object who inspires Astrophil to write; yet it is also true that "thy heart" may refer to the autonomous center of the author's inspiration, the desiring self.[21] This alternative reading implies that it is from one's own passions, rather than from love for a woman, that original poetry derives. As such, the first sonnet locates the poet's courtship of Stella in the interplay between conventional wooing of the beloved through praise and an unorthodox idolatry of the self through poetical feigning. By implying that the source of inspiration inheres in the poet's self-authorizing fantasies (rather than in the *Idea* of the beloved), Sidney's Astrophil attempts to shape a distinct sequence by distancing his verse from that of Petrarchan convention; this strategy is made evident by Astrophil's departures from the *Rime Sparse,* which, unlike *Astrophil and Stella,* begins with a direct address to its auditors:

> Voi ch'ascoltate in rime sparse il suono
> di quei sospiri ond'io nudriva'l core
> in sul primo giovenile errore,
> quand'era in parte altre'uom da quel ch'i'sono:

> You who hear in scattered rhymes the sound of these sighs with which I nourished my heart during my first youthful error, when I was in part another man from what I am now.[22]

It is not just that Petrarch, in these lines, reveals a proclivity for adjectives, while Astrophil prefers verbs; nor is it simply that the *Rime Sparse* is expressed as a series of memories, while *Astrophil and Stella* takes place in a continually unfolding present; it is also that these two works depend on differing aspects of the myth of Orpheus. The motifs of fragmentation that are scattered throughout Petrarch's sonnet (notably in the word "sparse" and the thematics of self-division) recall the language that Virgil and Ovid employ to describe Orpheus's fragmentation by the Thracian women. As in *The Courtier,* but less playfully so, the very act of speaking about passion is conceptualized as transgressive— an act that results in the fragmentation and scattering of the poet's words by Laura or by readers of the work.[23] This threatening and annihilating act can only be defended by projecting these images back onto the beloved. Astrophil, in contrast, is more concerned with the liberating aspects of his confessional utterances. As his final couplet makes evident, it is by rejecting established Petrarchan scripts that he is released from writer's block.[24] Against a Petrarchan metaphorics of sacrifice and fragmentation, Astrophil locates his poetic identity in a departure from literary tradition.

Yet if Sidney represents Astrophil as insistently deviating from the authoritative source, he also discloses this poet-protagonist's deep debt to the thematics of the *Rime Sparse,* particularly to Petrarch's meditations on originality and autonomy. As Robert Durling has noted, Petrarch established his own break from convention by excising narrative from his sonnet sequence, thus distinguishing his style from that of his literary father, Dante.²⁵ Fragmentation, then, is not simply the disabling, even castrating, effect of transgressive speech; it represents as well a constructive break from an authorizing past, including—as poem 4 makes clear—the authority of God's voice.²⁶ This early sonnet unfolds as an attempt to displace God's creation, Laura, by replacing her with Petrarch's artificial rendering of her. Petrarch's transgressive undertaking implicates him (or at least his persona) in the kind of sophistical poetics that Ovid's Orpheus represents—and that Plato condemns in *The Sophist;* for Petrarch, throughout the *Rime Sparse,* represents his persona as a deceiving artist who claims that his fantastical versions of the beloved equal, perhaps even surpass, the authentic original herself. Swerving from divine providence, platonic Truth, and the authority of Dante, Petrarch engages himself in an originary poetics that prefigures Astrophil's rebellion against Petrarch and establishes the Zeuxian poetics affirmed by Firenzuola's Celso and Castiglione's Magnifico.²⁷

This, of course, is the dilemma of the Renaissance sonneteer: any attempt to define himself as original—hence distinct from Petrarch—paradoxically implicates him in the originary project that Petrarch had already established. As John Freccero has articulated, Petrarch represents the desire for originality as the temptation to create a self-satisfying world of poetical feigning isolated from any problematic, self-fragmenting encounter with the Other—expressed variously as God, a literary predecessor, or, most often, the beloved.²⁸ Petrarch appears almost to celebrate his beloved's absence because he may fill the space left by her absence with his own controlled fantasies of her; she thus becomes his "idolo mio scolpito in vivo lauro" [idol (of mine) carved in living laurel (poem 30.27)].²⁹ This conscious representation of Laura as an idolatrous object of his poetic making (emphasized by the punning relationship between "Laura" and the poetic "laurel"), suggests that Petrarchan sequences may be read as dramas that portray how a male poet, threatened by his chaotic passion for the female Other, regains his autonomy by replacing the wild, elusive original with an artificial representation of her—a "snowy maiden" in place of each fleeing Florimell. Such a representation of creativity allows the poet to fantasize that he is the Horatian Orpheus who controls, even creates, his elusive beloved.

This reading of Petrarch as engaged in his own pursuit of autonomy problematizes Astrophil's attempt to distinguish his verse from "poore *Petrarch's* long deceased woes" (Sonnet 15.7). For Astrophil's early attempt to master Stella by making an idol of her recalls Petrarch's tendency to fragment and reshape the beloved alternately as a ship (poem 323), precious jewels (poems 46, 181), and a landscape (poems 116, 125, 126, 129). Similarly, in his ninth sonnet, Astrophil compares Stella's forehead to an "Alabaster" front, her mouth to a door of "Red Porphir," and her cheeks to "Marble, mixt red and white" (ll. 3–7). Astrophil's Zeuxian recasting of Stella as fetishized pieces of architecture invokes the metonym of Orpheus—Pygmalion. As Harry Berger says of this mythical artist, "His fear of loss or betrayal motivates Pygmalion's incarnation of desire into a semblance whose seductiveness lies precisely in its being fictive and therefore uncontaminated by the life process. . . . What he falls in love with is the manifestation of his art."[30] By replacing the elusive source of inspiration with his own artificial rendering of her, the poet is able to compensate for his problematic passion by worshipping his controlled version of the beloved.

Given Astrophil's dependence on Petrarch's vocabulary of poetical autonomy, what are we to make of his professed scorn for Petrarchan poetry? On the one hand, Astrophil's discursive rejection of Petrarch suggests that in the sixteenth century poets were already engaged in the politics of misreading. But what may at first seem a sophistical reduction of Petrarch's poetry (that parallels Petrarch's own attempt to reduce and control Laura) seems to be a conscious device employed by Sidney to set two inherited views of Petrarch against each other. On the discursive level we experience Astrophil's satire of conventional Petrarchism, a school whose dependence on terms like "bella" (lovely) and "dolce" (sweet) associate it with a traditional Neoplatonic praise of the beloved.[31] It is this perception of Petrarch's legacy that Astrophil mocks when he says that Stella speaks

> With so sweete voice, and by sweete Nature so,
> In sweetest strength, so sweetly skild withall,
> In all sweete stratagems sweete Art can show. (36.9–11)

Yet on the metaphorical and structural levels of the sequence, Astrophil gestures to Petrarch as a transgressive poet who inscribes in his sonnets a poetics of autonomy and originality. By gently mocking the Neoplatonic Petrarchism which followed Petrarch, Astrophil identifies his originary project with Petrarch's autonomous voice. Sidney is, in other words, shaping a poet-protagonist who turns from Neoplatonic conventions of Petrarchism and towards Petrarch's poems themselves, poems in which Petrarch's voice is consistently expressed as transgressive. Whether Astrophil himself is supposed to be aware of this doubling of Petrarch is unclear; but Sidney, at least, seems to be employing this strategy of identification as a means for celebrating poetical autonomy without in the process alienating his project entirely from literary authority.

STELLA'S ORPHIC AUTHORITY

If Sidney, paradoxically, bases Astrophil's claims to originality on the practices of a literary predecessor, this tactic is not atypical of Renaissance poetics. During a period when originality was associated with a return to origins, poets often distinguished their projects from those of their rivals by claiming to turn from misguided interpretations and toward an "authentic" reading of a literary work.[32] This is not to say that Sidney attempts to imitate the *Rime Sparse* in every possible way; rather that his most unexpected moves, in his sequence, depend on strategies that are more characteristic of the *Rime Sparse* than of the Petrarchan sequences that followed it. It is in fact from the *Rime Sparse* that we can trace one of the most distinctive characteristics of *Astrophil and Stella*—its conceptualization as a gendered debate that pits Astrophil's poetics of autonomy against Stella's Neoplatonic poetics.

Astrophil's attempt to gain the upper hand in the battle between the sexes is implied in his hypnotic repetition of Stella's name throughout the sequence— a repetition that recalls both Petrarch's obsessive invocation of the word "Laura" and Orpheus's echoing call to Eurydice in Virgil's and Ovid's versions of the tale.[33] This compulsive naming, which, according to Quint, attests to Orpheus's desire to replace the elusive Eurydice with the "memorializing artifact" that is her name, calls attention to Astrophil's desire to control and contain Stella with words.[34] But if Astrophil (like Ovid's Orpheus and like Petrarch) attempts to master his beloved by naming her, the sonnets in which he calls her name reveal an anxiety that, by invoking her, he is allowing her to disrupt his mastery of the sequence. By sporadically acknowledging Stella's ability to disrupt his master plan, Astrophil betrays a growing awareness that he can only write significant poetry if he compromises his autonomous project by allowing his beloved a say in how the sequence is to be shaped. As a result, the early poems either betray his loss of autonomy (Sonnets 2, 7, 14); reveal his dependence on Stella's inspiring powers (Sonnets 3, 6, 15); or reflect his inability to write poems on his own (Sonnets 1, 19, 34). Most often, Astrophil is forced to acknowledge his inability to outdo the two figures who rival his claims to poetic autonomy: first Nature (Sonnets 7, 9, 16), then, eventually, Stella herself.[35]

As Stella gains increasing influence over Astrophil, she eventually comes to usurp his poetic authority by taking on the Orphic voice of the sequence:

> IF *Orpheus'* voyce had force to breathe such musicke's love
> Through pores of sencelesse trees, as it could make them move:
> If stones good measures daunc'd, the *Theban* walles to build,
> To cadence of the tunes, which *Amphyon's* lyre did yeeld,
> More cause a like effect at leastwise bringeth:
> O stones, ô trees, learne hearing, Stella singeth. (Third Song, ll. 1–6)

If the first three and a half lines of this stanza introduce the conventional emblems of poetic virtuosity (Orpheus and Amphion), Sidney disrupts androcentric tradition with the last two words of the stanza; these announce that

Stella, not Astrophil, is the Orphic voice that shapes the sequence. In Virgil's story the masculine poet may animate stones and trees, but here a woman performs these magical transformations. In granting Orphic power to the female audience rather than to the male poet, Sidney may have been aware that he was doing something unusual, if not audacious, for he appears to be the only sixteenth-century English poet to have inverted the Orphic paradigm in this way.

The notion that certain women, because they are beautiful, virtuous, and spiritual, have authority over the men who love them is not, of course, alien to medieval and Renaissance literature; it appears in medieval courtly love poems, Petrarchan sonnets, and Neoplatonic philosophy.[36] In the Third Song, as in the other poems about Stella's artistic power, it is clear that the source of Stella's power is her adherence to the Neoplatonic aesthetic of a pure, abstract, and divine love that governs the universe; for Sidney associates Stella variously with virtue (Sonnets 25, 48, 52), chastity (Sonnets 42, 48, 61), and spiritual love (Sonnets 61, 62, 63)—qualities that are traditionally expressed as masculine. Stella is, indeed, a figure for "the heavenly Love [that] springs from a goddess whose attributes have nothing of the female, but are altogether male."[37]

Sidney departs from convention not so much by insisting on Stella's power over Astrophil (that notion is consistent with Petrarchism) as by making it increasingly clear as the sequence progresses that hers is an Orphic power—that she is, by implication, the author who governs the sequence. The notion that Stella's voice represents a magisterial masculine poetics is reinforced by the voices that she replaces in the sequence. The sequence begins as a sort of *psychomachia,* in which Astrophil's reason attempts to govern his emotions (Sonnets 4, 5, 10). As the sequence develops, however, a male friend takes over the role of reason, a friend that critics have identified with Fulke-Greville, Sidney's cautious and politic fellow writer (Sonnets 14, 21). Significantly, beginning with Sonnet 30, this figure is replaced by Stella, who takes on the voicings of reason, virtue, and authority: she now becomes the rival poet whom Astrophil emulates, competes against, and whose authority he attempts to displace.[38] Clearly, in *Astrophil and Stella,* traditional constructions of gender have been inverted: where Renaissance conventional wisdom saw woman as a passionate animal and man as the embodiment of reason and truth, the male poet here represents lust, while woman symbolizes a more heavenly, Orphic love. In fact, as Stella is increasingly linked with a sublime masculine love, Astrophil associates himself more and more with feminine lust.[39]

Unexpected as this reversal is, it has a significant precedent in Petrarch. For if the concept that the beloved represents Orpheus is not inherent to Petrarchism, Petrarch himself employed it in his sonnets. Although Petrarch (unlike Astrophil) usually compares himself to Orpheus, at times he notes that Laura

sospira
dolcemente, et s'adira
con parole che i sassi romper pono (359.68–70)

sighs sweetly and grows angry with words that could break the stone

or she may "far piangere un sasso" (286.14) [make a stone weep]. Petrarch's suggestion that Laura, like Horace's Orpheus, can wring emotion from stones clearly had a certain resonance for Sidney; if Sidney is not the only English Renaissance poet to suggest that his beloved is an artist, he is unique in implying that she has complete Orphic authority, and that the poet-protagonist is, by implication, a charlatan.

As Stella increasingly takes on the role of masculine poet, Astrophil comes to identify himself more with the feminized, subordinate audience of the work— the position into which he had originally hoped to place Stella. But Stella speaks,

With so sweete voice, and by sweete Nature so, . . .
That not my soule, which at thy foot did fall,
Long since forc'd by thy beames, but stone nor tree
By Sence's priviledge, can scape from thee. (Sonnet 36. 9, 12–14)

Stones and trees are, of course, the traditional Orphic audience. By associating himself with these aspects of nature, Astrophil reinforces our awareness that Stella is the Orphic power behind the sequence, whereas Astrophil is but its passive recipient.

Given Astrophil's tendency to identify himself as increasingly feminized, it is not surprising that he invokes the most natural means of creation—procreation.[40] By the end of his first sonnet he experiences labor pains, as he attempts to give birth to a poem; he repeats this experience when he complains that "my breast doth swell, / . . . my thoughts in labor be" (Sonnet 37, ll. 1–2), or when he states that "with my breast I oft have nurst" sighs (Sonnet 95).[41] Astrophil is following Renaissance convention when he adopts the conceit of pregnancy, but he repeats this imagery with such insistence from the first sonnet on as to call attention to the feminized nature of his creativity.

In A Defence the concept of the pregnant poet is for the most part empowering, particularly as Sidney suggests that a great poet may impregnate himself with his fertile imaginings. Astrophil and Stella, in contrast, presents a less idealized version of the pregnant poet; here, the poet exists as a hollow vessel in which gestate the inspiring ideas of Stella.[42] Astrophil's forty-fifth sonnet to Stella exemplifies the extent to which the distinctions between empowered masculine poet and subordinate female audience have collapsed:

STELLA oft sees the verie face of wo
   Painted in my beclowded stormie face:
   But cannot skill to pitie my disgrace,
Not though thereof the cause her selfe she know:
Yet hearing late a fable, which did show
   Of Lovers never knowne, a grievous case,
   Pitie thereof gate in her breast such place
That, from that sea deriv'd, teares' spring did flow.
   Alas, if Fancy drawne by imag'd things,
Though false, yet with free scope more grace doth breed
Then servant's wracke, where new doubts honor brings;
Then thinke my deare, that you in me do reed
   Of Lover's ruine some sad Tragedie:
   I am not I, pitie the tale of me.

This sonnet, one of the more complex of the labyrinthine sequence, blurs accepted distinctions between aesthetic categories. The poem begins conventionally enough by presenting the female beloved as the passive audience; but Astrophil disrupts convention when he portrays himself not only as a young poet but also as a "painted" representation—the latter, as Elizabeth Cropper has shown, is an image traditionally associated with the female beloved.[43] Astrophil calls attention to this confusion of identity at the end of the poem when he cries: "I am not I." He has erased his identity as subject, thus allowing Stella to turn him into a poetic "idol," a transformation dramatized by the metrical substitution of a trochee for an iamb ("I am") at this point in the sonnet. As the poet recognizes his loss of identity, the once passive Stella is placed in the shaping role that one normally associates with the author.[44]

On the surface, then, the poem is an elaborate device for attracting Stella's sympathy, but Astrophil, it turns out, seeks not so much her emotional as her sexual pity, a meaning enhanced when he asks her to pity his "tale" ("tail"). In this radical inversion of the poet-audience relationship, Astrophil indirectly reveals the source of his weakness as a poet: his insistence on a sexual relationship (a relationship from which Stella remains aloof) inspires him to deny all aspirations to honor and integrity in return for the prospect of one night in Stella's bed. By placing such emphasis on sexuality, he enacts a role more reminiscent of a maenad than of Orpheus; his feminine lust, deceit, and subversion cause him to write himself out of the position of masculine poetic authority.[45]

ARTISTRY AND THE BELOVED

We have seen that disclosures of the Orphic paradigm in *Astrophil and Stella* illuminate the interplay between Horace's magisterial, authoritative, and masculine Orpheus on the one hand, and Ovid's narcissistic, unconventional, and feminine Orpheus on the other. It might, then, appear that by aligning Stella with Horace's authoritative Orpheus, Sidney would have his readers accept the notion that women could be taken seriously as poets (even if this woman happens to be the fictional creation of a male poet). Undoubtedly the radical implications of associating Orpheus with Stella were not lost on Sidney, for the few references to the beloved as an artist in sixteenth-century lyrics tend to be based on feminine domestic arts rather than on masculine poetry. Wyatt, for instance, returns obsessively to his beloved's malignant powers of embroidery, while Gascoigne dwells on a woman singing a lullaby.[46]

Although these lyrics represent a significant departure from sonnet convention (the conventional beloved is more likely to look in the mirror or sit in a beautiful landscape than sew or sing), they nonetheless draw back from a radical interrogation of gender roles by maintaining traditional distinctions between feminine domestic arts and masculine authoritative poetry. In a similar but more elaborate way, Spenser's portrayal of Elizabeth Boyle as artist gestures to her extrinsic subjectivity without, finally, disturbing conventions of gender. In the *Amoretti*, composed about ten years after *Astrophil and Stella*, the beloved is compared to Penelope, weaver of tapestries. This representation, which would seem to grant Elizabeth a measure of poetical power, is, however, continually problematized. Looking back to Penelope's rhythm of weaving then unravelling her tapestries (to keep her suitors at bay), Spenser's Sonnet 23 ascribes the process of weaving to himself, while aligning Elizabeth exclusively with the act of unraveling:

> Such subtile craft my Damzell doth conceave,
> th'importune suit of my desire to shonne:
> for all that I in many dayes doo weave,
> in one short houre I find by her undonne. (ll. 5–8)[47]

If, in these lines, Spenser fleetingly praises the beloved for undoing his attempts to transform her into artifice, his verses characterize Elizabeth as a purely reactive artist, while validating Spenser's more constructive project. Elizabeth is finally absorbed into Spenser's artistic enterprise, as her destructive acts are what inspire Spenser to weave new verses into his sequence.

In Sonnet 71 Elizabeth *is* represented as weaving her own tapestry; yet this enterprise is again absorbed into the lover's sequence. In the first quartet

Elizabeth shapes her own interpretation of Spenser's sequence by weaving a tapestry that represents him as a predatory spider who has captured her in his web of words. Her woven work wittily inverts the terms of Sonnet 37, in which Spenser complains that he has been trapped by the web of Elizabeth's golden hair. Yet this interrogation of the lover's project by the beloved is ultimately contained by the poet-lover's words:

> But as your worke is woven all about,
>   with woodbynd flowers and fragrant Eglantine:
>   so sweet your prison you in time shall prove,
>   with many deare delights bedecked fyne. (ll. 9–12)

Spenser's ambiguous language opens up two distinct readings of these lines, both of which validate his poetical project. If we interpret "your worke" as Elizabeth's woven work, then these lines suggest that, by bordering her allegorical web with beautiful flowers, Elizabeth implies Spenser's ensnaring words are, ultimately, quite pleasant; her tapestry thus betrays her enjoyment of being transformed into artifice. If we read "your worke" as meaning Spenser's *Amoretti* (purportedly written for Elizabeth), then Spenser, playing on the popular pun between "flowers" and collections of poems (*florilegia*), suggests that if Elizabeth's tapestry is framed by Spenser's predatory words, this state of affairs is ultimately enjoyable to her. Both interpretations would seem to be borne out by Elizabeth's unconventional capitulation to Spenser's courtship in Sonnet 87.

This movement away from expressing the (female) artist's individual voice and towards absorbing her work into Spenser's all-encompassing project is in keeping with Spenser's poetics of assimilation. Whether it be the interlacing rhymes of his sonnets, the hermaphroditic figures in *The Faerie Queene,* or the references to a divinity who unites the fragments of sublunar experience, Spenser's poetry constantly looks to—even if it does not always find—a transcendent vision of harmony and unity.[48] In contrast, Astrophil's sonnets more often separate his transgressive voice from that of the authorizing beloved, a strategy that allows him, and, to an extent, Sidney to revel in this poetics of autonomy.

If Spenser and Sidney assign differing artistic roles to their beloveds, they nonetheless share an unconventional proclivity for allowing their beloveds a voice in their sequences.[49] Elizabeth speaks twice during the sequence. In Sonnet 29 she states that the laurel leaf does not so much symbolize Spenser's talents as a poet (as he would have it), as it affirms her power over him. In Sonnet 58 she sums up the lessons that she has been trying to teach her lover all along.[50] If these moments reinforce Spenser's tendency to present his beloved as more self assured and artistically inclined than are most of her predecessors, they do not attempt to outdo Elizabeth's predecessor, Stella, who is among the most talkative of sonnet heroines. Stella never speaks a word in the sonnets themselves, but she speaks extensively (for a sonnet heroine) in the songs that are interspersed throughout the sequence—uttering nine lines in the Fourth Song, 28 lines in the Eighth Song, and, in the last song, taking 18 lines to dismiss Astrophil.

In sonnet tradition only one other beloved (before Stella)—Laura—speaks more than does Stella.[51] Although relatively silent throughout most of the *Rime Sparse* (she speaks only twice before the 250th poem), Laura finds her voice with poem 250, when she announces her death to Petrarch. In poems 279, 330, 342, and 359 she compares her joys in heaven to Petrarch's sorrows on earth, while, in poem 362, she represents herself as a mediator between Petrarch and God. It is, again, by looking back to Petrarch—not to later conventions of Petrarchism (in which the beloved rarely speaks)—that Sidney is able to distinguish his writings from Petrarchan tradition.

Of course Stella's voice is somewhat different from Laura's. For one thing, Laura does most of her speaking after she has died; Petrarch, it seems, can only conceive of her as a speaking subject once her presence no longer problematizes his attempts to fashion fantastical idols of her.[52] Stella, in contrast, is much more present and alive to Astrophil, in part because she comes out of the somewhat carnal English sonnet tradition established by Wyatt and Gascoigne. In a sequence that is structured on debates between lover and beloved, fantasy and didacticism, it is not surprising that Stella also turns out to be more argumentative than Laura. She either opposes her aureate voice to Astrophil's seductive rhetoric (Fourth Song), or responds to Astrophil's "fancies" with didactic speech (Eleventh Song). Nowhere is her voice more significantly and quietly contestatory than in the Eighth Song, the poem in which she ends her affair with Astrophil. Indeed her final utterance so disrupts the trajectory of the song as to trigger an abrupt shift in narrative voice from third to first person:

> Therewithall away she went,
> Leaving him so passion rent,
> With what she had done and spoken,
> That therewith my song is broken. (ll. 101–4)

The final rhyming couplet affirms why it is that the beloved speaks so rarely in the lyric tradition: her spoken words fragment the poet's attempt to shape an autonomous world. Where Spenser questions convention by shaping a sequence in which the beloved unexpectedly gives in to her lover's desire, Sidney does so by forming a sequence out of the Renaissance debates on the nature of poetry, a sequence in which the voice of the beloved—identified as it is with the voice of convention—is at once what enables and problematizes the poet's contestatory voice.

ASTROPHIL'S POETICS OF TRANSGRESSION

Although Sidney disrupts convention by granting Orphic authority to his beloved and by representing his beloved as far more articulate and contentious than even Petrarch's Laura, his position is not as disinterested as these unexpected moves might at first suggest. Given that it is almost always through Astrophil's consciousness that we experience this drama of passion, it would seem that Sidney is not, finally, granting Stella the kind of poetical power that Astrophil claims she has; rather, the implication is that Astrophil is happy to grant Stella the traditional position of masculine authority because the feminine, or effeminate, position of deceit, subversion, and lust is more advantageous—at least from an aesthetic perspective. Sidney invests Astrophil with greater sympathy than Stella not in spite of, but rather because of his character's self-centered, deceitful, and sensual nature; these feminine traits, in fact, are common to most poet-figures in Sidney's works.[53] We have seen that, in *A Defence,* Sidney associates his poet-narrator with writers who are "mountebanks" and "paper-blurrers" (62, 63); similarly, in the *Arcadia*s he chronicles his hero's fall from a selfless, heroic way of life to a self-indulgent, deceitful existence—one which inspires him to dress like a woman and write poetry.[54] The implication is that deceit, subversion, and seduction all have something to do with poetic inspiration.

In other words, Sidney is associating Stella with Horace's conventional Orpheus (and with Neoplatonic Petrarchism) in order to illuminate, by contrast, the aesthetic implications of Astrophil's originary poetics—with which Sidney appears to be most in sympathy. By associating his fiction with subversion, deceit, and seduction, Astrophil is able to distance himself from conventional, authoritative, and accepted meanings of poetry. His enterprise recalls the playful rhetoric of such Renaissance fictions as *Orlando Furioso,* the *Decameron,* and *Pantagruel*—works that were at once praised for their originality and condemned for their immorality. In contrast, Stella's more virtuous, spiritual personality exemplifies a didactic, moral notion of fiction, one more in keeping with such works as the *Paradiso, Gerusalemme Liberata,* and *The Faerie Queene,* works that (despite their inherent ambiguities) claim the Word of God as their enabling authority.

To a large extent, Petrarch, too, would seem to be aligning his persona with prodigal Renaissance fictions. Throughout the sequence, his persona seems uncertain as to whether he should follow his beloved's virtuous example and accede to divine truths, or whether he should dwell on the sensual beauty of her body. This last preoccupation suggests that Laura all too often leads Petrarch away from the heavenly path, or, more accurately, that Petrarch stubbornly gazes on her lips, brows, and hair, even as Laura tries to teach him how to transcend his interest in the merely visible (poems 11, 29, 30, 34). Although Petrarch attempts to wrest himself from this obsession, he often remains helpless before it:

miserere del mio non degno affanno,
reduci i pensier vaghi a miglior luogo,
rammenta lor come oggi fuste in croce (62, 12–14)

have mercy on my unworthy pain, lead my wandering thoughts back to a better place, remind them that today you were on the Cross.[55]

Laura finally converts Petrarch to the spiritual path, but only after he has written 363 poems about her earthly beauty.

Yet if this persona frequently strays from the path of virtue, the language of repentance that consistently frames and contains his transgressive voice (language that echoes Augustine's *Confessions*) suggests that Petrarch is eager to identify his persona as, ultimately, eager to be virtuous. Astrophil, in contrast, rarely expresses any moral dilemmas. If Stella inspires at once sensual and virtuous thoughts in Astrophil, he has few compunctions about his obsession with Stella's form. More often, he aggressively insists on having Stella's body along with, or even instead of, her soul (poems 14, 48, 52, 61). This difference in moral attitude is dramatized in the quite different endings to the two sequences. Petrarch clearly rejects his sensual obsession with Laura in poem 366, replacing Laura with the Virgin Mary as the object of his affections. In contrast, Sidney's last poem in *Astrophil and Stella* suggests that Astrophil never transcends his passion for Stella: "in my woes for thee thou art my joy, / And in my joyes for thee my only annoy" (108. 13–14). This final couplet signals the continuation of his passion by mischievously repeating "joy"—a term rife with sexual connotations.[56]

That Petrarch's sonnet sequence comes to a close when he learns to gaze past Laura's features suggests why Astrophil never follows Petrarch's example. Astrophil recognizes the loose association between his creativity and the lust that Stella's sensual body awakens in him. His poems are after all material pieces, substitutes for the desired (if threatening) body of Stella: to transcend his fixation on Stella's corporeal beauty could signify a denial of his own creative efforts. When Astrophil cavalierly states, "Let *Vertue* have that *Stella's* self; yet thus, / That *Vertue* but that body graunt to us" (Sonnet 52. 13–14), he is, then, making an aesthetic as well as a sexual claim: he is allowing Stella to identify herself with a virtuous, icastic poetics of masculine truth and transcendence, if, in return, she will let him indulge in a sensual, fantastic and original poetics that draws its energy from feminine passion, deceit, and subversion. The ever-pregnant Astrophil identifies with these "feminine" attributes, since they stand in opposition to all that convention represents—didactic, authoritative, and (by implication) masculine constructions. Astrophil's paradoxical, perverse, and inverted poetics suggests that to fall into love and poetry is to rebel against conventional art, accepted morality, masculine reason, and society in general.[57] In fact, part of the reason that we often find the immoral Astrophil to be so engaging is that his subversive poetics has a strong rebellious and liberating—if also narcissistic—streak in it.

Yet in covertly celebrating Astrophil's originary project, Sidney charts the troubling—as well as liberating—implications of originality. For, in moving towards an autonomous self-definition (one that emerges from the poet's attempts to tame the threatening voice and presence of the beloved by transforming her into an idolatrous art object), Astrophil finds himself losing, rather than gaining, a centered sense of self.[58] Astrophil's greatest moments of self-confidence as poet and lover come not when he, Zeuxis-like, makes a blazon of his beloved (such an act leads, paradoxically, to a realization of the essential nothingness behind the artist's autonomous self); rather it occurs when Astrophil is in conflict or dialogue with Stella's authorizing voice. Originality in this work appears to have no intrinsic value: on its own it leads to a solipsistic and finally absurd fantasy of poetical empowerment. Instead, originality has value only insofar as it presents an alternative to convention. For all of his celebration of originality as a mode of rebellion and self-affirmation, Sidney seems to accept the limits of this heady poetics. By looking back to its origins in the *Rime Sparse,* his sonnet sequence (unlike Astrophil's poetry) finally draws back from the more troubling implications of originality by granting convention (embodied in Stella) a significant, if secondary, role in the work.

Astrophil's paradoxical desire to repress an external authority even as he depends on it, along with Sidney's insistence on a prodigal, effeminate alter ego, illuminates the ways in which Astrophil's dilated fantasy of desire is implicated in a larger aesthetics of originality. Invoking and exploiting the longstanding associations between the feminine and creativity (woman as muse and art object), Sidney shapes an apology for originality—an *apologue,* or fable that figures forth a powerful aesthetics of originality out of an apparent position of weakness (the traditional position from which an apologist makes his argument).[59] Such a conceptualization, however, depends on projecting an authoritative antagonist against whom the prodigal poet may rebel. It is, in part, because of this need that Sidney shapes a sonnet heroine who is almost unparalleled for her wit, energy, and powers of articulation; as such, her representation—a notable deviation from that of Petrarchan convention—reinforces Sidney's claims to originality. Yet the ambivalences and anxieties inscribed in the work gesture to the problematics inherent in shaping a poetics that depends so strongly on negation. Whether it be a negation of authority, of conventional truths, or even of masculinity, Astrophil's tendency to associate originality with negation, and, by extension, with absurdity, marks him as the product of a period when originality was not yet considered a *desideratum*. Drawing back from the radical implications of originality, Sidney locates the energy of his text not so much in the self-desiring poetics of Astrophil as in the fissures and gaps between the positions of Stella and Astrophil, authority and convention, Petrarchan convention and Petrarch's transgressive voice, in a self-perpetuating poetics of desire and contention.

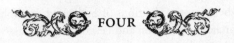

FOUR

Prose, Femininity,
and the Prodigal Triangle
in the *Decameron* and
The Old Arcadia

Although they are both early experiments in prose fiction, Boccaccio's *Decameron* and Sidney's *The Old Arcadia* are not normally paired with each other: Boccaccio's witty novelle are commonly identified with a middle class prose tradition that, in England, is taken up by Thomas Nashe, Barnabe Riche, and Thomas Deloney. In contrast, Sidney's elaborate prose style identifies him more closely with Elizabethan courtly writers like John Lyly and Edmund Spenser. But despite these salient differences in style, characterization, and literary influence, the *Decameron* and *The Old Arcadia* share one central preoccupation—a tendency to employ the medium of prose fiction to displace the patriarchal (oedipal) triangle, which they associate with conventional poetry. Where the paradigmatic patriarchal triangle consists of a youth vying with a father figure for the attention of the mother, Boccaccio and Sidney substitute a young woman for the mother, and hence represent the youth as deserving the female object of desire.[1] The father figure, by extension, is depicted as a grasping older man, unable to let go of his unauthorized hold over the young woman. Not surprisingly, the young woman is often represented as complicit in this plot of displacement: Boccaccio's and Sidney's female protagonists—frustrated by the sexual inactivity of their older husbands and lovers—willingly participate in their seduction from the authority figures who legally possess them.

This representation of woman's liberation from paternal authority might appear to be a profeminist defense of women; yet Boccaccio's *novelle* more accurately figure forth a fantasy of male adolescent prodigality. For, in these stories, a woman's value is ultimately determined by her willingness to ally herself with a younger, desiring man because of his skill in love-making and storytelling.[2] Indeed the youthful protagonists of the *Decameron* and *The Old Arcadia* often employ the medium of prose to claim both female character and feminine story for themselves. It is, for example, by telling a string of fictions that Pyrocles (the protagonist of *The Old Arcadia*) is able to seduce his beloved Philoclea from her watchful parents.

By reading the *Decameron* and *The Old Arcadia* as defenses of prodigal prose fiction, I am not arguing that Sidney was systematically influenced by Boccaccio: the *Decameron* is not a direct source for *The Old Arcadia* in the way that Jacopo Sannazaro's *Arcadia* and Jorge de Montemayor's *Diana* are; yet an awareness of Boccaccio's narrative strategies appears to inform Sidney's defense of fiction as a femininely inflected form.[3] What reinforces these intertextual resonances is the common positioning of both works within chirographic culture. As William Nelson has shown, a proclivity for structuring works around framing narrations (a structure that defines the *Decameron* and *The Old Arcadia*) is typical of texts produced during a period when works were generally read out loud to a larger audience.[4] The framing narrations in the *Decameron* conceptually reconstruct the intimate relations between minstrel/composer and immediate audience that were threatened by the transition from oral to manuscript culture. And if, unlike Boccaccio, Sidney was writing during the emergence of print culture, the exclusive circulation of his works in manuscript form (during his lifetime) speaks to his stronger identification with chirographic culture. Indeed, as I argue below, Sidney consciously constructs his work in such a way as to avoid any associations with the medium of print.

Boccaccio and Sidney, then, employ similar narrative techniques in order to celebrate their prodigal fictions within the circulatory exchanges of manuscript culture. Both privilege the upstart youth over the forbidding father; both affirm prose over poetry; both celebrate femininity; and both employ a framing narration to construct an intimate relationship with their conceptually female audience. These common techniques are, however, employed somewhat differently by each author. From the first words of the *Decameron*—where he subtitles his work the "Prencipe Galeotto"—Boccaccio announces that he is most interested in the notion of texts as mediators, or panders.[5] By celebrating analogies between women as mediators and the text as a pander between author and audience, Boccaccio suggests that disruptions of such mediations result in the idolatrous objectification of woman and text. Boccaccio specifically associates such disruptions with conventional patriarchal authority: in his novelle the authoritative male's control over the desired woman is analogous to a tendency by the patriarchal literary machine to fixate on conventional genres and styles. While Sidney (in *The Old Arcadia*) constructs a similar critique of patriarchy, he is more interested in exploring differences between conceptualizations of verse and prose; as a result, he focuses on oppositions between fluid, mediatory prose and fixed, idolatrous verse. In the prose sections of the work, Philoclea is depicted as an articulate, dynamic, sexually active heroine, while in the eclogue (verse) sections, she appears as a silent and passive piece of artifice.

It is through such layering of narrative space and fictional character that Boccaccio and Sidney investigate the possibilities inherent in conceiving prose as a femininely inflected construct. In each of his three narrative levels (framing narration, exchanges of stories between members of the *brigata,* and the novelle themselves) Boccaccio explores associations between femininity, sexuality, and textuality. In much the same way, Sidney takes us from his narrator's asides, to the dominant prose narrative, to the eclogue sections that conclude each book.[6] And, like Boccaccio, Sidney employs his framing structure to meditate on the associations between femininity, sexuality, and aesthetics. If, then, Boccaccio and Sidney characterize the relationship between prose and femininity in distinct ways, both employ their narrative frames to figure forth a defense of prose fiction and its erotically charged female characters during a time when the literary value of prose fiction and the cultural value of sexually active women were still in question.[7]

What finally distinguishes Sidney's project from Boccaccio's are the cultural implications associated with female audience and femininely inflected text. While Boccaccio validates vanguard prose and its unconventional female audience as a means for opening up his work to a wider audience, Sidney employs his female audience to draw back from associating his prose with the medium of print and with a growing middle-class readership, both of which threaten the hegemony of the predominantly aural court culture in which Sidney participated. The tension between the desire to align his work with the authority of dominant (often courtly) verse, and to represent himself as shaping a new, emergent prose deeply marks Sidney's text, as he attempts to represent himself as an innovative writer without opening up his text to a newer, middle class, audience.

I investigate the enabling and problematic implications of shaping femininely inflected narratives by exploring, first, Sidney's and Boccaccio's associations of patriarchy with sexual and textual idolatry: Sidney associates patriarchy above all with fetishized female characters and idolatrous verse; Boccaccio associates it with the repression of mediating female characters and texts—a repression

that he associates with idolatry. I then discuss how Boccaccio and Sidney figure
forth an alternative to idolatrous patriarchal fiction by promoting articulate
female mediators and the fluidity of feminized prose. The third section of the
chapter focuses on how this privileging of feminine narratives depends on conceptualizing a desiring female audience which displaces the traditionally male
audience of verse—an audience that these authors associate with the dissemination of conventional, idolatrous texts.[8] Yet if both texts express a cultural
desire to construct an alternative to traditional patriarchal literature, feminized
prose and its female audiences are ultimately put to distinct uses. For Sidney,
this audience enables him to close off his text from non coterie readers and
from the threatening encroachments of print; for Boccaccio, in contrast, it
opens up his writings to a heterogenous audience while conceptualizing a space
within which ambitious and educated commoners may be welcomed within
the courtly coterie.[9]

While Boccaccio's text clearly precedes—perhaps even serves as a template
for—Sidney's, I will begin my discussion with *The Old Arcadia.* Because it
comes later in the tradition, *The Old Arcadia* sets forth more self-consciously
symbolical associations between sexuality and textuality; as such it articulates
more clearly the paradigms of prodigal femininity that I explore in this chapter. Sidney foregrounds these associations when he presents us with his protagonist Pyrocles, who, having fallen in love, suddenly appears dressed as a woman
and uttering poetry. Pyrocles's boon companion, Musidorus, responds to his
friend's transformation by vehemently linking passion for women "with the
conceits of . . . poets" and with "making reason give place to sense, and man to
woman" (17.5, 20.11–12).[10] While Pyrocles responds with a spirited defense of
women and poetry, his amazonian costume is his most elemental defense: it
dramatizes how, in this work, femininity—or effeminate longing for a woman—
inspires creativity. I would add to this equation the suggestion that the narrator
himself is a kind of cross-dresser, for he closely associates himself with femininity throughout the work. One might say that the work sets forth a series of
shifting positions of male responses to femininity: if the narrator at times speaks
from the feminine position, he also speaks as male narrator to desiring female
audience; in much the same way Pyrocles is represented alternatively as effeminately identified with women and as a controlling male figure who idolizes
and fetishizes the female beloved.

IDOLATRIES OF WOMEN
AND TEXTS IN *THE OLD ARCADIA*

These shifting representations of male narrator and protagonist frequently respond to figurations of Philoclea, the heroine of *The Old Arcadia*. Indeed it is in her memory, the narrator declares, that "all this long matter is intended" (108.21).[11] But if we expect to learn about Philoclea's character in the eclogues dedicated to her, we are bound to be disappointed. Of the eleven poems that Pyrocles utters about Philoclea, only two provide us with any concrete information about her: the others tell us more about Pyrocles. One of these poems in fact calls attention to the self-contemplative nature of Pyrocles's passion:

> Over these brooks, trusting to ease mine eyes
> (Mine eyes e'en great in labour with their tears),
> I laid my face (my face wherein there lies
> Clusters of clouds which no sun ever clears).
> In wat'ry glass my watered eyes I see:
> Sorrow ill eased, where sorrows painted be. (118.15–20)

The poem, representing as it does Pyrocles's obsession with his image in a "wat'ry glass," betrays the narcissistic impulse behind these love poems, an impulse ironically underscored by the echoing language of the verses. In finding that passion for another inspires him to linger over his own beautiful face, Pyrocles is reenacting what, according to Renato Poggioli, is the classic pastoral moment—the moment of solipsistic self-surrender within the enclosure of the *locus amoenus*.[12]

Pyrocles is, of course, being not only classically pastoral but also fashionably Petrarchan when he writes verse that is purportedly about the beloved but is actually about himself. Like Astrophil—indeed, like Firenzuola, Nashe, and the Magnifico—he attempts to gain control over the elusive beloved and his own emotions by representing the beloved as an art object mastered by the poet. About this Zeuxian aesthetic—which in its extreme form yields the blazon—Roland Barthes comments that "the subject can only know the female body by its division and dissemination into anatomized parts: a leg, a breast, a shoulder, a neck, hands. . . . Fragmented, scattered, woman is but a kind of dictionary of fetishized objects. The artist . . . restructures that torn, dissected body . . . into a totalized body. . . . Yet . . . this redeeming body remains a fiction."[13] It is this controlled, fragmented, and reshaped idol that the poet worships—not the irreducible, elusive, subjective beloved. Philoclea in the eclogues represents an aesthetics that places great value on taming and effacing the source of inspiration by fragmenting it, then reshaping it into a showpiece of the poet's virtuoso skills.

Not surprisingly, it is in the blazons about Philoclea that the narcissistic underpinnings of Pyrocles's idolatrous makings are most evident, perhaps nowhere more so than when Pyrocles, overwhelmed by the force of his passion, fragments, then refashions Philoclea into discrete pieces of military hardware:

> Her loose hair be the shot, the breasts the pikes be,
> Scouts each motion is, the hands the horsemen,
> Her lips are the riches the wars to maintain,
> Where well couched abides a coffer of pearl,
> Her legs carriage is of all the sweet camp. (165.10–14)[14]

This extended blazon—in which the bodily parts of Philoclea are fragmented, then yoked violently together with such military paraphernalia as shot, pikes, and cannons—transforms the gentle and modest Philoclea into a glorious monument of poetical ornamentation. By rendering her as a series of ornamental phrases, Pyrocles (like Firenzuola before him) calls attention more to the author's virtuoso manipulation of structure and rhetoric than to the figure of Philoclea that he purports to represent. In fact the blazon appears to describe Pyrocles himself rather than Philoclea—for it is the aggressive and heroic Pyrocles (not the gentle Philoclea) who protects ladies, "disinherited persons," and kingdoms under siege (11.5).

But it is not only Philoclea who is transformed into a fetishized symbol of the poet's power; it is verse itself. As scholars of Sidney's work have noted with no little dismay, these formal, stilted, and convoluted pieces contain no apparent value beyond their virtuoso rhetorical schemas.[15] The words may call attention to their creator's stunning ability to shape intricate verbal patterns, but, like idols, they gesture to no transcendent meaning. Instead, both Philoclea and the verse that describes her are symptoms of a desire to control and master elusive femininity and creativity; both language and female character are represented as static symbols of the poet's powerful imagination. Verse, like Philoclea, has been reduced to a catalog of rhetorical parts, reintegrated by the master poet into a celebration of his dominance over elusive inspiration.

Overwrought as it may seem, Pyrocles's rhetoric is typical of Renaissance courtly poetry—of Shakespeare's narrative verse, of Lyly's *Euphues,* and, above all, of the Renaissance pastoral. Indeed, as Jeffrey Kittay and Wlad Godzich note, such a style is not just an expression of the poet's fantasy of autonomy; it is also a logical result of the transition from verse to prose: "Verse, as the displaced predecessor [of prose], poses particular problems. . . . In its emergent state, prose does not invariably confront verse directly but rather grants it a privileged position, one that nonetheless restricts the scope of verse by surrounding it. Verse seems intact, even highlighted or fetishized . . ., even though it has lost its deixis, which has now been transferred to prose."[16] Recalling Barthes's and Freccero's language about the fragmentation and fetishization of the female beloved, Kittay and Godzich articulate here how verse itself becomes idolized in an emerging prose culture: it has lost its deictic power to teach or even to signify, becoming instead a fixed symbol for the poet's mastery of inspiration and text, by means of his manipulation of words.

According to Kittay and Godzich, Sidney's aureate and fetishized poetry is symptomatic of a process that may be traced back to attempts to compose prose fiction in twelfth-century France. This process begins a shift away from the longstanding tradition of composing fiction in verse. Because of its mnemonic qualities, verse is almost automatically the medium for the oral dissemination of tales. Prose fiction does not develop until the establishment of a chirographic culture, and even then it only slowly replaces verse. Indeed, verse was so crucial a medium for telling tales in medieval culture that prose was often characterized as "derhyming." Yet with the increase of literacy from the fourteenth century on, mnemonic patterns of verse became less central to the dissemination of fiction; as a result, patrons began to express a growing interest in the novelty of prose fiction.[17] Kittay and Godzich argue that what appears to be largely an aesthetic problem—the problem of how to write fiction without depending on meter and rhyme—was a symptom of certain cultural changes, notably the transition from finding aesthetic authority in the minstrel's mnemonic, performative utterances to relocating authority in the written script, from which the minstrel would generate his performances. Although as a result, the minstrel lost status, the shift in emphasis from spoken word to written manuscript paved the way for notions of the *auctor,* whose authoritative words, inscribed permanently in ink, were (theoretically) not to be changed by reciters and circulators of his texts.[18]

Sidney's versiprosaic pastoral reveals a similar transitional structure. Although he is writing during a later transition—from a chirographic to a print culture—it is during a period when verse continues to be the dominant medium for fiction in England. Sidney self-consciously displaces the authority of poetry by fetishizing it and isolating it in the eclogue sections of the work. It is for this reason, I think, that Sidney presents his eclogues as if they are uttered by sudden inspiration to an audience—as if, in other words, they are products of a past oral culture. By situating these jewel-like pieces within a bygone era of orality, Sidney represents the idolatrous language of courtly verse as a thing of the past towards which he may look back nostalgically, even as his work expresses how verse has lost its almost incantatory power of presence within a chirographic culture.[19] In presenting verse and its idolatries of women as a once powerful form of utterance that has lost its power to signify, Sidney prepares his readers to turn to prose narrative and its more fluid female characters for pleasure and learning.

IDOLATRY AND EXOGAMY IN THE *DECAMERON*

While Boccaccio is less interested than Sidney in associating verse with idolatries of women, he shares with Sidney a tendency to associate idolatry with the desire to claim absolute possession over women and texts. For Boccaccio, texts, like women, should not be objects of possession, but rather agents of mediation, a notion that prefigures Lévi-Strauss's analogy between exogamy (mediating exchanges of women) and language—which is a "mediator in the formation of objects."[20] This analogy leads Lévi-Strauss to suggest, Philopole-like, that "the emergence of symbolic thought must have required that women, like words, should be things that were exchanged," and to note that abuses of language tend to be "grouped together with the incest prohibition, or with acts evocative of incest."[21] Like Lévi-Strauss, Boccaccio is interested not only in shaping analogies between exogamy and language, but also in exploring what happens when the system of exogamy breaks down—when the fluid mediation of women and words becomes fetishized and idolized by controlling men.

Perhaps Boccaccio's most explicit treatment of exogamy gone wrong is the story of Alatiel; the story might at first seem out of place in the narratives told during the Second Day, since these narratives are notable for figurations of empowered, articulate women.[22] Yet the story of Alatiel is not so much an exception as the extreme point of a continuum: for the stories of the Second Day develop from narratives about articulate, sexually empowered women, to stories about the problems that result when female sexuality is isolated from the female voice. The story of Alatiel (like others of this day) specifically attributes the objectification of women to such isolation.[23]

The story begins with an archetypal scene of exogamy: Alatiel is presented as a gift from the Sultan of Babylon to the King of Algarve in exchange for timely military aid.[24] Her ensuing voyage from Babylon to Algarve (on the other side of the Mediterranean) emblematizes the process of mediation, for she is to bridge the space between the two kingdoms. It is only when this process is disrupted by "fortune" that Alatiel's position shifts from that of agent to object of desire.

The resulting proliferation of scenes of seduction—scenes that focus on Alatiel's idolized, silenced, and ornamental body—suggests that the narrator's (Panfilo's) intent is to entertain his male readers by dwelling on violations and seductions of Alatiel.[25] From the moment that her first lover, Pericone, lingers over "le sue fattezze bellissime" (129) [her very fine features (172)] until the day when she finally encounters a man who can speak her language, it is almost exclusively through her beautiful body that she is defined and disseminated— a definition that from early on is associated with the loss of human identity.[26] The inexhaustible associations of Alatiel with the displayed and objectified body are epitomized by her encounter with the Duke of Athens. Because he cannot converse with Alatiel (she speaks only Arabic), Panfilo adds that the Duke "lei, sì come maravigliosa cosa, guardava" (133) [stared at her as if she were a marvelous thing (177)],[27] a vision that leads the Duke to perceive her as "sì bella cosa" (134) [so beautiful a plaything (178)] and "di questa felicità il pren- ze" (134) [a pleasure-giving object (178)].[28] Much as Sidney represents Pyrocles's blazons about Philoclea as narcissistic projections of self-love, so the story of Alatiel reveals how those who gaze upon Alatiel project upon her a common urge to possess and idolize elusive desire.

Yet the violent acts that frame these erotic scenes of display suggest that Boccaccio also critiques the objectification of Alatiel. His narrative retraces the classic plot of castration, as each male subject who gazes on the displayed body of Alatiel is made vulnerable to death and mutilation: the brothers fighting over Alatiel inflict numerous stab wounds on each other; the Prince of Morea is stabbed; the Prince of Constantinople is slaughtered by his rival. For Boccac- cio, it is not (as Nashe would have it) aggressive and articulate women who castrate men; it is aggressive men who castrate themselves by attempting to master the desired woman absolutely.

If, then, Boccaccio discloses how the display of the female body inspires fantasies of male autonomy and mastery, it is in part to show how this fantasy leads to the fragmentation, and, symbolically, castration, of the desiring male. Boccaccio's representation of castration here is not quite Freud's. Where, for Freud, castration results when the youth—by gazing on the desired woman— invites mutilation by the woman's legitimate male possessor, here it is the pos- sessor himself who is mutilated because of his unauthorized hold over the object of desire. Again, the classic oedipal triangle is deformed to fit the young claimant's fantasy of desire. Yet because each unauthorized theft of Alatiel places each claimant (temporarily) in the position of authority (a position which makes him vulnerable to being displaced by the next prodigal claimant) the story exemplifies how competition over the idolized female body yields a pathologi- cal narrative of repetition compulsion. Rapacious claims to the body of Alatiel become an ironic parody of exogamy: where Alatiel's presence should, accord- ing to Lévi-Strauss and Philopole, inspire homosocial bonds, it leads, instead, to self-destructive competition.[29]

Notably it is only when Alatiel regains her ability to speak—when she en- counters a man with whom she can communicate verbally as well as carnally—

that this pattern of murder, violation, and usurpation is transformed into a constructive narrative of female mediation. As Millicent Marcus has noted, it is when Alatiel meets her countryman Antigono that she regains her original identity as mediator.[30] By concocting a fiction, with his help, in which she claims to have spent her lost years in the convent of "san Cresci in Val Cava" (144) [St. Stiffen (189)], Alatiel reclaims her identity as the chaste daughter of the Sultan, and, by extension, as a legitimate member of the Muslim world. This identity allows her once more—this time successfully—to mediate between Egypt and Algarve.

Like a number of Boccaccio's prodigal protagonists, Alatiel's fiction-making talents allow her to represent herself as the culturally ideal woman while enabling her secretly to transgress cultural mores. By spinning a deceitful tale about her experiences abroad, she is able to represent herself as chaste, while nonetheless having experienced the transgressive pleasure of sleeping with a number of different men. Unlike Boccaccio's male protagonists, Alatiel employs fiction to affirm patriarchal authority rather than displace it—although she does so in such a way as to allow room for her own private pleasures. Clearly, Boccaccio is not interested in critiquing the system of exogamy; instead he employs the tale of Alatiel to distinguish between idolatrous (false) exogamy—which he associates with the objectification of women, and fluid exogamy—which he links with articulate and active female mediation.

The striking contrast between the silent, objectified, and ineffectual Alatiel (at the beginning and middle of the tale) and the articulate, mediating, and enabling Alatiel (at its conclusion) suggests that this narrative adumbrates analogical relations between the desire to claim a woman absolutely and the desire to claim a text as one's own. In both cases, rapacious competition between men disrupts constructive mediation. Certainly the story of Alatiel calls attention to a compulsion towards narrative, as well as sexual, repetition.[31] Panfilo signals a narrative obsession with Alatiel's body when he states, "essendo ella di forma bellissima, sì come già più volte detto avemo" (131) [As we have almost grown tired of repeating, the woman had the body of an angel (175)]. The story, he suggests, has exhausted itself by its repetitive structure: textual, like sexual, idolatry is represented as ultimately empty of interest and deictic meaning, pointing only to itself. Against this narrative of idolatry Boccaccio affirms Alatiel's mediating fiction, a witty, inventive mode of expression which associates subjective prose with a fluid form of exogamy that allows women to take a measure of control over the situations that they mediate.

As such, the story of Alatiel adumbrates somewhat different analogies between femininity, textuality, and idolatry than those expressed in *The Old Arcadia*. Where Pyrocles celebrates poetical mastery by scripting idolatrous eclogues, Panfilo's narrative discloses the self-destructive results of the desire to master and idolize texts and women. Where Philoclea is fragmented by her lover's fantasies of her, it is Alatiel's possessors who are fragmented by their own fantasies. Yet both narratives disclose how female characters, transformed into silenced, iconic emblems of male poetic mastery, become associated with isolated, solipsistic, and, finally, absurd fictionalizing. If, as we will see, Pyrocles avoids the castrating effects of idolatry, the fact that the eclogues are set off from the main body of the narrative gestures to their ultimate lack of significance.

PROSE AND FEMALE CHARACTER IN *THE OLD ARCADIA*

While Sidney seems less concerned than Boccaccio with the self-destructive implications of sexual and textual idolatry, the fact that these poems are predominantly marginalized within the eclogue sections, along with the fact that it is the character Pyrocles, rather than the narrator (who is more closely identified with the author), who utters these poems, suggests that Sidney, too, is distancing his narrative voice from the idolatrous poems which so delight his characters. Like Boccaccio, Sidney chooses instead to foreground a more fluid, complex relationship of lover to beloved and author to text. Boccaccio does so by characterizing women (for the most part) as articulate, mediating agents, rather than as silenced objects of representation; Sidney does so by aligning female interiority with the fluidity of prose. As a result, the narrator's prose version of Philoclea is radically different from Pyrocles's characterization of Philoclea in the eclogues.

The narrator's Philoclea is most strikingly elaborated in the reader's first encounter with her:

> But when the ornament of the earth, young Philoclea, appeared in her nymphlike apparel, so near nakedness as one might well discern part of her perfections, and yet so apparelled as did show she kept the best store of her beauties to herself; . . . her body covered with a light taffeta garment, so cut as the wrought smock came through it in many places (enough to have made a very restrained imagination have thought what was under it); with the sweet cast of her black eye which seemed to make a contention whether that in perfect blackness, or her skin in perfect whiteness, were the most excellent. (37.21–31)[32]

Although the language here appropriates conventional Petrarchan and pastoral vocabulary (Philoclea as "ornament" and "nymph"), the syntax expresses a radically different conceptualization of the heroine. If in the eclogues Philoclea appears as a static, manufactured object of the poet's imagination, here she is celebrated both as art object and as an elusive subject that cannot be wholly contained by the narrator's prose style; for by keeping "the best store of her beauties to herself," Philoclea engages in her own strategy of self-representation. Unlike Pyrocles, the narrator has surrendered some of the fantasy of absolute mastery to invoke, through a vocabulary of deixis, a subject that partially eludes the elegant rhetorical schema that would fix and contain her.[33] This more allusive means of representation would seem to suggest that Sidney (or his narrator) differs from his protagonist Pyrocles by identifying his writings with a feminist, or at least profeminist, perspective. But it is also true that this representation contains self-interested implications. In representing Philoclea, to an extent, as autonomous, Sidney characterizes prose as a style that deviates from the fixity of verse and moves toward a more dynamic and fluid mode of expression.

Yet Sidney appears to free Philoclea from the containment of the blazon only to fix her within conventional constructions of femininity, with phrases such as, "the tender Philoclea . . . was . . . apter to yield to her misfortune, having no stronger debates in her mind than a man might say a most witty childhood is wont to nourish"(369.30–34). The terms around which Sidney builds his description of Philoclea here—terms such as "tender," "yield," and "childhood"—imply that Philoclea is ready to take her place in the pantheon of such chaste, modest, and passive English heroines as Chaucer's Griselda or Shakespeare's Hero. But this description, though reductive, at least reveals an attempt to grant this character a measure of subjectivity, for Sidney creates a female character here that is neither a fetishized idol nor a projection of the poet's self-image.[34]

In fact, for all her conventional attributes, Philoclea often breaks out of early modern constructions of the feminine by engaging in a masculine dynamic of sight. As Philoclea deals with her sexual awakening and the concomitant desire to rebel against her parents, the narrator comments that Pyrocles's "two unrestrained parts, the mind and eye, had their free convoy to the delicate Philoclea, whose look was not short in well requiting it; although she knew it was a hateful sight to the marking eye of her jealous mother" (137.1–4).[35] Philoclea clearly disrupts the Renaissance convention of the ideal woman as one who, according to Brathwait, "hath made a covenant with her eyes never to wander."[36] No longer simply the Alatiel-like object of a male poet's gaze, Philoclea gains a measure of control within the narrative as she engages in her own semiotics of sight—one that allows her to express her awakening sexuality even as she appears to participate in the ideal of women as silent and chaste.[37]

Sidney's pervasive concern with presenting Philoclea as at least partly autonomous is perhaps most salient when he portrays her as a poet in her own right.

Although she is, for the most part, silent and silenced in the first book of *The Old Arcadia,* she composes a number of poems as the work develops. Like the verses uttered by the male protagonists outside of the eclogues, these verses, though highly ornamental, gesture toward an interiority that is not accessible in the eclogues uttered by Pyrocles (in part because these last poems are spoken to an audience). This presentation of Philoclea as at once versifier and object of verse demonstrates that, if Sidney is not interested in overturning cultural conventions of women, he is interested in complicating, stretching, and even questioning them. Although Philoclea never attains the level of authority that is granted to Musidorus and Pyrocles, she does occasionally achieve the status of poet.[38]

But if Philoclea in prose is endowed with a more subjective, even autonomous character than is her equivalent in verse, she nonetheless remains a trope for art. Much as Sidney employs Pyrocles's verse to associate both Philoclea and verse with fixation, idolatry, and convention, so Sidney (or his narrator) associates Philoclea and prose with fluidity, subjectivity and a questioning of convention. We may discern this latter aesthetics early in *The Old Arcadia,* where the prose narration seems to awaken Philoclea from her representation as static art object, for the narrator comments here that Philoclea's portrait is "drawn as well as it was possible art should counterfeit so perfect a workmanship of nature. For therein, besides the show of her beauties, a man might judge even the nature of her countenance, full of bashfulness, love, and reverence—and all by the cast of her eye—, mixed with a sweet grief to find her virtue suspected" (11.26–30). This is, of course, the standard description of a Renaissance virgin: she is beautiful, modest, and silent; but unlike the version set forth by Pyrocles in his eclogues, this description avoids the semiotics of idolatry and narcissism. Sidney in fact downplays Philoclea's physical attributes by focusing, instead, on a complex mixture of emotions that point to the underlying sexual tension in this modest heroine when she finds she has "her virtue suspected." The lack of physical description, along with the underlying sexual tension, reinforces the conceptualization of prose description as a more fluid and dynamic vehicle for characterization than idolatrous verse.

It may be that the narrator dwells on this ekphrastic description because, as Leonard Barkan comments, portraits at the threshold of romances frequently represent the "rhetorical strategy for the whole romance."[39] In the same way, this early description of Philoclea prepares us for our dual perspectives on her as at once art object and elusive subject. The narrator, by transforming static portrait into verbal prose description, enacts what Barkan calls the Ovidian strategy of ekphrasis, which "is grounded in a belief that the verbal description of a work of art unfolds into multiplicity and sequential time what the visual work itself captures frozen" (9). Reading Philoclea's portrait in light of Barkan's commentary, we can see that she is, Galatea-like, brought to life before our eyes, as the narrator initiates her transformation from art object into a subject that in part eludes the artist's mastering vision.[40]

Yet in making this indirect defense of prose fiction, Sidney is not pitting all verse against all prose. Instead, he is identifying lyric verse with a Petrarchan poetics of idolatry and his prose style with what might be termed an Ovidian narrative poetics.[41] Certainly the allusive and sexually charged Philoclea (in the prose sections) is as reminiscent of Ovid's self-willed and ambiguous heroines in the *Metamorphoses* and *Amores* as she is of Petrarch's alternately elusive and fetishized Laura. For Sidney, then, the movement from verse to prose entails moving from a Petrarchan to an Ovidian perspective—from a conventional aesthetics of idolatry grounded in the fetishization of the chaste beloved to an unconventional narrative of subjectivity generated by the developing sexuality of the beloved.[42] In the process Sidney compares lyric (which he associates with verse) to narrative (which he associates with prose), employing this opposition to figure forth the contrast between a static, idolatrous verse of the past ("Petrarchan") and fluid, allusive, emerging prose ("Ovidian").

PROSE AND SUBJECTIVE WOMEN IN THE *DECAMERON*

While Boccaccio is less interested than Sidney in setting forth distinctions between idolatrous poetry and fluid prose, the *Decameron* stages an analogous contrast between idolatrous and mediating texts. Like Sidney, Boccaccio does so by shaping analogies between fluid text and subjective female character. We have seen that it is particularly in travel narratives that Boccaccio discloses this poetics: against the ideal of travel-as-mediation suggested by Alatiel's journey from Egypt to Algarve, Boccaccio sets Alatiel's passive dissemination as a silenced, idolatrous object. It is in the early stories of the Second Day where Boccaccio most actively applies his poetics of constructive mediation. In tales like those of Martellino (which I will discuss later), Rinaldo d'Asti, and Alessandro, women actively transfer authority from an older, legitimate male to a younger, marginalized man. Yet what might at first imply that the best prodigal storyteller is a woman, encompasses a larger meditation on the Renaissance notion of *enargeia*—of the Ovidian speaking picture that creates a bond between male prodigal author and female audience.[43]

A similar dynamic is implied in the second story of the Second Day. The story strikingly resembles that of Alatiel, but with a shift in gender; for it focuses on a young man who, lost and wandering, becomes an object of desire. Boccaccio notes how the mistress of the Marquis, who succors the young dispossessed

Rinaldo, views Rinaldo as, "grande della persona, e bello e piacevole nel viso . . .
e giovane di mezza età" (83) [a fine, tall, handsome fellow in the prime of
manhood (125)]. The object of her gaze soon arouses in her "il concupiscevole
appetito" (83) [carnal instincts (125)]. What is notable about this description of
the female gaze is its lack of concern for the objectification of the gazed-upon
man. None of the figurations of castration associated with the female gaze in *The
Anatomie of Absurditie* or *The Courtier* appear here. Instead, objectification is
represented as a constructive first step towards the eventual empowerment of the
prodigal youth: so long as the articulate female allies herself with the objectified
male, the male object of desire is freed from subordination to patriarchal authority. What Boccaccio represents here is the ideal form of mediation in the
Decameron, in which a woman actively passes herself from the older, empowered
male, to the younger desiring man—a process that displaces male homosocial
bonds, replacing them with intimate alliances between a man and a woman.

The third story of this day plays even more curious games with gender inversion and female mediation. Here, after a number of setbacks, Alessandro gains
the daughter of the King of England from the King of Scotland—thanks to the
web of subterfuge woven by Alesandro's future wife. As in the story of Rinaldo,
the articulate woman at first objectifies the desiring youth, for she views him as
"giovane assai, di persona e di viso bellissimo" (88) [young, extremely good-
looking and well-built (130)]. But unlike the gaze of Rinaldo's lover, this gaze is
represented as masculine, for the princess, at this point, is disguised as a male
authority figure—an abbot. In itself her transvestism is not particularly significant; it is, after all, conventional to romance. But Boccaccio specifically calls
attention to associations between transvestism and homosexual desire here, by
keeping his readers in the dark about the abbot's actual gender. As a result, we
are invited to participate imaginatively in the forced seduction of a dispossessed young man by an older, male authority figure.

Boccaccio, I think, sets up this scene of homosexual seduction because it
emblematizes the problematics of textual authority that underlies the work. By
initially representing the young woman as an older man, Boccaccio suggests
that this is a narrative about an older man who abuses his position of authority
in order to establish his power over a subordinated youth and effeminize him.
Yet, at the very moment of sexual exploitation, this story is transformed into a
fantasy of oedipal prodigality, as the abbot reveals himself to be in fact a young
woman—who freely offers herself to the prodigal youth. A narrative of patriarchal power is thereby transformed into one about intimate relations between
two figures situated at the margins of patriarchy.

So long as we identify the abbot as a male authority figure, the tale represents
homosexuality (unexpectedly) as signifying the exploitative power of patriarchal

authority. However, when the abbot turns out to be a beautiful young woman, the story turns into a Boccaccian fantasy about the ways in which textual authority is granted to the prodigal narrator by means of the articulate woman's voice. For it is the princess who tells the story that convinces the pope to transfer authority from the "vecchissimo signore" (91) [very old man (133)] to whom she is engaged to the young, sexually active Alessandro.[44] Woman is represented less as an autonomous storyteller and more as a mediating agent who employs storytelling to transfer authority from patriarchal authority to prodigal youth.

Much as Sidney claims prodigal authority by championing fluid and subjective feminine prose, so Boccaccio sets up analogies between his complex female protagonists and Ovidian *ekphrasis*—what Aristotle and Sidney term a "speaking picture." For the story of the princess of England, like that of Alatiel, finally privileges speech over sight and script over icon (idol). Certainly the Princess of England is constantly associated with speech and freedom of movement. When Alessandro meets her (as abbot), we are told that "con lui cominciò piacevolmente a ragionare (89)" [began to converse amicably with him (130)]. The link between her speech and sexuality is reinforced by her self-assured seduction of Alessandro.

This contrast between gazed-upon and articulate women is carried over into the frame tale of the *Decameron,* where the female members of the *brigata* are represented as being just as articulate as are the men. Within this frame Boccaccio posits subtle differences between male and female modes of narration, differences that gesture to the subjectivity of female speakers. These differences are adumbrated in the narrative styles of the virtuous, witty Pampinea and the prodigal seductive Dioneo. If the stories told by Pampinea and Dioneo share similar characteristics (wit and rebellion against authority), Dioneo's stories are more likely to focus on the prodigal youth and less likely to depict dominant, articulate women.[45] In contrast, Pampinea is more likely to foreground an articulate, witty heroine, and to set forth an eventual accommodation with patriarchy, through marriage. Pampinea's version of the prodigal triangle is, then, much like that exemplified by Alatiel: she presents narratives in which women are often able to secretly cuckold their husbands. These narratives not only grant women a more significant role, but also allow them to act independently of patriarchy, even as they appear to affirm its conventions.

Boccaccio not only celebrates narratives of female empowerment but claims that women are, innately, better storytellers than are men:

de'laudevoli costumi e de'ragionamenti piacevoli sono i leggiadri motti. Li quali, per ciò che brievi sono, molto meglio alle donne stanno che agli uomini, . . . come che oggi poche o niuna donna rimasa ci sia, la quale o ne 'ntenda alcun leggiadro, o a quello, se pur lo 'ntendesse, sappia rispondere; general vergogna e di noi e di tutte quelle che vivono. Per ciò che quella virtù . . . hanno le moderne rivolta in ornamenti del corpo. . . .

Io mi vergogno di dirlo, . . . queste così fregiate, così dipinte, . . . come statue di marmo, mutole e insensibili stanno.(66)

good manners and pleasant converse are enriched by shafts of wit. These, being brief, are much better suited to women than to men, . . . Yet nowadays, to the universal shame of ourselves and all living women, few or none of the women who are left can recognize a shaft of wit when they hear one, or reply to it even if they recognize it. For this special skill, . . . has been replaced in our modern women by the adornment of the body. . . .

I am ashamed to say it, . . . but these over-dressed, heavily made-up excessively ornamental females . . . stand around like marble statues in an attitude of dumb indifference. (107–8)

Articulated by Pampinea, the passage defines wit (the key element of Boccaccio's prose style) as a feminine attribute, although one that few women continue to practice. This witty style—which certainly characterizes the speeches of Pampinea and the princess of England—is set against a current tendency by women to displace speech with ornamentation, a displacement that, according to Pampinea, yields idolized women like Alatiel or Pyrocles's version of Philoclea.[46] Speaking through a female character here, Boccaccio explicitly criticizes women who have internalized patriarchal ideals of women as silent, obedient objects. Significantly, this proem introduces the story of Master Alberto, whose feminine wit turns the table on a group of ladies. Alberto, Boccaccio suggests, is a version of himself: for just as Alberto refers to his aged yet desiring body as leeklike (white on top and green on the bottom), so Boccaccio compares himself to a leek in the proem to the Fourth Day. Pampinea's short, witty speech, then, shows how witty prose, once a woman's prerogative, has been absorbed by the prodigal male author, as a vital alternative to conventional, learned writing.

Boccaccio's adoption of Pampinea's female wit expresses a constant throughout the *Decameron:* rather than explicitly distinguish male from female ideals, Boccaccio privileges young men and women who are at once sexually desiring (even active) and know how to tell a good tale. It is in this sense that Sidney's and Boccaccio's prosaic women diverge from the articulate women that we have encountered so far. Jane Anger's narrator, Castiglione's Duchess, Pasquier's Charilée, and Sidney's Stella all balance chastity with speech—an act that is associated, symbolically, with gaining masculine authority. Indeed, in Anger's treatise, it is unruly men, not articulate women, who are effeminate, much as Castiglione implies that the Duchess is more masculine than is her sickly husband. In marked contrast, the desire for sexual experience turns Sidney's and Boccaccio's female protagonists into poets and storytellers. Desire inspires Philoclea to utter poetry, while it enables the Princess of England to narrate her story to the pope. For Boccaccio, indeed, it is the isolation of speech from sexuality that transforms male and female subjects into exploited objects of desire. This is why, for all his attention to women as objects, his stories depend, for a constructive resolution, on woman's recovery of her voice.

FANTASY AND THE FEMALE AUDIENCE

What complicates the dichotomy of idolatrous and subjective women and texts is the shifting notion of audience associated with these expressions of fiction. Boccaccio and Sidney both claim to write for a female audience; as such they represent themselves as speaking to a largely marginalized—hence unconventional and nonpatriarchal—audience. This claim is particularly transgressive given that, during the early modern period, fiction was often considered to be too morally questionable a genre for consumption by women.[47] Yet for all their affirmations of a female audience, both authors often associate the experience of reading with the act of looking upon the female form, an act that is identified with the male gaze.[48] A striking example of this act of "reading" is figured forth as Pyrocles gazes upon the sleeping Philoclea, "lying so upon her right side that the left thigh down to the foot yielded his delightful proportion to the full view" (231.3–4). While this erotic description affirms the awakening of Pyrocles's sexual and creative imagination (it immediately precedes his longest poem), it also illustrates how the privileging of the male gaze is associated with an idolatrous objectification of woman. It is interesting that this passage should immediately precede the Third Eclogues: for, as we have seen, it is in the eclogues that feminine subjectivity is effaced and fetishized; within the eclogue sections the predominantly female audience is silent, existing mainly to be "sweetly ravished" (82.18) or "stricken into a silent consideration" (152.20) by the verse which the male interlocutors utter. Much as Pyrocles's iconic verses about the gentle Philoclea mirror his own heroic self-image, so the female audience of the eclogues, like that of *The Courtier*, exists mainly to affirm the male speakers' homosocial system of verbal exchanges.[49]

Much the same dynamic is implied in Boccaccio's story of Cymon (first story of the Fifth Day), who

vide . . . dormire una bellissima giovane con un vestimento in dosso tanto sottile, che quasi niente delle candide carni nascondea, ed era solamente dalla cintura in giù coperta d'una coltre bianchissima e sottile. (355)

saw [asleep] a most beautiful girl, attired in so flimsy a dress that scarcely an inch of her fair white body was concealed. From the waist downwards she was draped in a pure white quilt, no less diaphanous than the rest of her attire. (407)

This vision of the half-clad Iphigenia, which strikingly resembles Pyrocks's vision of the transparently dressed Philoclea, changes Cymon "di lavoratore, di bellezza subitamente giudice" (355) [from a country bumpkin to a connoisseur of beauty (407)], a transformation that is specifically associated with reading the woman's body.[50] Yet while Cymon is transformed into a "connoisseur," Iphigenia herself is represented as little more than an Alatiel-like object of desire. But if such representations of the gazed-upon beloved affirm male fantasies of sexual and textual mastery, they also problematize this ideal. As Michael Sherberg has noted, the overdetermination of animalistic terms associated with Cymon, along with the vocabulary of victimization, even rape, associated with Iphigenia, interrogate the apparently idealized moment when Cymon is transfigured by gazing upon his object of desire.[51]

Much as Boccaccio's language problematizes its own idyllic scenario, so Sidney's narrative voice undermines the pleasures of the male gaze, as his protagonists encounter danger or suffer humiliation whenever they attempt to master their beloveds with look or gesture. In fact, Pyrocles's pleasurable gaze upon Philoclea's exposed thighs, which later leads to his seduction of her, is associated with emasculation, since, soon after this moment, the clownish servant Dametas steals Pyrocles's sword. For both Boccaccio and Sidney, then, a masculine mode of reading—associated as it is with envisioning woman/text as an object of idolatry—is at once pleasurable and deeply troubling; for it is linked with a superficial, exploitative mode of reading that endangers the integrity of the male subject as well as that of the female object of desire.

Perhaps because of the negative, even castrating, implications of the male gaze, Boccaccio and Sidney more often associate the awakening of the male creative imagination with the sight of the active, articulate beloved, rather than her silenced, iconic double. Sidney frequently creates descriptions of women that, like Philoclea's portrait, at once invite and frustrate the mastering impulse of the male gaze. This paradigm is exemplified in his representation of Philoclea, who (as I discussed above) inspires even "a very restrained imagination [to] have thought what was under [her diaphanous dress]." That the teasing gaps in Philoclea's wardrobe have something to do with the experience of reading is affirmed by Musidorus, who explains to Pyrocles that the "body and senses . . . are not only the beginning but dwelling and nourishing of passions, thoughts and imaginations" (372.19–21). As Musidorus's comment suggests, it is in the very interstices between Philoclea's "light taffeta garment" and her naked body that Sidney locates the reader's engagement in the dynamics of the text. Just as Pyrocles attempts to master Philoclea with his gaze only to find himself inevitably drawn into the very tableau that he would master from without, so readers are asked to risk their imaginative investment in the subjectivity of the text by completing for themselves suggestive descriptions of Philoclea.[52]

Boccaccio similarly avoids affirming the male gaze; rather than give us extended descriptions of a woman's body, he is more likely to present quick and allusive characterizations of women that foreground his female protagonists' ingenuity and wit (as well as beauty). But if such descriptions problematize the controlling perspective of the male gaze, they nonetheless assume the identification of the reader with the positions of male narrator and male characters, positions that weaken the authors' common rebellion against conventional, patriarchal structures; perhaps for this reason Boccaccio and Sidney also present us with an alternative, female audience of "belle donne" or "fair ladies," that at once affirms and displaces the priority of the masculine perspective.[53]

In itself, the acknowledgment of a female audience does not necessarily admit an alternative perspective to that of the narrator; we have seen that, in the eclogues, the female audience serves primarily to affirm the shepherd-poets' poetical perspectives. Indeed, the very analogy between woman and audience would seem to confirm Aristotelian ideals of women as passive, silent, and subordinate—much as (from the author's perspective) the ideal audience is at once silent and malleable. This analogy is initially affirmed in both *The Old Arcadia* and the *Decameron*. Philoclea is at first presented to us as a chaste, passive young woman who is carefully guarded by her parents. In much the same way, Boccaccio represents his female audience as passive, young women who, "Esse dentro a' dilicati petti, temendo e vergognando, tengono l'amorose fiamme nascose, . . . e oltre a ciò, . . . il più del tempo nel piccolo circùito delle loro camere racchiuse dimorano" (4) [out of fear or shame, conceal the flames of passion within their fragile breasts. . . . Moreover . . . they spend most of their time cooped up within the narrow confines of their rooms (46)]. But if this passage affirms Aristotelian notions of women as weak and subordinate, it also interrogates this perspective by representing this state of existence as the opprobious effect of oppression by parental figures, not as a cultural ideal. This critique of women's exploitation by men is not, of course, disinterested—it allows Boccaccio to promote himself as a champion of women—yet this designation does have liberating repercussions for the medieval/early modern woman reader. Not only does it question the assumption that women should be subject to the arbitrary drives of paternal or fraternal authority, but it constructs a female audience that—while dependent on the championing narrator—is witty, contains a measure of intellectual independence, and responds to the covert pleasures of texts.

While never granting his "fair ladies" a dominant voice in the text, Sidney, like Boccaccio, privileges a witty, bantering female reader who is alert to the covert implications of narrative. A characteristic aside to female readers is the narrator's commentary on the odd passion of the Duke and Duchess of Arcadia for Pyrocles, disguised as the amazon Cleophila: "But so wonderful and in effect incredible was the passion which reigned as well in Gynecia as Basilius (and all for the poor Cleophila, dedicated another way) that it seems to myself I use not words enough to make you see how they could in one moment be so overtaken. But you, worthy ladies, that have at any time feelingly known what it means, will easily believe the possibility of it" (49.21–27). The flirtatious tone of this passage foregrounds how the narrator depends on his audience's emotional participation in the story to bring his tale to life: indeed, for Sidney, the ideal author must create a sympathetic relationship with his readers by anticipating and bringing to the surface their buried emotions. Sidney's flirtatious tone, then, is directed towards a female audience who is at once alert to the narrator's covert implications and dependent on the narrator to anticipate her needs and desires.[54]

It is, however, within the prose narration that Sidney most elaborately sets forth his paradigm of author/audience dynamics—most notably in Prince Musidorus's courtship of Pamela. Disguised as the shepherd Dorus, Musidorus is unable to attain the attentions of Pamela, who believes that this lowly shepherd is unworthy of her attentions. And he cannot tell her that he is actually a prince because her guardians Dametas, Mopsa, and Miso never allow them any private moments together. Finally, Musidorus discovers how to communicate covertly with Pamela:

He began to counterfeit the extremest love towards Mopsa that might be. . . . Whereby, . . . [the counterfeiting made] Pamela begin to have the more consideration of him. . . . But the more she marked the expressing of Dorus's affection towards Mopsa, the more she thought she found such phrases applied to Mopsa as must needs argue either great ignorance or a second meaning in Dorus; and so to this scanning of him was she now content to fall, whom before she was resolved to banish from her thoughts. (99.1–17)

The words "scanning" and "second meaning" indicate that Pamela perceives Musidorus as a sort of text; or, more accurately, she recognizes that his passion for her is the hidden meaning of the apparently straightforward story he narrates. The story, then, receives the attention of such superficial readers as Dametas and Mopsa, but then leaves them behind, attracting a more subtle and sensitive reader to its intimate recesses.

Like Boccaccio's female readers and like the lady of the third story, Third Day, Pamela is "cooped up"; and like Aristotle's construction of women, she is to some extent malleable, predisposed to her suitor's words of love. But she is also an active participant in Musidorus's discourse; he only succeeds in awakening her love because she "let no word slip without his due pondering" (106.20–21). As Pamela reads between the lines of Musidorus's speech, Sidney carries forward Boccaccio's suggestion that writing and reading are akin to passion; for it is when she understands the covert meaning of Musidorus's text that "love began to revive his flames" (106.21–22).

In the *Decameron* this ideal of a discerning female audience is most clearly expressed between members of the *brigata,* a narrative space in which women are represented at once as storytellers and audience.[55] Differences between male and female perspectives are implied not only in women's narrations but in the women's responses to the stories that they hear. While clearly appreciating the wit behind the fabliaux, they are also aware that prodigal tales endanger women's reputations for honor and integrity. This tendency to at once applaud and interrogate the men's (particularly Dioneo's) narratives is most dramatically expressed in the ladies' responses to Dioneo's most pornographic tale, that of Alibech:

Mille fiate o più aveva la novella di Dioneo a rider mosse l'oneste donne, tali e sì fatte loro parevan le sue parole. Per che . . . la reina . . . levatasi la laurea di capo, quella assai piacevolmente pose sopra la testa a Filostrato, e disse:

—Tosto ci avvedremo se il lupo saprà meglio guidare le pecore, che le pecore abbiano i lupi guidati.—

Filostrato, udendo questo, disse ridendo:

—. . . e per ciò non ne chiamate lupi, dove voi state pecore non siete; . . .—

A cui Neifile rispuose:

—Odi, Filostrato, voi avreste, volendo a noi insegnare, potuto apparar senno, . . .—

Filostrato, conoscendo che falci si trovavano non meno che egli avesse strali, lasciato stare il mottegiare, a darsi al governo del regno commesso cominciò. (270–71)

So aptly and cleverly worded did Dioneo's tale appear to the virtuous ladies, that they shook with mirth a thousand times or more. And . . . the queen . . . removed the laurel from her head and placed it very gracefully on Filostrato's, saying:

"Now we shall discover whether the wolf can fare any better at leading the sheep than the sheep have fared in leading the wolves."

On hearing this, Filostrato laughed and said: . . . "But you have not exactly been behaving like sheep, and therefore you must not describe us as wolves . . ."

"Allow me to tell you, Filostrato," replied Neifile, "that if you men had tried to teach us anything of the sort, you might have learned some sense from us . . ."

On perceiving that the ladies had as many scythes as he had arrows, Filostrato abandoned his jesting. (319–20)

Like Sidney's, Boccaccio's speakers develop a rich and complex series of associations out of double entendre, flirtation, and verbal one-upmanship, language games in which the female audience is depicted as at once enjoying the inherent humor in the fabliau and employing wit to limit and contain prodigal male discourse. While such instances never finally subvert the prodigal perspective, they do affirm the notion that a female audience alert to the covert implications of a text will be quick to respond sharply to its attacks on women, as well as embrace its pleasures. The members of the *brigata* do so here by employing the castrating imagery of "falci" to counter Filostrato's phallic "strali." What the passage exemplifies, then, is how the male narrator who addresses a female audience must anticipate the responses that his tales will receive. Perhaps for this reason, Dioneo's tales tend to represent an extreme, rather than the norm of narration throughout the *Decameron:* most of the men—perhaps Boccaccio himself—ultimately modify their tales to fit the demands of the female audience.

This willingness to submit to the desires of the female audience reminds us that the promotion of female character, narrator, and reader has self serving implications for Sidney and Boccaccio. Above all, it allows these authors to represent themselves as original artists by aligning themselves with a female audience of prose, rather than the conventional male audience of verse. For this reason, I suggest that the concept of subservience to women is represented as far less problematic here than it is in texts such as *The Anatomie of Absurditie* and *The Courtier.*

Certainly Sidney is more likely to celebrate, rather than denigrate, the notion that the male author serves his female audience. Hence he dedicates his *Old Arcadia* to his sister, the Countess of Pembroke, whom he calls his "most dear, and most worthy to be most dear, lady" (3.1). Sidney patently replaces the conventional dedication to a powerful and authorized member of the court with an intimate address to his sister. If Philoclea's awakening sexuality is associated with creativity (both hers and Pyrocles's), the language of intimacy that binds sister to brother here takes on similar resonances. For if the work ("this child which I am loath to father") has no stated mother, Mary Sidney is, implicitly, its generator, at once its source of inspiration and the audience that imaginatively completes it (3.8–9). As Sidney tells her, "But you desired me to do it, and your desire to my heart is an absolute commandment" (3.9–10).[56] The eroticized interchange between brother and sister is almost literally enabled by the prose style of the text, or so Sidney would have us think; for he reminds his sister that the work was "being done in loose sheets of paper, most of it in your presence, the rest by sheets sent to you as fast as they were done" (3.16–17). The "loose sheets," which invoke the imaginative pleasure of Philoclea's loosely clad body, suggest a close relationship between textuality, sexuality, and the active participation of the feminized audience (men or women) in the production of the work. Indeed, the relationship (at once absent and present) between Sidney and his sister is mediated by the manuscript, which acts, Galahalt-like, as a go-between that facilitates intimate exchanges between brother and sister.

Having set up a close relationship between brother and sister via the intermediary of the romance text, Sidney extends this intimate audience of one by exhorting his sister to "keep it to yourself, or to such friends who will read it in the balance of goodwill" (3.11–12). This address entices the audience—male or female—to participate in covert exchanges between authorial brother and auditing sister, much as this audience was invited to speculate on the enigma of Philoclea's veiled body in the prose narrative. Unlike verse, whose iconic nature fixes and objectifies the female body, prose is expressed as a form that allows not only for subjective characters and fluid narrative, but for a female audience that becomes engaged in the intimate processes of textuality as well.

As we have seen, Boccaccio proposes much the same erotic relationship with his female audience when he represents his text as a pander between author and desiring female audience. But perhaps his most telling story about the advantages of subordinating the male self to women is that of Masetto of Lamporecchio (3.1). Like so many of Boccaccio's youthful male protagonists (and like Boccaccio's narrator), Masetto willingly objectifies himself so that he may sexually serve ladies. Pretending that he is mute, Masetto takes on a position as a gardener in a convent.[57] His apparent inability to speak essentially invites the nuns to consider him as effeminized, as a silenced, sexual object (the abbess in particular is entranced by the semi-naked Masetto's "cosa" [193].) Indeed all the nuns end up sleeping with Masetto because they believe that he will not be able to tell others about his sexual exploits. For his part, Masetto willingly turns himself into a sexual object in order to gain an eventual position of authority within this community of women: once the nuns find out that he can speak, they reward him financially for keeping silent about their sexual relationships with him. Eliciting at once a male fantasy of seducing virgins and a female fantasy of covert adultery (the women appear to follow the patriarchal ideal of chastity, while actually sleeping with the prodigal protagonist), the story sets forth the characteristic Boccaccian parody of the oedipal triangle by promoting a protagonist who cuckolds paternal authority—in this case, the Catholic church.

Filostrato's defense of Masetto's prodigality echoes Boccaccio's *apologia* for telling salacious tales—the need to serve women who have been unnaturally sequestered by paternal figures:

> assai sono di quegli uomini e di quelle femine che sì sono stolti, che credono troppo bene che, come ad una giovane è sopra il capo posta la benda bianca ed in dosso messale la nera cocolla, che ella più non sia femina, né più senta de' feminili appetiti, se non come se di pietra l'avesse fatta divenire il farla monaca. (188)

> There are a great many men and women who are so dense as to be firmly convinced that when a girl takes the white veil and dons the black cowl, she ceases to be a woman or to experience feminine longings, as though the very act of making her a nun had caused her to turn into stone. (234)[58]

Echoing Pampinea's comment that silent women are no better than statues, Panfilo proposes to release women from this objectified state by granting them sexual pleasure—much as the narrator proposes to liberate his cooped-up female readers by distracting them with sexually spiced tales.[59] If Masetto eventually gains a position of authority by anticipating and responding to the nuns' sexual fantasies, the narrator—and, I would argue, Boccaccio—hopes to gain authority outside of the patriarchal system by granting pleasure to his female audience.

This privileging of an intimate relationship between seductive male lover/ author and desiring female beloved/reader may illuminate one salient exception to Boccaccian sympathy for women—the infamous tale of Nastagio degli Onesti (5.8). Nastagio, spurned by the woman who loves him, retreats into a forest, where he witnesses a young girl fleeing a man and his hounds, who dismember her. The woman and young man turn out to be Dantesque spirits: when they were alive she spurned his advances, and, as a result, he committed suicide. The punishment (for her coldness and his suicide) is to enact daily this vicious scene of dismemberment. Nastagio eventually lures his beloved to the forest, where, witnessing the horrible punishment enacted upon the chaste woman, she relents and agrees to marry him. As Susanne Wofford notes, this story invites an allegory of reading the *Decameron;* not only does the tale go on to set forth a number of different witnesses (readers) to this terrifying spectacle, but the tearing apart of the woman's body is expressed as "graffiata" (405)—as a kind of writing.[60] For Wofford, this story gestures to the ways that Boccaccio's *novelle*, ostensibly written for the sexual liberation of women, indirectly teach women to subordinate themselves to the demands of patriarchy via marriage.[61] I would argue instead that this novella emblematizes the threat that chaste, young, aristocratic women pose to Boccaccio's prodigal aesthetics.[62] Nastagio is described several times as "un giovane" (403, 404) [a young man], the kind of prodigal protagonist whose purpose is to sexually liberate desiring young women from imposed chastity, and Nastagio's beloved is the kind of woman that the prodigal claimant usually saves—young, beautiful, and of "nobiltà . . . altiera" (404) [exalted rank (457)]. As such she represents a threat to Boccaccio's (or his narrator's) project of liberating rich young women from the oppression of patriarchy, along with the fantasy of advancement linked to pleasing aristocratic women. The story, then, is not so much about imposing the patriarchal institution of marriage upon young women, as it dramatizes the one kind of female audience—chaste, independent women—that threatens Boccaccio's project. Nastagio's beloved is thus punished by having projected upon her the threat of castration (fragmentation) that she poses for Boccaccio and his prodigal protagonists. In much the same way, this novella, unlike most others in the *Decameron,* is represented as a means of punishing, rather than pleasing, women. The tale ends by noting how "tutte le ravignane donne paurose ne divennero, che sempre poi troppo più arrendevoli a' piaceri degli uomini furono" (408) [the ladies of Ravenna in general were so frightened . . . that they became much more tractable to men's pleasures (462)].

If this story gestures to threats that certain female readers pose to Boccaccio's project, the narrator's overall sympathy for articulate, witty, and desiring female readers explains why such women are rarely associated with paradigms of castration in the *Decameron* and *The Old Arcadia.* Such instances are, for the most part, confined to scenes in which the desiring lover fixes and idolizes the beloved with his male gaze; yet we have seen that a metaphorics of castration nonetheless haunts conceptualizations of writing in both works. Although the anxiety of narrative castration is attenuated in Sidney's *Old Arcadia,* it is, nonetheless, a leitmotif of the prose narrative. For if, in the idealized space of the eclogues, Sidney's poet-protagonists shape idolatrous objectifications of women without being punished for such transgressions, in the prose sections his prodigal characters are condemned to death for sexually and narratively serving their ladies. This service is interpreted as a direct threat to patriarchy—embodied in the aged Basilius—for Pyrocles and Musidorus have claimed Basilius's daughters from him without his permission. The problematics of this prodigal desire is dramatized by Basilius's apparent and sudden death just at the moment when Pyrocles and Musidorus are stealing his daughters away from him. In a dramatic enactment of the return of the repressed, Basilius's advisor Philanax and Pyrocles's father Euarchus come upon the scene as substitutes for Basilius, and condemn the princes to death—a punishment, in Pyrocles's case, associated with castration (he is to be beheaded). If the providential reanimation of Basilius finally allows the protagonists to reclaim at once their masculinity and their women, the last minute nature of this intervention suggests that it is only in the narrative space opened up by fantasy that a prodigal narrator may secretly seduce the female audience from paternal vigilance, and even then he may not succeed.

Narrative castration is more strongly foregrounded in the *Decameron,* where Boccaccio complains that male critics and readers attempt to tear him apart, jealous of the intimate relationships he has kindled with his female readers.[63] This fear that prodigal narrations lead to censorship by patriarchal authority figures is at once playfully and problematically expressed in the story of Fra Alberto (4.2), who, unlike most of Boccaccio's prodigal protagonists, is severely punished for seducing a desiring woman by means of his fantastical tales. Alberto tells the rather dim Monna Lisetta that the Angel Gabriel will appear to her in the guise of Fra Alberto, because Gabriel has fallen in love with Lisetta and wishes to sleep with her. While the story is about a particularly nefarious prodigal protagonist (which explains why he is punished with such severity), it also unveils how difficult it is to shape Boccaccio's ideal relationship between prodigal author and female audience: such a relationship depends on a number of disparate elements, none of which the story of Fra Alberto fulfills. Where, for example, Boccaccio's narrator never even claims to participate in the patriarchal system, Fra Alberto exploits patriarchy by using his authoritative position as a friar to enable his seduction of Monna Lisetta. Equally problematic is the lady whom Fra Alberto chooses to serve. Unlike Boccaccio's ideal female audience, Monna Lisetta is clearly too stupid to notice that she is being oppressed by her husband and brothers; nor does she even attempt to read into the covert meaning of the tale that Alberto spins.[64] As a result, the relationship between narrator and female audience becomes a travesty of Boccaccio's aesthetics, as the prodigal protagonist employs the trappings of patriarchy to keep women in a subordinated position.

Perhaps the most troubling aspect of this story, from the narrator's point of view, is the breakdown of the notion of female patronage implicit in Boccaccio's representation of his female audience, the notion that, by serving a powerful lady (like the Princess of England), the narrator/protagonist will be elevated in status and protected from patriarchal authority. This fantasy is enhanced by analogies between Boccaccio's own status as a commoner and the often humble origins of male prodigal protagonists like Guiscardo (4.1), whom the aristocratic Ghismonda chooses because he was an "uom di nazione assai umile, ma per vertù e per costumi nobile" (283) [a man of exceedingly humble birth but notable in character and bearing (336)].[65] While this ideal of patronage by an aristocratic woman is affirmed in numerous stories, those of the Fourth Day depict its fragility. The story of Fra Alberto illustrates how a female patron may simply stand by stupidly as her "champion" is persecuted by the man who dominates her, while that of Guiscardo and Guismonda reveals how even a patroness who is powerful, articulate, desiring, and cunning, as Ghismonda is, cannot always protect her champion from being murdered by her even more powerful father.[66] Tancredi reinscribes the conventional oedipal triangle when he kills Guiscardo in order to regain possession of his daughter—an act that Boccaccio equates with sexual perversion.[67]

CLASS, GENDER, AND THE FEMALE AUDIENCE

Despite the anxieties that accompany fantasies of prodigal seduction, Boccaccio and Sidney clearly affirm an aesthetics of prose grounded in the sexual and textual service of the female audience. While this paradigm privileges an aristocratic female audience (the dominant group of female patrons in the early modern period), it is clear that, by addressing this subordinate group, Boccaccio is simultaneously opening up his work to other subordinate readers—those who share his own "humble" background.[68] This analogy is adumbrated shortly after the narrator expresses his sympathy for cooped-up female readers. Discussing the oppressive effects of the plague on Florence, Boccaccio notes how "Della minuta gente, e forse in gran parte della mezzana, era il ragguardamento di molto maggior miseria pieno; per ciò che essi, il più o da speranza o da povertà ritenuti nelle lor case" (12) [the common people and a large proportion of the bourgeoisie . . . presented a much more pathetic spectacle, for the majority of them were constrained, either by their poverty or the hope of their survival, to remain within their houses (55)]. Although this constraint is attributed narrowly to the plague, the contrast between aristocrats who are able to flee the infected town and the common people who are forced to remain within it, gestures towards the limited freedom of the non-aristocratic classes. These people, like Boccaccio's "racchiuse" (4) [cooped up (5)] fair ladies, are, as a result, in need of the kinds of distractions that (apparently) only Boccaccio's tales can offer. Certainly the proliferation of characters from the merchant class, a preference for native wit over worldly sophistication, and a proclivity for fabliaux speak to a non-aristocratic as well as aristocratic audience.

Where Boccaccio gestures to an association between an audience of women and (often) to one of commoners, Sidney, in significant contrast, insists on a female audience in order to avoid associating his prose poetics with the merchant class. The metaphorics of incest underlying Sidney's addresses to his sister suggests a desire to contain his text within the homogeneous courtly coterie that is linked with the "Sidney circle" (established in part by Sidney's aristocratic sister).

Indeed Sidney's reference to the "loose sheets" that he sends to his sister reaffirms that *The Old Arcadia* was conceived of as a coterie manuscript, not as a printed work generated for a heterogenous readership.[69] Yet if Sidney employs his female audience to maintain class distinctions, he nonetheless shares with Boccaccio a tendency to associate the female audience with fluidity and with a disruption of conventional boundaries. Sidney subtly mediates between his desire to embrace a prodigal, emergent prosaics and an equally strong desire to contain this experiment within a familiar courtly setting—a setting more commonly associated with verse.[70] For just as Sidney associates the fluid and permeable nature of his prose with sensuality, the intimate language of the dedication, along with the flirtatious asides to the "fair ladies," implicitly contains this relationship within a privileged circle of familiars.

If Boccaccio, unlike Sidney, gestures toward a larger audience, he nonetheless employs his audience of fair ladies to identify his narrator with the aristocratic court. For, in stories such as that of Guiscardo and Guismonda, the narrator makes pronouncements like, "La virtù primieramente noi, che tutti nascemmo e nasciamo iguali, ne distinse; e quegli che di lei maggior parte avevano ed adoperavano nobili furon detti" (288) [We are all born equal and still are, but merit first set us apart, and those who had more of it, and used it the most, acquired the name of nobles to distinguish them from the rest (338)]; such statements imply that a few desiring commoners may be raised in status by serving an aristocratic lady. For Boccaccio, it would seem, humble prose and the ladies who read it are a means for gaining access to the courtly coterie. If, then, Sidney addresses the courtly ladies to affirm the exclusive nature of the aristocratic coterie, Boccaccio addresses them to portray an ideal of upward mobility.

Whether they use the female audience in order to contain or open up boundaries between classes, Boccaccio and Sidney employ narrative techniques that ally them with the sort of dialogical structure that M. M. Bakhtin associates with the novel, a structure that in the *Decameron* and *The Old Arcadia* underlies the identification of elusive female characters with a fluid, generative prose narrative and with an audience that reads the work from a series of shifting narrative and gendered perspectives.[71] For if the reader—like the fair ladies who frame the text—is invited to enter into a flirtatious relationship with the male narrator, Sidney and Boccaccio also assume that the reader will at times identify with the male erotic imagination of the author. Boccaccio indirectly acknowledges such a dual readership in the sixth story of the Fifth Day, when Gianni and Restituta are tied to a stake:

Gli uomini tutti a riguardare la giovane si traevano, e così come lei bella esser per tutto e ben fatta lodavano, così le donne che a riguardare il giovane

tutte correvano, lui d'altra parte esser bello e ben fatto sommamente com-
mendavano. (393)

Whilst the men stood and gazed at the girl, unanimously praising her
shapeliness and beauty, so the women were all clustering around the youth,
expressing their warm approval of his fine figure and handsome features.
(447)

I suggest that this scene elucidates how readers, gendered alternately as masculine and feminine, are invited into an erotic experience of reading that is as
fluid and shifting as are the characterizations of the feminine in prose narrative. This is not to say that Boccaccio and Sidney, in a proleptic embrace of
democracy, give up all notions of textual and cultural authority. Rather than
embrace a larger audience (hence fulfilling what is, according to Bakhtin, the
logical extension of writing in dialogical prose), Sidney draws back from the
cultural implications of this semiotics by containing his works within a courtly
frame. And, while more open to an audience of commoners, Boccaccio finally
privileges those commoners who are cunning enough to move within courtly
circles. Nor does the authors' opening up of their texts to a variety of perspectives necessarily reveal an open-ended aesthetics; instead, it appears that Boccaccio and Sidney willingly give up a measure of authority to their audiences
in order to gain, in recompense, a more fluid form of expression that would
establish them as significant new voices in their national literatures.

PROSE AND CONSTRUCTIONS OF ORIGINALITY

Boccaccio's and Sidney's associations of prose with femininity are, I have suggested, products of a transitional period in the dissemination of literature.
While neither Boccaccio nor Sidney was writing during a transition from an
oral to an aural culture, they were composing their fictions during an analogously transitional era, an era during which courtly fiction began to shift from
predominantly aural, local, and versified productions (the oral recitation of
written texts within a semi-private courtly setting) to a larger dissemination of
texts beyond the author's immediate control, a shift even more radical during
Sidney's period of writing. Just as the problematic process of "derhyming"
reflects the gaps and ambivalences inherent in the shift from an oral to an
aural culture, so the contradictory encodings of the feminine in the *Decameron*
and *The Old Arcadia,* along with their complex narrative levels and defenses
of prose, suggest that Boccaccio and Sidney were attempting to determine

their own places in transitional periods. For if Boccaccio validates prose and its unconventional female audience, Sidney employs his female audience to draw back from associating his prose with the medium of print and with a growing middle-class readership.[72] Given that Boccaccio's self-positioning allows for a larger audience than does Sidney's, it is perhaps not surprising that his employment of prose should be even more radical than Sidney's—for Boccaccio almost entirely excludes poetry from his work. As a result, he is relatively unconcerned with opposing prose to poetry, preferring instead to establish prose as a mode of writing that enables the triangle of prodigal narrator, mediating text and desiring woman. Without entirely displacing Lévi-Strauss's cultural archetype of woman as mediator, Boccaccio's privileging of a female audience affirms woman as an active agent in her own right, not just as a passive object of mediation.

Shaping his *Old Arcadia* out of the Boccaccian alliance of prodigality, femininity and prose, Sidney focuses more on the stylistics of prose by defining, then marginalizing, verse as a fetishizing expression. It would, however, be simplistic to argue that, because he diminishes the power of verse in *The Old Arcadia,* he was content to abandon verse as a thing of the past. His delight in playing with definitions of verse and prose in *A Defence of Poetry* dramatizes his awareness that the hermeneutics of verse and prose is ultimately arbitrary—shifting in meaning depending on the cultural and aesthetic crises that generate them. Following through on the implications of Boccaccio's narrative strategy, Sidney's verse increasingly becomes the domain of the lyrical, of writing without an explicit narrative frame, while prose is associated with criticism and with such narrative forms as pastoral, romance, and epic. It is in this movement away from static, idolatrous verse and towards a more supple and complex prose style that Sidney engaged his writings in the provocative notion (for his time) that prose fiction—generally perceived to be a popular, even base, medium of expression—could be a worthwhile pursuit for the courtly artist as well.

Though more concerned with expressing prose as a style worthy at once of a merchant and aristocratic audience, Boccaccio precedes Sidney in associating supple prose and fluid femininity with originality—a concept that emerges out of Renaissance conceptualizations of prose and the feminine as subordinate (respectively) to verse and masculinity. To affirm the feminized space of prose is, then, to associate prose with subversive, problematic, and new voicings. That the authors' narrative voices ultimately frame and contain the many interior voices of the work reminds us that feminine characters in the work—provocative and subjective as they may be—are, finally, products of a certain prose style, a style that claims to be generated out of the collusion between the narrator's fertile imagination and an absent-present audience of fair ladies. Femininity and fiction seem, finally, to generate each other in these early experiments at authorizing prose fiction.

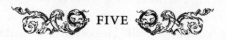

FIVE

"The Truest Poetry":
Gender, Genre, and Class in *As You Like It*
and *A Defence of Poetry*

One of the more puzzling aspects of *As You Like It* is its relative disinterest in dramatic action and plot. As Albert Gilman puts it, "Almost everything that is to happen happens in the first act; murders are attempted, ribs are cracked, and several major characters are packed off to the Forest of Arden."[1] Yet after this heady opening the play develops mainly as a series of debates on such diverse topics as the ethics of slaughtering deer, the nature of true love, and the virtues of rural retreat.[2] This tendency to interrupt action in order to stage protracted debates on a number of heterogeneous subjects suggests that Shakespeare, in composing *As You Like It,* was interested in transforming polemical literature like *A Defence of Poetry* and *The Anatomie of Absurditie* into drama, much as, in the *Diana, The Old Arcadia,* and *Orlando Furioso,* Montemayor, Sidney, and Ariosto had already turned debate literature into romance.[3] It is in the space of Arden that this transformation takes place—a pastoral space that (like other pastorals) is associated with the enclosures of fiction. For, in Arden one encounters "tongues in trees, books in the running brooks, / Sermons in stones."[4]

But the space of Arden is not just that of fiction in general; it is, I argue, specifically the space of Sidney's *A Defence of Poetry*—markedly alchemized into pastoral drama. For it is in the forest of Arden that Shakespeare at once affirms Sidney's defense of poetical feigning and interrogates Sidney's contention that English drama (because it is deficient in generic and class boundaries) is the least poetical of all literary genres. By representing Arden as a Sidneian "speaking picture" Shakespeare suggests the opposite—that drama is the preeminent genre for realizing Sidney's theories about poetry (the Renaissance catch-all term for poetry, fiction, and drama in general).[5] He does so most markedly by substituting for Sidney's male poet-narrator the deceitful and seductive Rosalind—his *figura* for the medicinal powers of fantasy and drama, and, by extension, for the fantastical space of Arden.

In maintaining that *As You Like It* is a dramatization of *A Defence of Poetry*, I am not suggesting that Shakespeare gets his plot from Sidney—we know that the story of *As You Like It* comes mainly from Thomas Lodge's *Rosalynde;* nor am I proposing that Shakespeare's philosophical ideas about poetry consistently derive from Sidney—for a number of ideas articulated in *As You Like It* and *A Defence of Poetry* emerge from shared ideas about poetry inherited from Plato, Plotinus, Boccaccio and Fracastoro. What I am arguing is that Shakespeare repeatedly frames his discourse with rhetoric and imagery that are decidedly Sidneyesque: if *A Defence* begins with Pugliano's elaborate praise of horses (17), *As You Like It* begins with Orlando's complaints about his brother's overpraise of his horses (1.1.10–33). If Sidney goes on to discuss the "golden" poetry of the past (24) by contrasting it with its present "fallen" state (18), Shakespeare describes the "golden world" of the forest of Arden (1.1.118–19) by contrasting it with the degraded state of the court. And if Sidney complains of "bastard poets . . . [who] post over the banks of Helicon, till they make the readers more weary than post-horses" (63), Rosalind says of Orlando's poetry that it is "the very false gallop of verses" (3.2.113). Both works, then, begin with highly praised horses and idle young men, then proceed to golden worlds and galloping verse.[6] By transforming *A Defence of Poetry* from polemical text to dramatic script, Shakespeare overturns the assumptions of antidrama treatises, as he suggests that it is drama—not the genres of criticism, lyric, and pastoral in which Sidney so famously dabbled—that is the best vehicle for Sidney's *A Defence of Poetry.*[7]

FEIGNING THE FOREST OF ARDEN

My investigation of *As You Like It* begins at the one scene about which some scholars *have* noted the influence of *A Defence of Poetry*—Touchstone's courtship of Audrey in act 3, scene 3.[8] This scene of clownish wooing might at first seem to have little to do with Renaissance debates on the nature of fiction, but, like so many of Shakespeare's fools, Touchstone is a product of the court, and, as such, of courtly debates:

> Touchstone: *Truly,* I would the gods had made thee poetical.
> Audrey: I do not know what "poetical" is. Is it honest in deed and word? Is it a true thing?
> Touchstone: No, *truly;* for the truest poetry is the most feigning, and lovers are given to poetry; and what they swear in poetry may be said as lovers they do feign.
> Audrey: Do you wish then that the gods had made me poetical?
> Touchstone: I do, *truly;* for thou swear'st to me thou art honest. Now if thou wert a poet, I might have some hope thou didst feign. (3.3.15–27; emphasis added)[9]

Aside from "poetry" and "poetical," the most repeated words in this passage are "truly" and "true," words that call to mind Sidney's paradoxical response to the accusation that poets are liars. As Sidney puts it, "*truly,* I think *truly,* that of all writers under the sun the poet is the least liar . . . for the poet, he nothing affirms, and therefore never lieth" (52; emphasis added).[10] Poets, in other words, are not liars, since they freely admit that they lie. As such, Sidney's response differs notably from that of previous defenders of poetry. True poetry, for Boccaccio, is "a fair and fitting garment" that veils the truth of God from ignorant people and blasphemers.[11] Fracastoro's defense is that poets are not liars, but rather perfectors; while Castelvetro defends poetry by distinguishing between poets who follow Aristotelian rules and versifiers who abuse these essential rules.[12] All these writers defend poetry by representing its fictive nature as either protecting divine truths, leading to divine truths, or following inherited, conventional forms. Sidney, in contrast, celebrates poetry as a series of self-confessed and seductive lies that point to no transcendent or hermetic meaning, but that move readers to virtue by means of the poet's inventive skills.

Touchstone confirms his debt to Sidney's representation of lying (fiction) by repeating Sidney's ironic references to "truly" and by revealing his seductive intentions to Audrey. These echoes of Sidneian language and theory suggest that Touchstone's courtship of Audrey is its own "miniature defense of poetry," a defense in which Touchstone temporarily personifies a fantastical poet while Audrey personifies the icastic audience to whom his seductive rhetoric is addressed.[13] Audrey's persona is linked with truth, chastity, and lack of ornamentation; for she is plain in looks as in language.[14] But her honest nature is somewhat denigrated in this scene, associated as it is with reductive mimesis: she can only view "poetical" as a "thing." She is, in other words, the kind of audience who on "coming to a play, and seeing *Thebes* written in great letters upon an old door, doth believe that it is Thebes" (*A Defence,* 51). For Shakespeare and Sidney, an audience that (like Audrey) is too ignorant to distinguish between literal and metaphorical concepts is also incapable of experiencing the "enriching of memory, enabling of judgement, and enlarging of conceit" that should epitomize the experience of reading, watching, or listening to fiction (*A Defence,* 28).[15] Both authors, then, suggest that the purpose of fiction is to seduce an audience away from narrow, literal thinking by opening up the audience's imagination. This is what distinguishes Touchstone's fictive rhetoric from the lies of villains like Oliver and Duke Frederick: not only does Touchstone let Audrey know that his intentions are not fully honorable, but, unlike the deceptive practices of Duke Frederick, Touchstone's lies give pleasure to their victims.

FANTASY AND THE BOUNDARIES OF DRAMA

So far, then, Sidney and Shakespeare (or at least Sidney's narrator and Touchstone) seem to be on the same poetical track: both represent fiction as a device that draws the audience away from narrow, literal thinking; both suggest that the way to achieve this end is by lying seductively while calling attention to these lies. This poetics gestures to a strong homosocial bond between deceased literary critic (Sidney) and living playwright (Shakespeare), a bond enabled by a common project of seducing the reader/audience with pleasant lies. But Shakespeare's embodiment of his defense in Touchstone and Audrey also problematizes the close, poetical relationship between the two authors, as Shakespeare transforms Sidney's quite didactic text into a dialogue between two clownish characters. This strategy, I suggest, allows Shakespeare to frame and contain Sidney's aesthetic statements in such a way as to foreground the performance of Sidney's poetics over its rhetoric.[16] By scripting Sidney's literary criticism as a comic interlude between a courtly fool and a country bumpkin, Shakespeare paves the way for his own playful defense of drama—one, I argue, that discredits Sidney's stridently elitist criticism of English drama as deficient in structure, content, and decorum.

Sidney's strongly worded stance against English drama is somewhat surprising, given that *A Defence* reads like a treatise on poetry in search of a drama to represent it. Certainly Sidney seems to be aching to transform poetry into drama when he says things like, "hear old Anchises speaking in the midst of Troy's flames, or see Ulysses in the fulness of all Calypso's delights . . . let but Sophocles bring you Ajax on stage, killing or whipping sheep and oxen" (33). Such emphatic references to actions, sounds, sights, and gestures (not to mention to the "stage" itself) call attention to the dramatic deficiencies of the written word, suggesting that drama may indeed be the preeminent forum for Sidney's project of awakening the reader's imagination.[17] Indeed Sidney affirms almost indefatigably that fiction has no value unless it has successfully "moved" the audience with lively "speaking pictures."[18] The purpose of "moving" is, as he puts it, "not only to make [prince] . . . Cyrus, . . . but to bestow a Cyrus upon the world to make many Cyruses" (24). In other words poetry exists to entice readers—inspired by the author's words—to model themselves on such idealized heroes as Cyrus. This is why so much of *A Defence* depends on the language of seduction and deceit: pleasurable rhetoric and fantastical plots are crucial mediums for enticing the reader into this conversion experience.

Yet despite his ongoing affirmation of dramatic characterization, Sidney shows little sympathy for the work of English dramatists.[19] As O. B. Hardison and others have noted, Sidney turns from earlier affirmations of the "high flying liberty" of poetical language to become insistently rule-oriented when he discusses English drama, making statements like: "Our tragedies and comedies (not without cause cried out against), . . . [observe] rules neither of honest civility nor skilful poetry" (22, 65). Using *Gorboduc* as his primary example, Sidney excoriates drama for its deficiencies in the unities of time, place, and action (65); in the process he condemns the kind of romance plays that Shakespeare would soon be writing: "Now you shall have three ladies walk to gather flowers: and then we must believe the stage to be a garden. By and by we hear news of shipwreck in the same place: and then we are to blame if we accept it not for a rock. Upon the back of that rock comes out a hideous monster with fire and smoke: and then the miserable beholders are bound to take it for a cave" (65).

Sidney's insistence that drama should radically limit itself to neo-Aristotelian rules and plausible plots is something of a puzzle, for it appears to contradict his earlier affirmation that the greatness of a poet inheres in his ability to "freely range."[20] One could argue, of course, that Sidney, like Boccaccio, Pasquier, and, later, Shakespeare, liked to shape works out of internal debates and, hence, contradiction; this stance would explain why he appears to make one point only to contradict it with its opposite. But this does not in itself explain why Sidney should reserve particular spleen for the aesthetic abuses of drama. The answer, nonetheless, is fairly obvious: Sidney—writer of romance, pastoral, entertainment, lyric, translations, and criticism—never dabbled in drama, because drama (except for masques and closet dramas) was considered to be beneath aristocratic aspirations.[21] In other words, English drama is excluded and excoriated because it has not yet achieved courtly status.

I focus on this point because Sidney appears to conceptualize genre here as a kind of metonym for class by shaping an analogous relationship between the unruly and undifferentiated nature of romance plays and the broad theatrical spaces of Elizabethan drama, liminal spaces that contrast strongly with the more carefully delimited space of the Elizabethan court (or the Countess of Pembroke's estate).[22] Indeed, Sidney shows particular scorn for plays that disrupt class boundaries—that are "neither right tragedies, nor right comedies, mingling kings and clowns" (67).[23]

If Sidney is concerned, even obsessed, with delimiting the generic and class boundaries of English drama, Shakespeare shows little concern with either problem, at least within the Forest of Arden. Perhaps for this reason his pastoral drama differs from the pastorals of his Elizabethan contemporaries, which are most often represented as hermetic sites that enclose within them idle, aristocratic shepherds and swains.[24] Shakespeare's Arden, far more porous than the pastorals of Spenser, Sidney, and Drayton, allows room at once for duke and servant, idealized shepherd and impoverished swain, wintry scenes and verdant landscapes. As such, it figuratively recalls not so much the Elizabethan court as the public theater, a space in which (temporarily) aristocrat and commoner, actor and audience, art and experience might encounter each other. By shaping an Arden in which, if not kings and clowns, at least dukes and fools meet, Shakespeare implies that it is in the broader theatrical world rather than the circumscribed space of the courtly coterie that the poet can most powerfully employ seductive fantasy to engage his audience imaginatively in his poetical world.

This is not to say that Shakespeare successfully effaces all class distinctions. Not only does Arden contain its own courtly hierarchy-in-exile, but Shakespeare's representation of the mentally limited Audrey demonstrates his own prejudice against audiences who do not share his background as an urbane, educated, and prosperous commoner. Shakespeare, in other words, has successfully dismantled the aristocratic prejudices of Sidney's *A Defence of Poetry* only to inscribe his own, proto-bourgeois, leanings in his play.[25] Nonetheless, the popularity of his plays with the non-aristocratic classes along with the sympathy with which he depicts some of his uneducated characters, suggests a desire to conceptualize the theater as a place which draws and depends on a heterogenous audience.

THE FEIGNING AND SEDUCTIVE ROSALIND

What I have sketched out so far is Shakespeare's ambivalent response to *A Defence of Poetry,* one that emerges from intersecting issues of class and aesthetics. On the one hand Shakespeare critiques Sidney's aristocratic prejudices against drama by suggesting that the heterogenous nature of English drama is what makes drama significant, not, as Sidney would have it, "defectuous" (65). On the other hand, the play strongly affirms Sidney's poetics, particularly his notion that fiction is a seductive and deceitful force whose purpose is to enrich the audience's imagination.[26] It is, ultimately, via the unruly and sexually ambiguous figure of Rosalind that Shakespeare embodies his poetical project of affirming drama as the ideal medium for Sidney's poetics of seduction.

Rosalind's very sexuality speaks to Shakespeare's ambivalent relationship to Sidney. If her status as a woman recalls Sidney's tendencies to associate fiction with femininity (with both positive and negative implications in *A Defence* and, more constructively, in *The Old Arcadia* and *Astrophil and Stella*), Sidney himself represents his poet-protagonists as men, suggesting his ultimate inability to construe feminine fantasy as a stable site of identification for male poets. Against Sidney's comments (in *A Defence*) that "effeminateness" characterizes weak English poetry, Shakespeare represents femininity and effeminacy as enabling constructs that, along with seduction and deceit, bring *enargeia* to Sidney's abstract poetical notions (61).

Critical perspectives on Rosalind as female protagonist may be divided, roughly, into three camps: those who affirm Shakespeare as a feminist (or proto-feminist) by pointing to his creation of an intelligent and articulate heroine; those who argue that the ultimate subjugation of Rosalind to a man speaks to Shakespeare's inability to transcend patriarchal codes; and, most frequently, those who characterize Shakespeare's representation of Rosalind as feminist, but not fully so.[27] I would like to propose a fourth reading by suggesting that while Shakespeare affirms Rosalind's articulate and unruly nature, he does so not from a feminist perspective but rather from self-interested motives—from a desire to represent the dramatist as an innovative, emergent author, and he does so by associating the dramatist with an antipatriarchal, anti-authoritative, and, hence, feminine or effeminate (via Ganymede) aesthetics.

It is by juxtaposing Renaissance debates on poetry with those on the nature of women that Shakespeare calls attention to the aesthetic implications of shaping a female poet-protagonist who serves, to a large extent, as the male playwright/actor's mouthpiece—as the main *figura* for creating, directing and acting in the space of Arden. My purpose, in emphasizing this point, is not so much to look at the boy actor behind this female character (as a number of critics have recently done), but at one man behind this "woman"—Shakespeare.[28] Shakespeare, one might say, masquerades his male self with a female persona who shares his proclivities for puns, wit, and acting, and he does so to suggest an alternative to the dominant aristocratic and masculine poetics that he associates with *A Defence of Poetry*. Like Boccaccio, in other words, Shakespeare metaphorically castrates (feminizes) his male persona in order to avoid the patriarchal convention of identifying with his literary father who, in this particular scenario, he projects as Sidney.

Shakespeare's poetics of femininity-as-masquerade yields a two-pronged representation of Rosalind: an ongoing desire by the male authorial self to curb his female protagonist's independence (by marrying her off at the end) co-exists with what one might call the ultimate male fantasy—the liberation from biological and patriarchal determinism associated with having a penis; hence the tendency to represent Rosalind both as poet-protagonist and object of male fantasy. If, then, Rosalind is not Shakespeare per se, she is a site onto which Shakespeare can project fantasies of liberating the authorial self from the dominant patriarchal poetics of the period, and from biology as well.[29]

Certainly the process by which Shakespeare scripts the development of Rosalind is not unrelated to the process that a young author must undergo before he can distinguish himself as an emerging and significant writer. Before she can become the protagonist of the play, Rosalind must displace her main, male rival for the role of protagonist, Orlando, whose speech, actions, and even poetry dominate the first part of the play.[30] To displace Orlando is to take on a strategy somewhat analogous to Shakespeare's attempted displacement of his male rival, Sidney, one that emerges from an initial identification with Sidney. This early scene of identification is adumbrated as, we have seen, *As You Like It* and *A Defence of Poetry* initially present their male protagonists in a similar light: not only are both comically overshadowed by horses, but both refer to themselves as "idle."[31] By shifting from an initial identification with the threshold poet-persona—the male, Sidneyesque Orlando—to a stronger focus on the female prosaic Rosalind (Orlando's "Other"), Shakespeare, enacts his own desire to turn away from authoritative works like *A Defence of Poetry.* Indeed, when Rosalind emerges as heroine—in the Forest of Arden—her primary function is to engage in a series of contentious and competitive dialogues with or about Orlando, dialogues that, until the last few lines of the play, represent her as mastering this initial candidate for hero. As such, she may well represent Shakespeare's fantasy of displacing Sidney—perhaps the most read, quoted, and respected English writer during the 1590s (when Shakespeare apparently wrote *As You Like It*).

Rosalind's strategy of displacement and mastery is based above all on a critique of conventional lyric poetry; indeed her first unruly act in the forest is to anatomize, then dismiss, Orlando's poetry—a fairly simple task, given Orlando's tendency to express his passion in somewhat clumsy verse:

From the east to western Inde,
No jewel is like Rosalind.
Her worth, being mounted on the wind,
Through all the world bears Rosalind. (3.2.88–91)

Of the many infelicitous aspects of this verse, Touchstone and Rosalind focus on its irregular meter. Touchstone (Rosalind's alter ego) contends that, "This is the very false gallop of verses; why do you infect yourself with them?"—a phrase that recalls both Sidney's disparagement of galloping verse and his comment that English poets are "infected" with the disease of bad writing (*As You Like It*, 3.2.113–14; *A Defence*, 63).[32] After echoing Touchstone's sentiments, Rosalind dwells on the general dullness of Orlando's lines, by commenting, "O most gentle pulpiter, what tedious homily of love have you wearied your parishioners withal" (3.2.155–56).[33] Her lines echo Sidney's comment about the dullness of English love lyrics: "But truly many of such writings as come under the banner of unresistable love, if I were a mistress, would never persuade me they are in love, so coldly they apply fiery speeches"—language that Sidney also associates with bad preachers (69–70). Certainly Orlando's mistress has been left cold by his verse, a reaction that leaves room for Rosalind's preferred form of fiction—witty prose dialogue.[34]

If Rosalind and Touchstone echo the language of *A Defence* here, they do so in order to discredit it by promoting the witty rhetoric of comic repartee over the courtly genres that Sidney affirms. Sidney, we have seen, also critiques the plodding, conventional nature of many English lyrics, but, unlike Rosalind, he does so not by discrediting the lyric per se but rather by advocating a renewal of this genre with the kind of lively and witty lyrics epitomized by *Astrophil and Stella*.[35] Sidney, indeed, implies that the way to bring *enargeia* back to the lyric is to remove it from an academic setting and return it to the precincts of the Elizabethan court, for "I have found in divers smally learned courtiers a more sound style than in some professors of learning" (72). Rosalind and Touchstone imply the opposite. They discredit the traditional love lyric by associating it with courtly language—a language that they represent as desiccated, outdated, and, thus, needing renewal from a space outside the court—a place like Arden, with its close affinities to the English stage.

The critical modus operandi of Touchstone and Rosalind is not just to call attention to the infelicities of Orlando's lyrical style, but also to associate Orlando's verse with the impersonal dissemination of manuscripts. This may not be the first association one makes with manuscripts: Sidney, we have seen (in *The Old Arcadia*), employs the idea of the manuscript to suggest intimate relationships between writers and readers (in order to distinguish manuscript dissemination from the more impersonal form of print); but in *As You Like It* manuscripts are impersonally disseminated, at least in comparison to the intimacies of dramatic dialogue. Orlando's poems are, after all, anonymous texts that are discovered hanging in trees. Against this impersonal dissemination, Rosalind re-inscribes the language of presence by turning from conventional lyric and toward dramatic and fully present prose dialogues between lovers (and between actors and their audiences). Under the aegis of Rosalind, the courtly love lyric gives way to dramatic, witty prose dialogue—dialogue that, interestingly enough, captures much of the wit and allusiveness of Sidney's prose style. Rosalind and Touchstone, in other words, seem to be suggesting what Sidney can never quite utter in *A Defence*—that the future of fiction lies in supple and witty prose dialogue, not in the traditional courtly lyric.

Certainly the verbal and narrative power of the play is strongly associated with Rosalind's witty prose. It is, after all, through the medium of her seductive words that Rosalind manages to marry off most of the characters. This rhetorical power is also associated with—perhaps even inseparable from—her seductive looks. The close symbolization between beautiful words and a beautiful woman recalls Sidney's claim that, "who could see virtue would be ravished with the beauty of her thoughts" (47). Shakespeare gives an ironic twist to this statement when he embodies "virtue" as Rosalind—at once chaste and seductive, honest and feigning, masculine (*vir*) and feminine. In the process he unveils what is both celebratory and problematic about virtue as Rosalind—Rosalind's ability to seduce women as well as men. It is, apparently, Rosalind's beauty and eloquence that inspire Phebe to exclaim, "Sweet youth, I pray you chide a year together, / I had rather hear you chide than this man woo" (3.5.64–65).[36] Phebe's experience is, of course, in an inverse relationship to that of the Renaissance audience: she is erotically attracted to a boy who turns out to be a woman; Renaissance audiences were instead presented with attractive women who turned out to be boys. In either case, the effect is the same—the suggestion that the erotic attractions of poetical feigning problematize normative heterosexual equations.[37]

Of course one could argue that Rosalind does not so much problematize heterosexuality as multiply its possibilities for the Elizabethan audience. As Stephen Orgel and Peter Stallybrass have noted, the boy actor / female character combination enabled the boy actor to erotically attract the female members of the audience while the female character he projected (Rosalind) excited male members; in much the same way one might say that Phebe is drawn to Rosalind's disguise as a boy, not to the woman behind this costume.[38] But what this transsexual dynamics suggests above all is an ongoing tendency among Renaissance authors to slip from femininity to effeminacy—from Rosalind to Ganymede. This staging of effeminacy as an extension of femininity (and vice versa) has two implications. First (as other critics have proposed), it suggests that Rosalind's attractions lie not so much in her identity as an effeminate boy or feminine woman, as they do in her very sexual ambiguity;[39] by extension, Shakespeare suggests here that the poetics of fantasy is best performed by slippages between femininity and effeminacy. The point is not, then, whether Rosalind attracts hetero- or homosexual desire, but about the ways that fantasy's seductive powers inhere in constantly shifting sexual positions that are always unmasculine (feminine or effeminate) and, hence, subversive of patriarchal convention.[40] For Shakespeare, it would appear, the power of drama inheres in its ability to disrupt dominant ideologies of class, gender, and aesthetics—to enact what Penny Gay calls the "fantasies of transgression" that audiences experience through theatrical performances (14).[41]

The burden of representing the erotic transgressions of androgyny on stage has, perhaps, become more onerous since the Restoration—when productions of *As You Like It* effaced, to a degree, sexual ambiguity by having an actress (rather than a young man) play Rosalind. Transvestism, of course, remains present in the play—in Rosalind's disguise as Ganymede; but the play loses the intricate layerings implied in having a boy actor pretend to be a woman who is pretending to be a boy.[42] For one thing, this more complex and confusing representation of gender identity contrasts strongly with the poetics of Sidney's *A Defence;* Sidney seems as troubled by "mingling" genders as he is by "mingling kings and clowns." This at least is what Sidney implies when he tropes effeminacy negatively in *A Defence.* If Rosalind's ambiguous gender identity is what promotes her creativity, for Sidney it generates bad poetry.

By characterizing English fiction, including drama, as weak and effeminate, Sidney is affirming the perspective of most antidrama writers, who often represent poetical transvestism as threatening the very foundations of their culture, particularly its dependence on stable notions of patriarchy, sexuality, and gender. It is, for these authors, the transgressive eroticism of androgyny that moves the audience to unvirtuous and unauthorized thoughts; or as Stephen Gosson puts it, the "Theaters, . . . rather effeminate the minde as prickes unto vice, then procure amendement of maners as spurres to vertue" (19). Much as women, according to Nashe, contaminate men with their feminine ways, so androgynous characters on stage easily infect the audience with the vices that they embody.

While contemporary theater critics put a positive spin on the notion that theatrical bodies are invested with "the rhetorical power to move," Renaissance antidrama critics viewed the representation of bodies on stage as moving the audience in dangerously seductive ways.[43] Characteristic of this stance is Philip Stubbs's strong declaration against comedy, about which, he thunders, "The matter and ground is love, bawdrie, cosenage, flattery, whordome, adulterie: the Persons, or agēts, whores, queanes, bawdes, scullions, knaves, Curtezans, lecherous old men, amorous yong men, with ſuch like of infinit varietie. . . . For ſo often, as they goe to thoſe howſes where Players frequēt, thei go to Venus pallace and ſatās ſynagogue to worſhip devils, and betray Chriſt Jeſus."[44] What Shakespeare celebrates—the heterogenous nature of the theatrical experience—is precisely what, for Stubbs, is its preeminent threat to his culture, its ability to entice the audience into a variety of illicit sexual acts.

If the varied hetero- and homoerotic fantasies associated with Rosalind alarmed antidrama critics, Shakespeare closely aligns them with the liberating experience of fantasy. Phyllis Rackin has found in *As You Like It* a celebration of fantasy as a feminine construct, for

> In an androcentric culture, the female principle is negative, like . . . the concept of feminine gender that allows the male to define itself as masculine. . . . Fantastic drama reverses this equation, locating the reality principle within the world of art rather than outside it, creating an antiworld where object becomes subject and the feminine can be characterized as real. Realistic art, by contrast, strives to replicate within itself the hierarchical relations that its society has defined as natural.[45]

It is because she is at once woman and effeminate boy that Shakespeare figures forth Rosalind as his emblem for fantasy—for an alternative to patriarchal experience. Other associations of Rosalind, her seductive rhetoric and deceitful appearance, are also related to fantasies of androgyny. Just as fantasy, in most poetical treatises, is necessary for moving the audience to virtue yet is considered vicious when it becomes an end in itself, so the erotic androgyny of Rosalind effects a constructive movement towards marriage yet potentially subverts this institution if homoerotic attraction or unruly femininity becomes an end in itself. It is in the performance of this feminine/effeminate character that Shakespeare embodies his notion that drama, because it interrogates traditional lyric forms and coterie "aristocratic" aesthetics, is the preeminent forum for embodying Sidney's notions about poetical "moving" and freedom.

THE APRON OF THE STAGE

In the sense that she emblematizes the constructive yet problematic eroticisms of femininity, effeminacy, and fantasy, Rosalind is an emblem for this project as a whole. Like Boccaccio, Pasquier, and Sidney (in his lyrics and romances) Shakespeare celebrates these subversive traits in part because they are associated with aesthetic alternatives to patriarchal truths and convention. This is arguably why Shakespeare associates Rosalind so strongly with the emergent genre of drama by calling attention to the boy actor behind the female character. His action recalls Boccaccio's strategy of displacing the Dantesque epic with the novella and its sexually aware heroines, or Sidney's displacement of the Petrarchan lyric with prose fiction and its seductive women (before rewriting notions of the lyric in *Astrophil and Stella*).

These diverse imbrications of fantasy with gender and originality are, however, circumscribed at the end of these works, as the authors prepare their audience's return to patriarchal experience. Boccaccio ends his *Decameron* with his most conventional, chaste, and silent heroine—Griselda; Pasquier's characters move from the garden to the court in order to debate the masculine topic of the ideal military leader; while Sidney's putative audience of "fair ladies" in *The Old Arcadia* simply disappears. In much the same way Shakespeare ends *As You Like It* with Rosalind's entrance into the patriarchal world of marriage.[46]

The one exception to this pattern is *Astrophil and Stella*. At the end of his sequence Astrophil refuses the conventional "farewell to love," preferring to affirm his unrequited love for Stella even as he confesses the impossibility of consummating this love. His final couplet illustrates at once the advantages and shortcomings inherent in refusing conventional closure. By stating, "in my woes for thee thou art my joy, / And in my joys for thee my only annoy" (108.13–14), Astrophil affirms his final triumph over Stella's authoritative, conventional voice by celebrating a poetics of liminality—a poetics associated with sexuality and prodigality. Yet the ambiguous and paradoxical language of this couplet, along with its direct address to Stella, reminds us of the extent to which Astrophil depends on the conventional voice of Stella as a site from which he may express his prodigal poetics. While affirming a marginalized place from which to write transgressive verse, Astrophil's poetry betrays a dependence on a conventional, if femininely inflected, invocation and imitation.

If Sidney's is the only work I have explored that openly resists the return to patriarchal closure and convention, it is nonetheless true that resistance is encoded as well in the other prodigal works that I have investigated here. Boccaccio's stories may end on a conventional note, but his ensuing epilogue affirms his poetics of prodigal seduction; in much the same way *Monophile* moves from feminine to masculine topics, yet the apparent inclusion of Charilée in the ensuing debate on the nature of war keeps open the possibility of including an articulate, female voice within the courtly coterie; and if *The Old Arcadia* returns to male rule and conventional marriage, the author's suggestion of a sequel involving the adventures of the heroine's daughter allows for the possible reemergence of feminine, prodigal, and unruly fictions. What these diverse endings hint at is not so much an inevitable return to patriarchal convention as an ongoing tension between dominant patriarchal codes and the continuing pressure against these codes implied in feminine or effeminate fantasy.

That, at least, seems to be the implication of the epilogue to *As You Like It*, which has its own, quite famous, response to the problem of closure. By stepping out onto the apron of the stage, Rosalind at once maintains her identity as a female character and reminds her audience of the boy actor who plays her.

As such, her epilogue reveals a consistent attempt to mediate between the open-ended and prodigal flavor of feminized fantasy and the limited authority of experience and convention suggested by the male actor behind Rosalind.

Given Shakespeare's constant invocation of, dependence on, and rebellion against Sidney's *Defence,* it is not surprising to discover echoes of Sidney's final *peroratio* in Rosalind's epilogue. Sidney's narrator ends his treatise by conjuring "you all that have had the evil luck to read this ink-wasting toy of mine, . . . no more to scorn the sacred mysteries of poesy . . . but to believe . . . themselves [poets] . . . they will make you immortal by their verses" (74–75). Portraying poetry as at once weak ("ink-wasting") and all-powerful ("immortal"), Sidney calls attention to the contingent nature of poetical feigning, to the ways in which poetry's immortality depends on the reader's willingness to be seduced and deceived by poetry.[47] The language of conjuration associated with the poet's rhetorical power calls attention both to the tremendous potential of fantasy to move the reader and its radical dependence on the willingness of the reader to accept its premises.

The boy actor's epilogue depends on a similar mix of power and contingency, one that depends on a Sidneian language of conjuration:

My way is to conjure you, and I'll begin with the women. I charge you, O women, for the love you bear to men, to like as much of this play as please you; and I charge you, O men, for the love you bear to women (as I perceive by your simp'ring, none of you hates them), that between you and the women the play may please. If I were a woman I would kiss as many of you as had beards that pleas'd me, complexions that lik'd me, and breaths that I defied not; and I am sure, as many as have good beards, or good faces, or sweet breaths, will for my kind offer, when I make curtsy, bid me farewell. (Epilogue.11–23)

The epilogue highlights a problem recently articulated by performance theorists—how a powerful stage character is deeply dependent on the whims of the theatrical audience.[48] Employing the same language of conjuration and belief that Rosalind used to prepare the couples for their ultimate union with each other (5.2.56–65), the character Rosalind and the boy actor who plays her express an analogous desire to conjoin the male and female members of the audience. Again, it is the actor's androgyny that gives him/her the potential to effect this union.[49] Calling attention to Rosalind's erotic attraction to men ("If I were a woman I would kiss . . . you") and the boy actor's attraction to women ("for the love you bear to men"), the actor attempts the same sort of transference that Rosalind enacts so well in Arden by (following Boccaccio's lead) representing the text as a kind of pander that unites men with women.[50] Through the

eroticized medium of prose, the boy actor at once enacts the necessary movement from fantasy to experience and affirms Shakespeare's (and Sidney's) fantasy that the poet, by creating a fictional hero like Cyrus, will "make many
Cyruses" (*A Defence,* 24). Shakespeare's version is to bestow a Rosalind upon
the world of the audience in order to convert the audience into the poetics of
passion and femininity/effeminacy staged by Rosalind.

It is through such poetical moving that Rosalind and the boy actor who
plays her engage the language of feigning and seduction to conjure, temporarily, the magical forest of Arden, an imaginative space in which author and audience may enter into an intimate, transgressive relationship with each other. In
thus incarnating Sidney's language as Audrey and Touchstone, Rosalind and
Orlando, boy actor and audience, Shakespeare dramatizes the theater's vivid
power of presence. For it is as the fantastical Rosalind that poetry "giveth so
sweet a prospect into the way, as will entice any man to enter into" the feigned
Forest of Arden (*A Defence* 39–40). In acting out the dynamics between fantasy and experience via the mediatory space of the theatrical apron, Shakespeare
implies that it is in the very public precincts of the stage rather than in the
private manuscript culture of the English court that Sidney's aesthetics of fantastical moving may most powerfully and seductively be expressed.

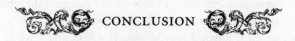

Illusions of Originality

he poetical politics of *As You Like It*—its radical reconceptualizations of Sidney's *A Defence of Poetry*—speak to an ongoing desire to trope an influential male predecessor as conventionally patriarchal. This strategy enables the emergent author to represent himself as feminine (or effeminate), and, by implication, original. In *As You Like It* such a strategy makes it possible for Shakespeare to transform his predecessor's defense of poetry into a defense of drama. For English Renaissance polemicists, I have noted, drama was considered to be a particularly suspect form of expression because (unlike poetry) it acts out lies: characters who claim to be one kind of person, even one kind of sex, turn out to be something else altogether. Shakespeare indirectly replies to such charges (via Touchstone's dialogue with Audrey) by suggesting that drama, like other fictions, calls attention to its deceptive practices; hence it demystifies its seductive rhetoric. Nonetheless, antidrama, like antifiction, polemicists had a point; for the diverse male writers I looked at all celebrate the unruly, deceptive, and seductive powers of fiction, despite the strategies of demystification inscribed in these authors' fictions.

Throughout this book I have considered how the celebration of seductive and deceitful fantasies closely aligns fantasy with Renaissance constructions of

femininity and effeminacy. As I noted in the introduction, this association between aesthetics and gender has been overlooked until recently because scholars
of fiction normally construe fantasy as an aesthetic construct, while scholars of
gender view gender as a cultural construct. By looking at conceptual points of
convergence between fantasy and femininity, I affirm how the act of writing
fiction during the early modern period was always imbricated in a cultural construction of the authorial self as masculine, feminine, or effeminate. When male
authors promote feminine or effeminate alter egos (such as Rosalind or Pyrocles),
they are not simply experimenting with genre, or even presenting a protofemi-
nist platform; they are attempting to rewrite cultural constructs of patriarchal
truth and experience, even if contingently and ambivalently so. It is this pur-
poseful representation, even perhaps identification, of the authorial self with
"deviant" femininity and effeminacy that holds together the heterogenous conceptualizations of the self promoted by these authors.

Boccaccio's *Decameron*, I have noted, acts as a kind of template for this common project by staging the prodigal claimant's relationship to patriarchy as a
series of mutations of the classic oedipal paradigm. Rather than represent protagonists who, by giving up claims to the desired woman (a woman who belongs to an authoritative man), eventually gain another girl and the phallus,
Boccaccio's protagonists revel in their "castrated" position by serving the desired woman directly (thus circumventing any dependence on the patriarch).
Pasquier changes the terms of this oedipal mutation slightly, as his rebellion
against Castiglione depends on mimicking much of *The Courtier*, while displacing the male hegemony of speech in the earlier treatise with the articulate
and unruly words of Charilée.

Sidney likewise takes on Petrarchan tradition in *Astrophil and Stella* by promoting an unusually articulate sonnet-heroine, a strategy which allows him to
celebrate, unexpectedly, the effeminization of his poetical alter-ego (much as
Pasquier represents himself as a kind of hermaphrodite). In *The Old Arcadia*
Sidney takes this scene of rebellion a step further by, literally, dressing his hero
as a woman and (following Boccaccio's unruly lead) by representing literature
as a series of flirtations with a female audience that turns away from the traditional, idealized audience of literature—masculine, serious and learned. Shakespeare, we have seen, suggests that drama is the preeminent medium for
celebrating feminine/effeminate fantasy; he does so by staging the transformation of boy actor into female character, a process that, within the fantastical
realm of the theater, unleashes the provocatively liberating and subversive poetics of fantasy.

Ambivalences inherent in these authors' elaborations of fantasy remind us
that fantasy is, for these authors, at once a site of power and weakness. Because
these writers had not yet been accepted within the patriarchal academy, their

scriptings of fantasy as feminine or effeminate allowed them to claim an alternative authority associated with female patrons and audiences, also outside of the academy. But, throughout these texts a strong dependence on women is often associated with castration, or, at least effeminacy. While castration is unexpectedly celebrated as a sign of liberation from patriarchal convention, its strong cultural associations with weakness, even loss of selfhood, makes it a difficult trope to affirm unproblematically. The "nothingness" of the nonmale body, of fantasy, and even of originality problematizes the notion that deviations from patriarchal truths have any substantive significance and influence of their own.

This ambivalent celebration of unruly genres, genders, and poetics adumbrates certain quite marked distinctions between Renaissance responses to gender and aesthetics and our own conceptualizations of these constructs. The fourteenth through sixteenth centuries are a period during which fiction was commonly viewed as an insidiously influential form of expression (hence the number of treatises dedicated to condemning, or, at least, containing its influence). Just as many treatises were written in an effort to contain the subversive influence of unruly women. But perhaps most alien to current ways of thinking is the notion that originality should be considered a suspect way of thinking. The authors I study, with their unusual proclivities for fantasy, femininity (or effeminacy), and originality, seem to be somewhat "modern" in their thinking and writing. What marks them as odd, from contemporary perspectives, is the often defensive or audacious rhetoric associated with an affirmation of these traits—one that betrays their awareness that they are alienating themselves from the dominant aesthetics of the period.

One might say, then, that the texts I have looked at limn out notions of gender, genre, and aesthetics that became dominant in later centuries. Already, for instance—in seventeenth-century cavalier poetry—associations between fantasy and femininity are troped far more openly and affirmatively than they are in the texts I have studied. And, of course, by the late eighteenth century, authors had laid the groundwork for romantic affirmations of originality that continue to dominate discussions of aesthetics even within our postmodern era. It might appear, then, that the proclivity for writing in the vernacular and prose shared by most of the authors I have looked at predicted the kinds of writing that dominate twentieth-century fiction. But one need only look at the rhetoric of these works to see that we cannot read them as gesturing clearly to late modern thought. Sidney's and Boccaccio's preference for narrative frames, like Pasquier's, Sidney's, Anger's, and Nashe's interest in poetical treatises, speak to an aural era—when manuscripts, much like playscripts, were written on the assumption that they would most likely be read out loud to an audience.

The alien (to us) nature of this form of textual dissemination is analogous to the somewhat odd construction of women and effeminacy in the period. If, for example, we tend to stereotype effeminacy as a manifestation of homosexual desire, the authors I have studied tend to associate it with overheated heterosexuality, with a desire for women so strong that it leads men to abandon their position of authority. Equally estranging is these authors' conceptualization of fiction; for they betray how certain situations that we find "realistic" in Boccaccio and Shakespeare—such as empowered, sexually active women—were considered to be so rare during this period as to become associated with fantasy.

Indeed it is often unclear to what extent the authors themselves were willing to support their subversive notions of identity outside of the field of fantasy. Yet their very scripting of these fantasies, and the popular and heterogenous readership that they attracted, made these unconventional gendered positions conceptually possible; hence they provided a foundation which promoted and sustained alternative constructions of gender. These authors are not revolutionaries, but they provided positions from which women and fiction writers could promote themselves as deserving power and influence not only within fantasy but within patriarchal experience as well.

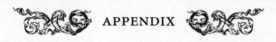

Parallel Passages Between
A Defence of Poetry
and *As You Like It*

A DEFENCE OF POETRY	AS YOU LIKE IT
Then would he add certain praises, by telling what a peerless beast the horse was, the only serviceable courtier . . . that if I had not been a piece of a logician . . . he would have persuaded me to have wished myself a horse. (17)	His horses are bred better, for besides that they are fair with their feeding, they are taught their manage, and to that end riders dearly hir'd; but I (his brother) gain nothing under him but growth. (1.1.11–14)
I will give you a nearer example of myself, who (I know not by what mischance) in these my not old years and idlest times. (17–18)	Marry, sir, I am helping you to mar that which God made, a poor unworthy brother of yours, with idleness. (1.1.32–34)
Nature never set forth the earth in so rich tapestry as divers poets have done; neither with so pleasant rivers, fruitful trees. . . . Her world is brazen, the poets only deliver a golden. (24)	They say many young gentlemen flock to him every day, and fleet the time carelessly, as they did in the golden world. (1.1.116–19)

A DEFENCE OF POETRY	AS YOU LIKE IT
And if in neither of these anatomies he [poetry] be condemnable, I hope we shall obtain a more favourable sentence. (28)	I speak but brotherly of him, but should I anatomize him to thee as he is, I must blush and weep, and thou must look pale and wonder. (1.1.155–58)
Is it then the Pastoral poem which is misliked? . . . Is the poor pipe didained, which sometime out of Meliboeus' mouth can show the misery of people under hard lords or ravening soldiers. (43)	My master is of churlish disposition, And little reacks to find the way to heaven By doing deeds of hospitality. (2.4.80–82)
There is no art delivered to mankind that hath not the works of nature for his principal object, without which they could not consist, and on which they so depend, as they become actors and players, as it were, of what nature will have set forth. (23)	All the world's a stage, And all the men and women merely players; They have their exits and their entrances, And one man in his time plays many parts, His acts being seven ages. (2.7.139–43)
For now, as if all the Muses were got with child to bring forth bastard poets, without any commission they do post over the banks of Helicon, till they make the readers more weary than post-horses. (62–63)	This is the very false gallop of verses; why do you infect yourself with them? (3.2.113–14)
But truly many of such writings as come under the banner of unresistable love, if I were a mistress, would never persuade me they were in love: so coldly they apply fiery speeches. (69–70)	O most gentle pulpiter, what tedious homily of love have you wearied your parishioners withal. (3.2.155–6)
Let but most of the verses be put in prose, and then ask the meaning, and it will be found that one verse did but beget another, without ordering at the first what should be at the last; which becomes a confused mass of words, with a tingling sound of rhyme. (64–65)	Ay, but the feet were lame, and could not bear themselves without the verse, and therefore stood lamely in the verse. (3.2.169–71)

A DEFENCE OF POETRY

but truly, I think truly, that of all writers under the sun the poet is the least liar . . . Now, for the poet, he nothing affirms, and therefore never lieth. For, as I take it, to lie is to affirm that to be true which is false. (52)

and know whether she [Nature] have brought forth so . . . valiant a man as Orlando (24)

I conjure you all that have had the evil luck to read this ink-wasting toy of mine, . . . to believe, with Aristotle, . . . to believe, with Bembus, . . . to believe, with Scaliger, . . . (74–75)

AS YOU LIKE IT

No, truly; for the truest poetry is the most feigning (3.3.19–20)

And nature, stronger than his just occa-
sion,
Made him [Orlando] give battle to the
lioness,
Who quickly fell before him (4.3.129–31)

Believe then, if you please, that I can do strange things. I have, since I was three year old, convers'd with a magician (5.2.58–60)

My way is to conjure you, and I'll begin with the women. (Epilogue.10–11)

Notes

Introduction: Prodigality, Effeminacy, Fantasy

1. Margaret Cavendish, *Poems, and Fancies* (Providence: Brown University Women Writers Project, Version 0.1, 1991), 2.

2. My slippages from "fantasy" to "poetry" and "fiction" follow Renaissance usage. Renaissance writers tend to employ "poetry" or "imagination" when they refer to fiction as a neutral or constructive concept and to use the term "fantasy" when it takes on negative connotations (I discuss the negative implications of fantasy below). Throughout this study, references to "male" and "female" refer to biological sexes, while "masculine" and "feminine" refer to gendered, metaphorical or cultural attributes that are usually associated with "male" and "female" (respectively) but may also be applied to opposite sexes, to cultural constructions, or to certain aesthetic notions.

3. For studies of this modesty topos as it is employed by Renaissance women writers, see Fiora A. Bassanese, "Gaspara Stampa's Poetics of Negativity," *Italica* 61 (1984): 335–46; Margaret Ferguson, "A Room Not Their Own: Renaissance Women as Readers and Writers," in *The Comparative Perspective on Literature: Approaches to Theory and Practice,* ed. Clayton Koelb and Susan Noakes (Ithaca: Cornell University Press, 1988); Katherine Usher Henderson and Barbara F. McManus, introduction to *Half Humankind: Contexts and Texts of the Controversy about Women in England, 1540–1640* (Urbana: University of Illinois Press, 1985); and Ann Rosalind Jones, *The Currency of Eros: Women's Love Lyric in Europe, 1540–1620* (Bloomington: Indiana University Press, 1990).

4. With the exception of Boccaccio, all the authors I focus on wrote primarily during the sixteenth century. For the sake of simplicity, I therefore at times refer to this cluster of writers as sixteenth-century writers. I discuss below my reasons for including Boccaccio in this list.

I employ the term "patriarchy" loosely to signify a culture in which laws, politics, marriage, and other cultural institutions are predominantly in the hands of men. By extension I use the term to indicate, as well, certain structures that are associated with patriarchy—such as Claude Lévi-Strauss's representation of traditional exogamy (in *The Elementary Structures of Kinship,* trans. James Hearle Bell, John Richard von Strumer, ed. Rodney Needham [Boston: Beacon Press, 1969]). While this practice is an imprecise use of the traditional meaning of "patriarchy," it is the term most commonly employed by scholars to describe the dominant structures of sixteenth-century culture. On the problematics of this term, see especially, Gayle Rubin, "The Traffic in Women: Notes on the 'Political Economy' of Sex," in *Toward an Anthropology of Women,* ed. Rayna R. Reiter (New York: Monthly Review Press, 1975).

5. A number of critics have written on how articulate women writers were associated with subversion and deceit; see especially, Elaine V. Beilin, *Redeeming Eve: Women Writers of the English Renaissance* (Princeton: Princeton University Press), xiii–xxiv ff.; and Margaret Patterson Hannay, introduction to *Silent but for the Word: Tudor Women as Patrons, Translators, and Writers of Religious Works* (Kent, Ohio: Kent State University Press, 1985), 4–14.

6. On women patrons during the Renaissance, see Pamela Joseph Benson, *The Invention of the Renaissance Woman: The Challenge of Female Independence and the Literature and Thought of Italy and England* (University Park: Penn State University Press, 1992), 10–14 and passim; Michael G. Brennan, *Literary Patronage in the English Renaissance: The Pembroke Family* (London: Routledge, 1988), 9–18 and passim; John N. King, "Patronage and Piety: The Influence of Catherine Parr," in Hannay, ed., *Silent but for the Word,* 43–60; Mary Ellen Lamb, "The Countess of Pembroke's Patronage," *English Literary Renaissance* 12 (1982): 162–79; and Jon A. Quitslund, "Spenser and the Patronesses of the *Fowre Hymnes,*" in Hannay, ed., *Silent but for the Word,* 184–202.

7. I employ the term "prodigal" not to signify its common meaning of "extravagant" but rather as it is used by Richard Helgerson, in *The Elizabethan Prodigals* (Berkeley: University of California Press, 1976)—to refer to the "prodigal son" motif of youthful rebellion against authority. I discuss the relationship of this book to Helgerson's text later in the introduction.

Whether or not the four writers I focus on were fully heterosexual is not the focus of my argument here; rather, I look at the gender position with which they appear to have identified themselves as writers. While scholars have not recently made a claim for Shakespeare as homosexual, his strong interest in homoeroticism has been the subject of numerous studies; see, for instance, Joel Fineman, "Fratricide and Cuckoldry: Shakespeare's Doubles," in *Representing Shakespeare: New Psychoanalytic Essays,* ed. Murray M. Schwartz and Coppélia Kahn (Baltimore: Johns Hopkins University Press, 1980), 74ff.; Stephen Greenblatt, *Shakespearean Negotiations: The Circulation of Social Energy in*

Renaissance England (Berkeley: University of California Press, 1988), 86–93; Bruce R. Smith, "Making a Difference: Male/Male 'Desire' in Tragedy, Comedy, and Tragi-Comedy," in *Erotic Politics: Desire on the Renaissance Stage,* ed. Susan Zimmerman (New York: Routledge, 1992), 133–40; and Valerie Traub, *Desire and Anxiety: Circulations of Sexuality in Shakespearean Drama* (London: Routledge, 1992), 117–44. For a similar perspective on Sidney, see Katherine Duncan-Jones, *Sir Philip Sidney: Courtier Poet* (New Haven: Yale University Press, 1991), 239–42; and Bruce R. Smith, *Homosexual Desire in Shakespeare's England: A Cultural Poetics* (Chicago: University of Chicago Press, 1991), 139–45.

8. See Thomas Laqueur, *Making Sex: Body and Gender from the Greeks to Freud* (Cambridge: Harvard University Press, 1990).

9. Contemporary theorists continue to make the same analogies between masculine heterosexuality and authoritative writings. Lee Edelman, for instance, makes a distinction between writing, which he tropes as heterosexually masculine, and orality, which he associates with other states or constructs, such as male homosexuality (*Homographesis: Essays in Gay Literary Cultural Theory* [New York: Routledge, 1994], 9).

10. See especially Benson, *The Invention of the Renaissance Woman;* Philippa Berry, *Of Chastity and Power: Elizabethan Literature and the Unmarried Queen* (London: Routledge, 1989); Henderson and McManus, introduction to *Half Humankind;* Katharine Eisaman Maus, "A Womb of his Own: Male Renaissance Poets in the Female Body," in *Sexuality and Gender in Early Modern Europe: Institutions, Texts, Images,* ed. James Grantham Turner (Cambridge: Cambridge University Press, 1993); and Louis Adrian Montrose, "*A Midsummer Night's Dream* and the Shaping Fantasies of Elizabethan Culture: Gender, Power, Form," in *Rewriting the Renaissance: The Discourses of Sexual Difference in Early Modern Europe,* ed. Margaret W. Ferguson, Maureen Quilligan, and Nancy J. Vickers (Chicago: University of Chicago Press, 1986).

11. One exception is Patricia Parker, particularly her *Literary Fat Ladies: Rhetoric, Gender, Property* (London: Methuen, 1987), 55, 56.

12. See Bernard Weinberg, *A History of Literary Criticism in the Italian Renaissance* (Chicago: University of Chicago Press, 1961), 2:1013ff.; and Baxter Hathaway, *The Age of Criticism: The Late Renaissance in Italy* (Ithaca: Cornell University Press, 1962), 16–17, 75–76, 120–25, and passim. For studies of fantasy during the Renaissance sharing a similar perspective, see Murray W. Bundy, "'Invention' and 'Imagination' in the Renaissance," *Journal of English and Germanic Philology* 29 (1930): 541–45; Daniel Javitch, *Proclaiming a Classic: The Canonization of "Orlando Furioso"* (Princeton: Princeton University Press, 1991), 18, 38, 142, and passim; Robert L. Montgomery, *The Reader's Eye: Studies in Didactic Literary Theory from Dante to Tasso* (Berkeley: University of California Press, 1991), 16ff.; and William Rossky, "Imagination in the English Renaissance: Psychology and Poetic," *Studies in the Renaissance* 5 (1958): 49–73. As Marga Cottino-Jones notes, contemporary scholars on fantasy tend to note how fantasy is associated with a subversion of dominant, mimetic discourse; Cottino-Jones and others have not, however, pursued the gendered implications of this construction of fantasy. See Cottino-Jones, "Desire and the Fantastic in the *Decameron:* The Third Day," *Italica* 70 (1993): 1. Among scholars who share Cottino-Jones's perspective are Brian Atterbery (*Strategies of Fantasy* [Bloomington:

Indiana University Press, 1992]), Rosemary Jackson (*Fantasy: The Literature of Subversion* [London: Methuen, 1981]), and Eric S. Rabkin (*The Fantastic in Literature* [Princeton: Princeton University Press, 1976]).

13. See Linda Woodbridge, *Women and the English Renaissance: Literature and the Nature of Womankind, 1540–1620* (Urbana: University of Illinois Press, 1984); and Constance Jordan, *Renaissance Feminism: Literary Texts and Political Models* (Ithaca: Cornell University Press, 1990). For similar perspectives, see Benson, *The Invention of the Renaissance Woman;* Catherine M. Dunn, "The Changing Image of Woman in Renaissance Society and Literature," in *What Manner of Woman: Essays on English and American Life and Literature,* ed. Marlene Springer (New York: New York University Press, 1977); Henderson and McManus, introduction to *Half Humankind;* Ruth Kelso, *Doctrine for the Lady of the Renaissance* (Urbana: University of Illinois Press, 1956); Glenda McLeod, *Virtue and Venom: Catalogs of Women from Antiquity to the Renaissance* (Ann Arbor: University of Michigan Press, 1991); and Katherine J. Roberts, *Fair Ladies: Sir Philip Sidney's Female Characters* (New York: Peter Lang, 1993), 1–26. Melinda Gough has made this connection between fantasy and femininity in her paper "'Effeminate Wantonness,' or 'The Companion of Camps'?" (presented at the annual meeting of the Shakespeare Association of America, Albuquerque, New Mexico, April 1994), as has, to an extent, Frances Dolan, in her article, "Taking the Pencil Out of God's Hand: Art, Nature, and the Face-Painting Debate in Early Modern England," *PMLA* 108 (1993): 224–39.

14. These two readings (often a mixture of both) are articulated in a number of studies; but see especially Linda Bamber, *Comic Women, Tragic Men: A Study of Gender and Genre in Shakespeare* (Stanford: Stanford University Press, 1982); Catherine Belsey, "Alice Arden's Crime: *Arden of Faversham* (c. 1590)," in *Staging the Renaissance: Reinterpretations of Elizabethan and Jacobean Drama,* ed. David Scott Kastan and Peter Stallybrass (New York: Routledge, 1991); Benson, *The Invention of the Renaissance Woman;* Greenblatt, *Shakespearean Negotiations;* Rosemary Kegl, *The Rhetoric of Concealment: Figuring Gender and Class in Renaissance Literature* (Ithaca: Cornell University Press, 1994), chap. 3; Montrose, "*A Midsummer Night's Dream*"; and James Nohrnberg, *The Analogy of "The Faerie Queene"* (Princeton: Princeton University Press, 1976).

15. See especially Alan Bray, *Homosexuality in Renaissance England* (1982; reprint, New York: Columbia University Press, 1985); Gregory W. Bredbeck, *Sodomy and Interpretation: Marlowe to Milton* (Ithaca: Cornell University Press, 1991); Mario DiGangi, *The Homoerotics of Early Modern Drama* (Cambridge: Cambridge University Press, 1987); Marjorie Garber, *Vested Interests: Cross-Dressing and Cultural Anxiety* (1992; reprint, New York: Harper Perennial, 1993); Jonathan Goldberg, *Sodometries: Renaissance Texts, Modern Textualities* (Stanford: Stanford University Press, 1992); Janel Mueller, "Lesbian Erotics: The Utopian Trope of Donne's 'Sapphoe to Philaenis,'" in *Homosexuality in Renaissance and Enlightenment England: Literary Representations in Historical Contexts,* ed. Claude J. Summers (New York: Harrington Park Press, 1992); Eve Kosofsky Sedgwick, *Between Men: English Literature and Male Homosocial Desire* (New York: Columbia University Press, 1985); and Traub, *Desire and Anxiety.*

16. This list to some extent overlaps with the previous one. See especially Bredbeck, *Sodomy and Interpretation;* DiGangi, *The Homoerotics of Early Modern Drama;* Goldberg, *Sodometries;* and Jean Howard, "Sex and Social Conflict: The Erotic Politics of *The Roaring Girl,*" in Zimmerman, ed., *Erotic Politics.*

17. As such my project runs counter to studies like Peter C. Herman's *Squitter-wits and Muse-haters: Sidney, Spenser, Milton, and Renaissance Antipoetic Sentiment* (Detroit: Wayne State University Press, 1996), which focus on negative conceptualizations of effeminacy and emasculation in Renaissance texts.

18. Plato, *Sophist,* trans. F. M. Conford, *The Collected Dialogues of Plato, Including the Letters,* ed. Edith Hamilton and Huntington Cairns, Bollingen Series, vol. 71 (Princeton: Princeton University Press, 1961).

19. For a more extensive treatment of Plato's conceptualizations of fantasy, see Murray Wright Bundy, *The Theory of the Imagination in Classical and Medieval Thought* (1927; reprint, N.p.: Norwood Editions, 1976), 33–47, and passim; see also Montgomery, *The Reader's Eye,* 23–29, and passim.

20. For more detailed investigations of the influence of Aristotelian notions about women on Renaissance writers, see Henderson and McManus, introduction to *Half Humankind,* 4–20; Jordan, *Renaissance Feminism,* 29–34; Ian Maclean, *The Renaissance Notion of Woman: A Study in the Fortunes of Scholasticism and Medical Science in European Intellectual Life* (Cambridge: Cambridge University Press, 1980), 2–10, and passim; and Woodbridge, *Women and the English Renaissance,* 15, 19, 25, and passim.

21. Aristotle writes specifically about female animals here, but later writers employed this passage to characterize human women as well. Aristotle is not, of course, the only authority that Renaissance writers drew upon to make these claims, but he is the authority most often claimed by writers.

22. See Aristotle, *Politics,* trans. Benjamin Jowett (1923; reprint, New York: The Modern Library, 1943), 1:1; and *Physica (Physics),* trans. R. P. Hardie and R. K. Gage, *The Basic Works of Aristotle,* ed. Richard McKeon (New York: Random House, 1941), 1:9.

23. While *eikastiké* is not exactly the same as "didacticism," Renaissance theoreticians tended to define them similarly. In Sidney's *A Defence of Poetry,* for example, *eikastiké* refers primarily to literature that teaches the reader to act morally. See Sir Philip Sidney, *A Defence of Poetry,* ed. J. A. Van Dorsten (Oxford: Oxford University Press, 1966), 54. All subsequent references to *A Defence of Poetry* are by page number to this edition of the text.

24. Francesco Barbaro, *Directions for Love and Marriage,* anonymous translation (London, 1677), 49. On Barbaro's representation of women, see also Ann Rosalind Jones, "City Women and Their Audiences," in Ferguson et al., eds., *Rewriting the Renaissance,* 299–300, 306–7; Jordan, *Renaissance Feminism,* 40–47; and Peter Stallybrass, "Patriarchal Territories: The Body Enclosed," in Ferguson et al., eds., *Rewriting the Renaissance,* 127.

25. Giovanni Boccaccio, *Boccaccio on Poetry Being the Preface and the Fourteenth and Fifteenth Books of Boccaccio's Genealogia,* ed. and trans. Charles G. Osgood (1930; reprint, Indianapolis: Liberal Arts Press, 1956), 48.

26. If, influenced by the example of Plato, medieval and Renaissance attacks on fantasy focused on its base associations, some critics, influenced by Aristotle, defended fantasy by presenting it as a crucial force that mediates between sensation and abstract truths. But even for those who saw fantasy as constructive, its associations with mere sensation (lust) and appearance (lies) led them to interpret it as a force that could easily be abused. This is why Giacopo Mazzoni, despite his defense of sophistical rhetoric, admits that "the species of sophistic condemned by the philosopher is that which misdirects the intellect with falsehood and the will with injustice" (*On the Defence of the Comedy of Dante*, trans. Robert L. Montgomery [Tallahassee: University Presses of Florida, 1983], 83).

27. Stephen Gosson, *The School of Abuse: Containing a Pleasant Invective against Poets, Pipers, Players, Jesters, &c.* (1841; reprint, New York: AMS Press, 1970), 10.

28. Where contemporary writers are most likely to describe fantastical fictions as those that are antimimetic, Renaissance writers (without wholly discarding this notion) were more likely to define fantasy as any work that promotes illusion, deceit, seduction, and, by extension, sexual fantasies. This is why, for example, Ariosto's *Orlando Furioso* was commonly characterized as fantastical while Tasso's *Gerusalemme Liberata*—which contains its own share of fantastical figures—was almost universally considered to be a serious, didactic piece of literature.

29. While my psychoanalytic reading of prodigal fictions is deeply influenced by Freud and Lacan, I am not trying to present a narrowly Freudian/Lacanian reading of these fictions. Quite often, as this paragraph suggests, Renaissance prodigal writers shape their own versions of classic psychoanalytic paradigms.

30. Robert Con Davis, "The Discourse of the Father," in *The Fictional Father: Lacanian Readings of the Text*, ed. Robert Con Davis (Amherst: University of Massachusetts Press, 1981), 13.

31. I am aware that most texts fall in between the extremes of purely "patriarchal" and purely "prodigal" fiction. My own emphasis in this project is on texts whose narratives fall predominantly, if not wholly, within the prodigal paradigm.

32. Giovanni Boccaccio, *Decameron*, ed. Enrico Bianchi, in *Giovanni Boccaccio: Decameron, Filocolo, Ameto, Fiammetta*, vol. 8 of *La Letteratura Italiana: Storia e Testi*, ed. Raffaele Mattioli, Pietro Pancrazi, and Alfredo Schiaffini (Milan: Riccardo Ricciardi Editore, 1969), 4. All subsequent references to *Decameron* are by page number to this edition of the text. Giovanni Boccaccio, *The Decameron*, trans. G. H. McWilliam (London: Penguin Books, 1972), 46. Unless otherwise noted, all translations of *The Decameron* come from this translation of the work.

While I have elided references in this passage to mothers, mothers are represented here as clearly identifying with an oppressive patriarchy by colluding with brothers, fathers, and husbands to repress the sexuality of the desiring young women. Interestingly, Luce Irigary all but echoes Boccaccio's language here when she states that "women are marked phallically by their fathers, husbands, procurers" (*This Sex Which Is Not One*, trans. Catherine Porter, with Carolyn Burke [Ithaca: Cornell University Press, 1985], 31).

33. Boccaccio himself was not a young man when he wrote the *Decameron* (he was, in fact, pushing forty). Yet (as I discuss in chapter 4) he insists throughout this work on

his intellectual, emotional, and sexual youthfulness—one that positions him as at least metaphorically prodigal. For a somewhat different discussion of the oedipal paradigm in the *Decameron,* see Mihoko Suzuki, "Gender, Power, and the Female Reader: Boccaccio's *Decameron* and Marguerite de Navarre's *Heptameron,*" *Comparative Literature Studies* 30 (1993), 238. On the ways that Boccaccio's narrator differs from his predecessors, see Millicent Joy Marcus, *An Allegory of Form: Literary Self-Consciousness in the "Decameron,"* vol. 18 of *Stanford French and Italian Studies* (Saratoga, Calif.: Anma Libri, 1979), 14; and Giuseppe Mazzotta, *The World at Play in Boccaccio's Decameron* (Princeton: Princeton University Press, 1986), 10–11, 16–17, 66–67, and passim.

34. Boccaccio's most salient example of the oppressive father figure is Tancredi in his first story of the Fourth Day. I discuss such figures in more detail in chapter 4.

35. As such, these texts mutate as well the Girardian triangle of rivalry between men over a woman, as it is expressed in *Deceit, Desire, and the Novel: Self and Other in Literary Structures,* trans. Yvonne Freccero (Baltimore: Johns Hokins University Press, 1965). For René Girard, the desired woman is ultimately less significant than the rivalrous and emulative relationship between men over the desired woman; while this homosocial paradigm remains significant in the prodigal texts I study, their authors quite often critique this paradigm as conventional and patriarchal, displacing it with a greater attention to the subjectivity of the desired woman.

36. Marjorie Garber, *Vice Versa: Bisexuality and the Eroticism of Everyday Life* (New York: Simon and Schuster, 1996), 160.

37. The pandering implications of this subtitle have been discussed by a number of critics. See especially Lance Donaldson-Evans, "The Narrative of Desire: Boccaccio and the French *Decamerons* of the Fifteenth and Sixteenth Centuries," *Neophilologus* 77 (1993): 541–45; and Mazzotta, *The World at Play,* 13–14.

38. On this notion, see also Mary Ellen Lamb, "The Cooke Sisters: Attitudes toward Learned Women in the Renaissance," in Hannay, ed., *Silent but for the Word,* 113.

39. In the same way, the *Decameron* insists on the usually pleasurable reaction of the female members of the *brigata* to the stories that they hear. Boccaccio takes special pains to note that while the women often voice disapproval of erotic tales, their smiles betray their essential enjoyment of these stories.

40. On Boccaccio's dedication of *Concerning Famous Women,* see Benson, *The Invention of the Renaissance Woman,* 10–13. Pasquier wrote while the French court was under the influence of Marguerite de Navarre and while the Dames de Roches were important patrons of the arts; Sidney had two aunts who were important patrons of the arts, as well as his sister, to whom he dedicated his *Arcadia.* On the growing influence of women during the Renaissance as readers and patrons, see Brennan, *Literary Patronage in the English Renaissance,* xi–xii, 8, 12ff.; Dorothy Connell, *Sir Philip Sidney: The Maker's Mind* (Oxford: Clarendon Press, 1977), 19, 68; Duncan-Jones, *Sir Philip Sidney: Courtier Poet* 143, 176, 192, and passim; Suzanne Hull, *Chaste, Silent, and Obedient: English Books for Women, 1475–1640* (San Marino, Calif.: Huntington Library, 1982), 1–28ff.; Dennis Kay, introduction to *Sir Philip Sidney: An Anthology of Modern Criticism,* ed. Dennis Kay (Oxford: Clarendon Press, 1987), 21–28; Caroline Lucas, *Writing for Women: The Example*

of Woman as Reader in Elizabethan Romance (Milton Keynes, Eng.: Open University Press, 1989), 1–7ff.; Margaret Spufford, *Small Books and Pleasant Histories: Popular Fiction and Its Readership in Seventeenth-Century England* (Athens: University of Georgia Press, 1981), 13–14ff.; and Louis B. Wright, "The Reading of English Renaissance Women," *Studies in Philology* 28 (1931): 149–56. I discuss this kind of audience in more detail in chapter 4.

41. The strong link in these fictions between celebrating the feminine and fulfilling the male writer's prodigal fantasies complicates umbrella commentaries, like Irigaray's, that "Woman, in this [patriarchal] sexual imaginary, is only a more or less obliging prop for the enactment of a man's fantasies" (*This Sex Which Is Not One*, 25). While this comment may hold true for the conventional oedipal narrative, the tendency of male prodigal writers (like Boccaccio) to turn from this patriarchal plot leads to a celebration of independent and unruly female characters—even as these authors employ such characters to project their own fantasies of authorial achievement.

42. On paradigms of castration in the *Decameron*, see also Suzuki, "Gender, Power, and the Female Reader," 237–38. Suzuki argues that this metaphorics of castration by male authority figures veils underlying anxieties of castration by active, articulate women.

43. Meredith Skura, *The Literary Use of the Psychoanalytic Process* (New Haven: Yale University Press, 1981), 97. (Skura is referring to Hamlet here.) Margaret Ferguson has written on a very similar passage to this one in Boccaccio's *Genealogia Deorum*. See her *Trials of Desire: Renaissance Defenses of Poetry* (New Haven: Yale University Press, 1983), 182. I discuss this passage further in chapter 4.

44. I discuss the paradigm of Orpheus in greater detail in chapters 1, 2, and 3.

45. See especially the stories of Day Three.

46. Boccaccio never states explicitly who these envious men are, but his language implies that they are rival, powerful male writers.

47. Nancy J. Vickers has traced much the same process of defensive self-fragmentation in the lyrics of Boccaccio's contemporary and mentor, Petrarch. See her "Diana Described: Scattered Women and Scattered Rhyme," in *Writing and Sexual Difference*, ed. Elizabeth Abel (Chicago: University of Chicago Press, 1982).

48. The two are, of course, closely related, but a difference in focus on the father or on the woman as representing the threat of castration yields a quite different narrative and poetics on the part of the writer.

49. Jacqueline Rose, introduction (2) to *Feminine Sexuality: Jacques Lacan and the École Freudienne*, ed. Juliet Mitchell and Jacqueline Rose, trans. Jacqueline Rose (New York: Norton, 1985), 49. This kind of thinking is most playfully and famously articulated in Shakespeare's sonnet 23, in which the young man's addition of a "something" (penis) to his "nothing" (the concavity of the vagina) transforms him from woman to man. On this issue, see also Irigaray, *This Sex Which Is Not One*, 23; and Jacques Lacan, "God and the *Jouissance* of The Woman: A Love Letter," in Mitchell and Rose, eds., *Feminine Sexuality*, 144ff. This sense of female nothingness is, in part, a projection by men of their essential nothingness, as Lacan suggests in "Aggressivity in Psychoanalysis," in *Écrits: A Selection*, trans. Alan Sheridan (New York: Norton, 1977), 10ff.

50. Phyllis Rackin, "Androgyny, Mimesis, and the Marriage of the Boy Heroine on the English Renaissance Stage," *PMLA* 102 (1987): 33–34. I discuss this passage in greater detail in chapter 5.

51. Margaret Tyler, "The Mirror of Princely Deeds and Knighthood," in *Renaissance Woman: A Sourcebook: Constructions of Femininity in England,* ed. Kate Aughterson (London: Routledge, 1995), 235.

52. See chapter 5 for a more detailed discussion of gender and fantasy in this play.

53. This notion has been most famously articulated by David Quint in *Origin and Originality in Renaissance Literature: Versions of the Source* (New Haven: Yale University Press, 1983). I discuss his theories in more detail in chapter 3.

54. Robert Con Davis makes a similar point when he writes that narratives in which the protagonist avoids encounters with the father figure yield "a narcissistic world outside of family and culture" ("The Discourse of the Father," 11). This kind of thinking is strongly influenced by Augustinian theology, particularly Augustine's association of God with creation and the devil with nothingness. See especially *Confessions* 7.12. On Renaissance anxieties about originality, see also Thomas M. Greene, *The Light in Troy: Imitation and Discovery in Renaissance Poetry,* vol. 7 of *The Elizabethan Club Series* (New Haven: Yale University Press, 1982); John Guillory, *Poetic Authority: Spenser, Milton, and Literary History* (New York: Columbia University Press, 1983); William Kerrigan, "The Articulation of the Ego in the English Renaissance," in *The Literary Freud: Mechanisms of Defense and the Poetic Will,* ed. Joseph H. Smith (New Haven: Yale University Press, 1980); and Jacqueline Miller, *Poetic License: Authority and Authorship in Medieval and Renaissance Contexts* (New York: Oxford University Press, 1986).

55. Boccaccio became a highly respected humanist scholar; Pasquier became one of the most notable lawyers during the French civil war period; Shakespeare, as Helgerson puts it, "bought his father a coat of arms and bought himself the second largest house in Stratford" (*The Elizabethan Prodigals,* 13); and Sidney, posthumously, became one of England's exemplary heroes.

56. See Victor Turner, *The Forest of Symbols: Aspects of Ndembu Ritual* (Ithaca: Cornell University Press, 1967), 93; and idem, *From Ritual to Theatre: The Human Seriousness of Play* (New York: Performing Arts Journal Publications, 1982).

57. The liminal aspect of Sidney's life has been commented on by a number of scholars. See especially, Duncan-Jones, "Sir Philip Sidney's Toys," in *Sir Philip Sidney; an Anthology of Modern Criticism,* 62; Alan Hager, *Dazzling Images: The Masks of Sir Philip Sidney* (Newark: University of Delaware Press, 1991), 1–2ff.; Helgerson, *The Elizabethan Prodigals,* 124–58; Richard McCoy, *Sir Philip Sidney: Rebellion in Arcadia* (New Brunswick: Rutgers University Press, 1979), 1–7ff.; Maureen Quilligan, "Sidney and His Queen," in *The Historical Renaissance: New Essays on Tudor and Stuart Literature and Culture,* ed. Heather Dubrow and Richard Strice (Chicago: University of Chicago Press, 1988), 171–96; and Alan Sinfield, *Faultlines: Cultural Materialism and the Politics of Dissident Reading* (Berkeley: University of California Press, 1992), 88–90.

58. Margaret Ferguson articulates a similar perspective on Sidney in *Trials of Desire,* 152–62.

59. While Helgerson stresses works that yield an eventual reconciliation with and submission to the dominant culture, I am more interested in fictions that affirm rebellion so strongly as to problematize any such reconciliation.

60. As the debates on the nature of poetry reveal, the very profession of writing fiction had long been considered morally suspect; hence, simply writing fiction could make one a prodigal. On this problem see especially Helgerson, *Elizabethan Prodigals*, 5; and Ferguson, *Trials of Desire*, 161.

61. On the culturally threatening aspects of affirming femininity, see also Herman, *Squitter-wits and Muse-haters*, 14ff.

62. Boccaccio, of course, is the one writer I deal with who is not writing during the sixteenth century. But his deep involvement in shaping debates on the natures of poetry and femininity and his creation of fictions that develop out of this mode of thinking serve as a significant prototype for the kinds of concerns about fiction and femininity that become more common in the sixteenth century.

63. On this cultural semiotics of chastity, see Ferguson, "A Room Not Their Own," 93–116.

64. This problem is discussed by Benson in *The Invention of the Renaissance Woman*, 12.

65. An exception to this pattern is chapter 4, where I explore ways in which Sidney adopts Boccaccio as a model for rebellion. I discuss the ways in which *A Defence of Poetry* is an Italianate text in chapter 5.

1. SIDNEY, NASHE, ANGER, AND THE RENAISSANCE AESTHETICS OF EFFEMINACY

1. Agnolo Firenzuola, *On the Beauty of Women*, ed. and trans. Konrad Eisenbichler and Jacqueline Murray (Philadelphia: University of Pennsylvania Press, 1992), 31. All subsequent references to *On the Beauty of Women* are by page number to this edition of the text.

2. Elizabeth Cropper, "The Beauty of Woman: Problems in the Rhetoric of Renaissance Portraiture," in Ferguson, et al., eds., *Rewriting the Renaissance*, 175–76. Cropper expresses this metaphorical relationship between women and art as Zeuxian by nature. This kind of thinking is particularly popular in Italian aesthetic treatises. See especially Barbaro, *Directions for Love and Marriage*, 49ff.; Castelvetro, *Castelvetro on the Art of Poetry: An Abridged Translation of Lodovico Castelvetro's Poetica d'Aristotele Vulgarizzata et Sposta*, ed. Andrew Bongiorno (Binghamton: Medieval and Renaissance Texts and Studies, 1984), 300; as well as Firenzuola. I elaborate more fully on the artistic ideal of fragmentation and reunification in chapter 3.

3. Barbaro, *Directions on Love and Marriage*, 18. This passage has been discussed, as well, by Jones, in "City Women and their Audiences," 299–300; by Ferguson, in "A Room Not Her Own," 99; and by Stallybrass, in "Patriarchal Territories," 127. The desire to envision woman as a malleable object is perhaps best exemplified by Nancy

Vickers's comment that artists like Benvenuto Cellini used their models both as inspirations for painting and as objects of sexual pleasure ("The Mistress in the Masterpiece," in *The Poetics of Gender*, ed. Carolyn G. Heilbrun [New York: Columbia University Press, 1986], 21).

4. Shakespeare, *A Midsummer Night's Dream*, ed. Anne Barton, in *The Riverside Shakespeare*, ed. S. Blakemore Evans (Boston: Houghton Mifflin, 1974), 1.1.47–50.

5. This pattern describes, for instance, George Puttenham's *The Arte of English Poesie*, the anonymous *The Schoolhouse of Women* (probably by Edward Gosynhill), and Philip Stubbs's *The Anatomy of Abuses*.

6. Sidney's *A Defence of Poetry* is considered to be his first major text, written when he was around twenty-seven years old; *The Anatomie of Absurditie* is Nashe's first published piece of writing, written when he was twenty-two years old; and *Jane Anger* may be Anger's first and only published piece. There is of course, some discussion as to whether or not Anger was a woman; see, for instance, Henderson and McManus, *Half Humankind*, 22–23. Most scholars, however, agree that she was a woman writer.

7. While I will not continue to place quotation marks around "masculine," "feminine," or "effeminate," it should be clear that I use these terms throughout to designate metaphorical or constructed notions, not essential or universal characteristics of gender.

8. The notion that poets, inflamed by their desire for women, become effeminate (subordinate to women) is a constant in most Renaissance treatises against poetry and drama. See, for instance, Stephen Gosson, 11ff. G. Gregory Smith theorizes that it is as a defensive move against this notion that Sidney characterizes poets as soldiers (*Elizabethan Critical Essays* [Oxford: Oxford University Press, 1904] 1: xxix).

9. The problematics of Queen Elizabeth's identity as a female "king" has been well charted in the last twenty years. See especially Marie Axton, *The Queen's Two Bodies: Drama and the Elizabethan Succession* (London: Royal Historical Society, 1977); Montrose, "*A Midsummer Night's Dream*"; Christopher Pye, *The Regal Phantasm: Shakespeare and the Politics of Spectacle* (London: Routledge, 1990); Roy Strong, *The Cult of Elizabeth: Elizabethan Portraiture and Pageantry* (London: Thames and Hudson, 1977).

10. See the introduction, where I outline this aspect of aesthetic history.

11. Gosson, *The School of Abuse*, 18. See also Roger Ascham, *The Scholemaster*, ed. Edward Arber, English Reprints, vol. 10 (Birmingham, Eng., 1870), 6.

12. Sidney articulates this concern about censorship when he discusses the pastoral genre. See *A Defence of Poetry*, 43–44.

13. Sidney's aesthetic theories are not, of course, all of his own devising, as his frequent references to Greek, Roman, and Italian rhetoricians, philosophers, and literary critics make clear. But many of these ideas came to English literary critics of the late sixteenth century through the filter of *A Defence of Poetry*.

14. This dependence has been overlooked by scholars writing on this treatise, until the last few years. For a pre-1990s reading of this gendered aesthetics, see Edward Berry, "The Poet as Warrior in Sidney's *Defence of Poetry*," *Studies in English Literature 1500–1900* 29 (1989): 26–33; and my "Ruptured Closure" (Ph.D. diss., University of Virginia, 1990, 13–21). For more recent treatments of this issue, see Dolan, "Taking the Pencil out

of God's Hand," 224; Gough, "'Effeminate Wantonness' or 'the Companion of Camps'?";
and Herman, *Squitter-wits and Muse-haters,* 84–93. M. J. Doherty, in *The Mistress-
Knowledge: Sir Philip Sidney's "Defence of Poesie" and Literary Architectonics in the
English Renaissance* (Nashville: Vanderbilt University Press, 1991), also recognizes the
gendered aesthetics of *A Defence,* although she posits a poetics of androgyny that is
distinct from other current readings of *A Defence* (including mine).

15. Nashe suggests that his work was influenced by Sidney's when he ends his *Anatomie of Absurditie* by naming Sidney as the only good British poet. Certainly Nashe's
echoes of Sidney's oblique references to Queen Elizabeth and the similarities inherent
in their final perorations suggest that Nashe may well have had Sidney's treatise in
mind when he shaped his own work on fantasy and femininity.

16. Throughout this discussion I strongly associate "poetry" with "fiction," since,
like most of his contemporaries, Sidney uses the term "poetry" to describe fictional
works that are written in either verse or prose.

17. Ronald Levao, *Renaissance Minds and their Fictions: Cusanus, Sidney, Shakespeare*
(Berkeley: University of California Press, 1985), 163 (Levao does acknowledge that to a
great extent such inconsistencies are conscious on Sidney's part); Stephen Greenblatt,
Shakespearean Negotiations, 116. On such frustrations with *A Defence* in particular, see
Elizabeth Sewell, *The Orphic Voice: Poetry and Natural History* (New York: Harper and
Row, 1971), 74–76; and O. B. Hardison, "The Two Voices of Sidney's *Apology for Poetry,*"
English Literary Renaissance 2 (1972): 83–99.

18. By overlooking this stance critics like Hardison have even suggested that *A Defence
of Poetry* was written during two different periods—an early period, when Sidney was
deeply influenced by Platonic philosophy, and a later period, when he became more
interested in Aristotelian aesthetic philosophy ("The Two Voices of Sidney's *Apology for
Poetry,*" 83–99). One critic who does examine inconsistency as a conscious strategy in *A
Defence* is Ferguson, in *Trials of Desire,* 137–62.

19. On the trope of the "nurse" in *A Defence of Poetry,* see also Lynne Dickson,
"Sidney's Grotesque Muse: Fictional Excess and the Feminine in the Arcadias," *Renaissance Papers* (1992): 43. The problematics of fantasy and sexuality are hinted at in the
opening sections to *A Defence,* but they are not developed until later in the treatise.

20. Throughout *A Defence* Sidney refers to Nature as "she." On this passage, see also
Dolan, "Taking the Pencil out of God's Hand," 225.

21. Sidney appears to be following the poetics of Giacopo Mazzoni here, who distinguishes between a superior virtuous fantasy and an inferior seductive fantasy (*On the
Defense of the Comedy of Dante,* 79–83, 97–98).

22. In place of "seduction" Sidney employs the word "moving," to suggest that
poetry inspires the reader to higher, moral purposes.

23. There are two exceptions to this paradigm in *A Defence.* One is the examples of
"the prophetess Sibylla" (21) and "Deborah with her hymns" (25). These examples
represent notable women per se, rather than femininely inflected metaphors. The
other exception is of female historical characters who are transformed into art objects.
I discuss these below.

24. See Gosynhill, *Mulierum Paean;* Elyot, *The Defence of Good Women;* and Edward More, *A Lytle and Bryefe Treatyse Called The Defence of Women, and Especially of Englyshe Women, Made Agaynst The Schole Houuse of Women,* in vol. 2 of *Selected Pieces of Early Popular Poetry Republished Principally from Early Printed Copies* (London, 1817).

25. Lodovico Castelvetro, *Castelvetro on the Art of Poetry,* 301.

26. This same concept is repeated in Sidney's example of Canidia (35).

27. On the masculine gender of Sidney's conceptual audience, see Berry, "The Poet as Warrior in Sidney's *Defence of Poetry*"; and Gough, "'Effeminate Wantonness.'"

28. See also *A Defence,* where the narrator states that "poetry ever sets virtue so out in her best colours, making Fortune her well-waiting handmaid, that one must needs be enamoured of her" (37). The origins of this concept of poetical seduction are, of course, in Plato's *Symposium,* where it is the beautiful young man who initiates the lover's seduction into virtue. Its most influential articulation during the Renaissance is the oration by Castiglione's Bembo in Book 4 of *The Courtier.* For a different, more sexualized reading, of such passages in *A Defence,* see Dolan, "Taking the Pencil out of God's Hand," 227.

29. Boccaccio, *Boccaccio on Poetry (Genalogia Deorum Gentilium),* 35.

30. Puttenham, *The Arte of English Poesie,* ed. Gladys Doidge Willcox and Alice Walker (Cambridge: Cambridge University Press, 1936), 18. On negative conceptualizations of poetry in the Renaissance, see also Peter C. Herman, *Squitter-wits and Muse-haters,* 13–29ff.; Richard A. Lanham, *The Motives of Eloquence: Literary Rhetoric in the Renaissance* (New Haven: Yale University Press, 1976), 29ff.; and G. Gregory Smith, introduction to *Elizabethan Critical Essays,* xiv–xxi.

31. Puttenham, *The Arte of English Poesie,* 66. I will not discuss here other negative representations of "feminine" poetry in this section of *A Defence*—such as Sidney's reference to Muses who bring forth "bastard poets" (63) or to drama as an "unmannerly daughter" (69). These allusions, for the most part, reinforce those of England and Queen Elizabeth as problematic stepmothers to poets (which I discuss below). Among the many scholars who have discussed associations between Queen Elizabeth and unruly or threatening women, see especially Benson, *The Invention of the Renaissance Woman,* 235, 245, 248, and passim; Berry, *Of Chastity and Power,* 61, 65ff.; Ferguson, *Trials of Desire,* 160–61; Montrose, "*A Midsummer Night's Dream,*" 79–81; Pye, *The Regal Phantasm,* 34, 68–73, and passim; and Stallybrass, "Patriarchal Territories," 123–42. For a reading of Elizabeth's relationship with Sidney as at once playful and antagonistic, see Sally Minogue, "A Woman's Touch: Astrophil, Stella, and 'Queer Vertue's Court,'" *English Literary History* 63 (1996): 555–68.

32. This was, to a large degree, true. As C. Wright Mills has argued, Elizabeth preferred to encourage others to patronize poetry rather than pay poets out of her own pocket (*Power, Politics, and People,* ed. Irving Louis Horowitz [New York: Oxford University Press, 1963], 406). See also Brennan, *Literary Patronage in the English Renaissance,* 6.

33. See also Edward Berry, "The Poet as Warrior in Sidney's *Defence of Poetry,*" 31–32; and Ferguson, *Trials of Desire,* 160–62, for discussions of how Sidney indirectly slights Elizabeth for her lack of patronage to poets.

34. The very denseness of this passage suggests that Sidney is criticizing Queen Elizabeth in the only safe way possible—via circumlocution. On this passage, see also Edward Berry, "The Poet as Warrior in Sidney's *Defence of Poetry,*" 32. Dickson ("Sidney's Grotesque Muse," 43) interprets this passage somewhat differently, as an expression of Sidney's vexed relationship to the notion of an exterior, perhaps noncourtly, audience.

35. On Renaissance associations between women and pacifism, men and war, see especially Jordan, *Renaissance Feminism,* 168.

36. For an interesting reading of Sidney's association of poetry with warlike manoeuvres, see Gough, "'Effeminate Wantonness' or 'the Companion of Camps'?" 1–4.

37. In James M. Osborn, *Young Philip Sidney: 1572–1577* (New Haven: Yale University Press, 1972), 502–3. On this letter, see also Roger Kuin, "Sir Philip Sidney: The Courtier and the Text," *English Literary Renaissance* 19 (1989): 268; and Louis Adrian Montrose, "Celebration and Insinuation: Sir Philip Sidney and the Motives of Elizabethan Courtship," *Renaissance Drama* 8 (1977): 17. Connell discusses letters from Languet with similar arguments in *Sir Philip Sidney,* 99.

38. Interestingly, this seems to have been the period when Sidney was composing *Astrophil and Stella,* which also contains a condemnation of arranged marriages.

39. Sidney's resistance to this marriage has been discussed by most biographers of Sidney; see especially Katherine Duncan-Jones, *Sir Philip Sidney: Courtier Poet,* 61, 89, 156ff.; Roger Howell, *Sir Philip Sidney: The Shepherd Knight* (Boston: Little, Brown, 1968), 62, 65, 67ff.; and Richard McCoy, *Sir Philip Sidney: Rebellion in Arcadia,* chap. 1. For an overview of the dating of *A Defence,* see especially Berry, "The Poet as Warrior in Sidney's *Defence of Poetry,*" 23.

40. A similar contention is made by Helgerson (*Elizabethan Prodigals,* 143) and David Kalstone (*Sidney's Poetry: Contexts and Interpretations* [Cambridge: Harvard University Press, 1965], 136). See also my "Ruptured Closure," 7–77. I discuss how this paradigm informs *Astrophil and Stella* in chapter 3 and *The Old Arcadia* in chapter 4.

41. Sidney, characteristically, takes liberties with Plato's definitions of *eikastiké* and *phantastiké.* On his redefinitions of these terms, see M. J. B. Allen, "Sidney's *Defence* and the Image Making of Plato's *Sophist,*" in *Sir Philip Sidney's Achievements,* ed. M. J. B. Allen, Dominic Baker-Smith, and Arthur Kinney (New York: AMS Press, 1990), 97–103.

42. Thomas Greene, *The Light in Troy,* 3.

43. Most likely *The Anatomie* preceded *Jane Anger,* so a case may well be made for Anger as responding to Nashe. On the dating of these texts, see especially Lynne A. Magnusson, "Nicholas Breton Reads Jane Anger," *Renaissance Studies* 7 (1993): 292, 294–95; and Ronald B. McKerrow, ed., *Works of Thomas Nashe* (London: Sidgwick and Jackson, 1910), 4:1. Unlike Magnusson, who suggests that Nashe may well have influenced Anger (295), McKerrow argues that neither influenced the other (4:2–3).

44. G. R. Hibbard essentially makes this point when he argues that *The Anatomie* is "Badly organized" (*Thomas Nashe: A Critical Introduction* [London: Routledge and Kegan Paul, 1962], 11). See also Marie Couton, " *The Anatomie of Absurditie:* Portrait of the Satirist as Compiler," *Cahiers Élizabéthains* 37 (1990): 17; Devon Hodges, *Renaissance Fictions of Anatomy* (Amherst: University of Massachusetts Press, 1985), 36; and

McKerrow, *Works of Thomas Nashe,* 4:1. While Antoine Demadre acknowledges the loose organization of *The Anatomie,* he states that this kind of structure was typical of university writing of the period (*Essais sur Thomas Nashe* [Salzburg: University of Salzburg Press, 1986], 63, 170).

45. Sarah Kofman, *The Enigma of Woman: Woman in Freud's Writings,* trans. Catherine Porter (Ithaca: Cornell University Press, 1985), 95–96.

46. Thomas Nashe, *The Anatomie of Absurditie,* vol. 1 of *Works of Thomas Nashe,* ed. R. B. McKerrow (London: Sidgwick and Jackson, 1910), 6. All further references to *The Anatomie of Absurditie* are by page number to this edition of the text.

47. Gosson, *The School of Abuse,* 10.

48. For an extended discussion of the Classical and Renaissance tradition of associating the art of Zeuxis with writing, see Thomas M. Greene, *The Light in Troy,* 62.

49. See, for instance, Ascham, *The Scholemaster,* 3–4.

50. The number of Renaissance tales about women who turned into men and, conversely, men who became women illuminate and crystallize this kind of thinking. On such fluid gender transformations, see Greenblatt, *Shakespearean Negotiations,* 66–93; and Maclean, *The Renaissance Notion of Woman,* 38–39. On Renaissance male anxieties that desire for women leads to the effeminization of men, see Sedgwick, *Between Men,* 35.

51. It is interesting that this problem is not even an issue in *A Defence of Poetry.* Sidney, for example, condemns Queen Elizabeth not for being too aggressively masculine but rather for not being aggressive enough as a patron and warrior.

52. As such the passage points as well to woman's covering up of her essential, castrated self—an act of covering that, according to Nashe, she employs in order to represent herself as "something," hence as masculine.

53. *The Schoolhouse of Women,* in Henderson and McManus, eds., *Half Humankind,* ll. 76–77.

54. Dolan, "Taking the Pencil Out of God's Hand," 229–32.

55. *The Proude Wyves Pater Noster,* in vol. 2 of *Selected Pieces of Early Popular Poetry Republished Principally from Early Printed Copies* (London: 1817), ll. 177–78.

56. Ibid., ll. 83–84.

57. It is interesting that women themselves made the same analogies between ornamental dress and writing fiction. Cavendish, we have seen, makes this claim in her introduction to *Poems and Fancies.*

58. See Freud's "Medusa's Head," vol. 5 of *Collected Papers,* ed. Lytton Strachey, trans. Joan Rivière (London: Hogarth Press, 1950), 105. Nashe makes his buried allusion to Medusa explicit several sentences later, when he adds, "Did not mercilesse *Minerua,* turne the hayres of *Medusa,* whom shee hated, into hyssing Adders?" (16).

59. Freud, "Medusa's Head," 105. Freud goes on to comment that the figure of the Medusa represents at once a scene of horror—gesturing as it does towards castration, and of solace—as Medusa's snakelike hair serves as a figurative (and overdetermined) substitution for one's possible castration. Nashe, of course, is less interested in the idea of solace.

60. For Lacan, the emergence of the gaze as a site of aggressivity and control results from its primal association with power by the pre-verbal child. See his "Aggressivity in Psychoanalysis," 11. The associations between the Medusa, the gaze, and male representations of the feminine have been most famously discussed by Laura Mulvey, in *Visual and Other Pleasures* (Bloomington: Indiana University Press, 1989). My own discussion of these three elements in the *Anatomie of Absurditie* has been illuminated by her exploration of these issues; however, my focus on the different ways that Nashe employs figurations of Medusa to shape a paradoxically enabling aesthetics of castration is not as rigorously psychoanalytical as Mulvey's model, for it depends, as well, on Renaissance theories of gender and fantasy.

61. On the problematics inherent in troping woman as mediatress, see chapters 2 and 4.

62. See Lacan, "Aggressivity in Psychoanalysis," 10–12. See chapters 2 and 3 for a more thorough discussion of the symbolic significance of Orpheus in Renaissance literature.

63. This concept, of course, is something of a Renaissance cliché, expressed most famously in Petrarch's *Rime Sparse*.

64. On female patrons rewriting men's works, see Hannay, introduction to *Silent but for the Word*, 4–5.

65. Richard Braithwait, *The English Gentlewoman* (New York: Da Capo Press, 1970), 84.

66. On associations between the monarch's sight and his or her power over the people, see especially Pye, *The Regal Phantasm*, 66–73.

67. Interestingly, Sidney has his poet-protagonist, Astrophil, identify with Echo in *Astrophil and Stella*. For a discussion of this identification, see chapter 3.

68. Jonathan V. Crewe, discussing Nashe's *An Almond for a Parrot* makes a similar point about the ways in which Nashe's language often replicates the very forces he claims to argue against. See *Unredeemed Rhetoric: Thomas Nashe and the Scandal of Authorship* (Baltimore: Johns Hopkins University Press, 1982), 33–34. See also Couton, "*The Anatomie of Absurditie*," 18–20; and Hodges, *Renaissance Fictions of Anatomy*, 36–49.

69. Nashe, here, is specifically referring to Philip Stubb's *Anatomy of Abuses,* but, as I have mentioned, this reference describes Nashe's writing as well. The notion that an author is contaminated by the subject matter that he presents in his works is a Renaissance concept as well; it appears, for example, in Speroni's *Apologia dei dialoghi* of 1584. For a discussion of ideas of contamination in Speroni's treatise, see Virginia Cox, *The Renaissance Dialogue: Literary Dialogue in Its Social and Political Contexts, Castiglione to Galileo* (Cambridge: Cambridge University Press, 1992), 29–30. The apparent self-consciousness of such moments would seem to problematize Hibbard's contention that "The claim that the *Anatomy* contains merriment of any kind is bogus" (*Thomas Nashe*, 11).

70. Mulvey, *Visual and Other Pleasures*, 14. Although Nashe himself may not have explicitly associated the threats of femininity with castration, the self-consciousness inherent in his many references to Medusa, spilling of ink, blinding, and cuckoldry would

suggest, at least, that Nashe closely associated these figures with female usurpation of male sexual and sensual prerogatives.

71. Jane Anger, *Jane Anger, Her Protection for Women,* in *The Women's Sharp Revenge: Five Women's Pamphlets from the Renaissance,* ed. Simon Shepherd (New York: St. Martin's, 1985), 32. All subsequent references to this text are by page to this edition of *Jane Anger.*

72. The contention that men have misused their position of privilege is fairly traditional to defenses of women. We find similar statements in Sir Thomas Elyot, *The Defence of Good Women,* ed. Edwin Johnston Howard (Oxford, Ohio: Anchor Press, 1940), 1ff.; Goysnhill, *Mulierum Paean,* 158ff.; and More, *A Lytle and Bryefe Treatyse,* 98ff.

73. On Anger's tactics of redirecting the meaning of men's misogynistic language, see also Kate Aughterson, introduction to *Renaissance Woman: A Sourcebook, Constructions of Femininity in England* (London: Routledge, 1995), 5.

74. Gosson, for example, makes this analogy (*The School of Abuse,* 13ff.). See also Lanham, *The Motives of Eloquence,* 29.

75. Shakespeare, *Hamlet, Prince of Denmark,* ed. William Farnham, in *William Shakespeare: The Complete Works,* edited by Alfred Harbage (Baltimore: Penguin Books, 1969), 3.1.50–52.

76. For Anger, it is men who are unnatural, for their "tongues sting against nature" (41).

77. See also Anger's assertion, "but grace was first given to a woman, because to Our Lady: which premises conclude that women are . . . wiser than men" (40).

78. On this point see also Lynne A. Magnusson, "'His Pen with my Hande': Jane Anger's Revisionary Rhetoric," *English Studies in Canada* 17 (1991), 271ff.

79. Magnusson, in "'His Pen With my Hande,'" also comments on such inversions. See especially page 273.

80. While Anger is not the first writer to defend women in this way, she is certainly among the first. Henricus Cornelius Agrippa's treatise, *Declamation on the Nobility and Preeminence of the Female Sex,* makes a similar claim.

2. EXCHANGES OF WOMEN AND WORDS: ETIENNE PASQUIER'S REWRITING OF *THE COURTIER*

1. Pasquier is best known for his *Recherches de la France,* a loose collection of essays on the meaning of France and its traditions; he is also known for his *Lettres Amoureuses,* an epistolary proto-novel. For an overview of Pasquier's life and accomplishments, see Clark L. Keating, *Etienne Pasquier* (New York: Twayne, 1972); Suzanne Sweany, *Estienne Pasquier et Nationalisme Littéraire* (Paris: Champion-Slatkine, 1985); and Dorothy Thickett, *Estienne Pasquier: The Versatile Barrister of Sixteenth-Century France* (London: Regency Press, 1985). While the printed edition of the text is *Le Monophile,* I have followed the current convention of referring to it as *"Monophile."*

2. Thickett, *Estienne Pasquier,* 22; Keating, *Etienne Pasquier,* 28. Most scholars who discuss Pasquier's works either ignore *Monophile,* or, like Sweany, devote one sentence to it (*Estienne Pasquier et Nationalisme Littéraire,* 7).

3. For more extended discussions of the conventions of Renaissance dialogue, see Peter Burke, *The Fortunes of the "Courtier": The European Reception of Castiglione's "Cortegiano"* (1995; reprint, University Park: Penn State University Press, 1996), 19–22; Virginia Cox, *The Renaissance Dialogue,* 1–21; Daniel Javitch, *Poetry and Courtliness in Renaissance England* (Princeton: Princeton University Press, 1978), 18–48; Wayne Rebhorn, *Courtly Performances,* 92, 103; and Jon Snyder, *Writing the Scene of Speaking: Theories of Dialogue in the Late Italian Renaissance* (Stanford: Stanford University Press, 1989), 1–38ff. On the popularity of *The Courtier* in sixteenth-century France, see Burke, *The Fortunes of the "Courtier,"* 63–64, 73–74, 76; and Pauline M. Smith, *The Anti-Courtier Trend in Sixteenth Century French Literature* (Geneva: Librarie Droz, 1966), 26ff.

4. Certainly *Monophile* was considered readable enough in its time to have been translated by Geoffrey Fenton into English within twenty years of its publication.

5. *The Courtier* had been translated into French in 1542, thirteen years before Pasquier completed *Monophile.*

6. As such, Pasquier participates in a general re-conceptualization of the French court as Italianate that took place during the mid to late sixteenth century. On this conceptualization, see especially Ellery Schalk, "The Court as 'Civilizer,' of the Nobility: Noble Attitudes and the Court in France in the Late Sixteenth and Early Seventeenth Centuries," in *Princes, Patronage, and the Nobility: The Court at the Beginning of the Modern Age,* ed. Ronald G. Asch and Adolf M. Birke (Oxford: Oxford University Press, 1991), 248–49; R. J. Knecht, "The Court of Francis I," *European Studies Review* 8 (1978): 1–22; and Jean Jacquart, *François Ier* (Paris: Fayard, 1981), 379–84. On reactions against the Italianate influence over the French court, see Smith, *The Anti-Courtier Trend in Sixteenth Century French Literature,* 26ff. This "Italianate" notion of the court is ascribed to a parallel movement in France from older, military conceptualizations of the aristocracy, to more recent conceptualizations of aristocrats as courtiers. On this shift in France, see especially Jacquart, *François Ier,* 379–84; Knecht, "The Court of Francis I," 83–104; and Schalk, "The Court as 'Civilizer' of the Nobility," 249.

7. Baldesar Castiglione, *Il Libro del Cortegiano,* ed. Bruno Maier (Turin: Unione Tipografico-Editrice Torinese, 1964), 146. All subsequent references to *Il Libro del Cortegiano* are by page number to this edition of the text. Baldesar Castigione, *The Book of the Courtier,* trans. George Bull (Harmondsworth: Penguin Books, 1967), 81. All subsequent references to the translated text are by page number to this edition of the translation. Throughout this chapter I have also used Bull's English translation of characters' names in *The Courtier.* Burke mentions this passage in *The Courtier* without suggesting that it was used as a paradigm for later writers; see *The Fortunes of The "Courtier,"* 82.

8. On this representation of Duke Federico, see also Arthur Kinney, *Continental Humanist Poetics: Studies in Erasmus, Castiglione, Marguerite de Navarre, Rabelais, and Cervantes* (Amherst: University of Massachusetts Press, 1989), 94.

9. Castiglione is being somewhat devious here; for if the discussion about Francis I is said to have take place before Francis I ascended the throne, Castiglione added this comment to his work well after Francis I had become a king known for his patronage of the arts. In fact, Castiglione claims that Francis I influenced his writing of *The Courtier*. On this claim, see Burke, *The Fortunes of the "Courtier,"* 58. On Francis I's patronage of the arts, see R. J. Knecht, *Renaissance Warrior and Patron: The Reign of Francis I* (Cambridge: Cambridge University Press, 1994), 424-77; Smith, *The Anti-Courtier Trend in Sixteenth Century French Literature,* 20; and Raymond B. Waddington, "The Bisexual Portrait of Francis I: Fontainbleau, Castiglione, and the Tone of Courtly Mythology," in *Playing with Gender: A Renaissance Pursuit,* ed. Jean R. Brink, Maryanne C. Horowitz, and Allison P. Coudert (Urbana: University of Illinois Press, 1991), 107ff.

10. Etienne Pasquier, *Le Monophile* (Paris, 1555), 1. All subsequent quotations from *Monophile* are by page number to this edition of the text. All translations from *Monophile* are mine. (I have modernized the Renaissance spellings of "ſ" to "s" and "u" to "v" in *Le Monophile*).

11. The one exception to this tendency in *Monophile* is the character Philopole, whose misogynistic utterances I discuss below.

12. *The Courtier,* of course, has its own radical moments; my point is that Pasquier's strategy is to highlight conservative moments in *The Courtier* so as to foreground, by contrast, *Monophile*'s innovatory structure and content.

13. On the self-protective aspect of *The Courtier,* see Frank Whigham, *Ambition and Privilege: the Social Tropes of Elizabethan Courtesy Theory* (Berkeley: University of California Press, 1984), 5ff., as well as Whigham's "Interpretation at Court: Courtesy and the Performer-Audience Dialectic," *New Literary History* 14 (1983): 623–39. Burke notes that Castiglione himself imitated this strategy of self-protection by circumscribing the role of commoners, increasingly, as he rewrote *The Courtier* (*The Fortunes of the "Courtier,"* 36). On this movement towards self-protection in the French court, see Schalk, 254–57. On this tendency in European courts in general, see Ronald G. Asch: "Introduction: Court and Household from the Fifteenth to the Seventeenth Centuries," in Asch and Birke, eds., *Princes, Patronage, and the Nobility,* 4.

14. Evidently Pasquier succeeded in this manoeuvre, for if he never achieved aristocratic status, he retained a prestigious position in the French court, which flourished in part through his ability to engage the interest of women like Marguerite de Navarre and the Dames des Roches. For a view of women in *The Courtier* as powerful in their own right, see especially Wayne A. Rebhorn, *Courtly Performances: Masking and Festivity in Castiglione's "Book of the Courtier"* (Detroit: Wayne State University Press, 1978), 126–30.

15. On the situation of influential women in the French court, see also Waddington, "The Bisexual Portrait of Francis I," 106ff. *The Courtier,* of course, also attracted the attention of women readers; see Burke, *The Fortunes of the "Courtier,"* 47–51.

16. For a more extended discussion of how the movement from Duke Federico to Duke Guidobaldo symbolizes the decline of the Italian aristocratic warrior, see Thomas M. Greene, "*Il Cortegiano* and the Choice of a Game," in *Castiglione: The Ideal and the*

Real in Renaissance Culture, ed. Robert W. Hanning and David Rosand (New Haven: Yale University Press, 1983), 11; and John C. McLucas, "Amazon, Sorceress, and Queen: Women and War in the Aristocratic Literature of Sixteenth-Century Italy," *The Italianist* 8 (1988): 34–35. Javitch, in *Poetry and Courtliness,* attributes this sense of decline not so much to military weakness as to the loss of autonomy that accompanied the erosion of feudal systems (46).

17. Arthur Kinney also discusses the problem of the courtier's ornamental role, although he does not look at its gendered implications. See Kinney, *Continental Humanist Poetics,* 91–92.

18. On Ottaviano's condemnation of courtly effeminacy, see also Javitch, *Poetry and Courtliness,* 40–42; and Rebhorn, *Courtly Performances,* 128–29.

19. Natasha Korda has argued, interestingly, that this concern with effeminacy, or at least "lack," is inscribed within the very concept of "sprezzatura"—the essential virtue, for Castiglione, of the courtier. See her "Mistaken Identities: Castiglio(ne)'s Practical Joke," in *Desire in the Renaissance: Psychoanalysis in Literature,* ed. Valeria Finucci and Regina Schwartz (Princeton: Princeton University Press, 1994), 44–45.

20. On the symbolical associations between military weakness and effeminacy, see Javitch, *Poetry and Courtliness,* 40–49; Jordan, *Renaissance Feminism,* 77–79; and Rebhorn, *Courtly Performances,* 42–43.

21. On the Duchess as an enabling presence, see Valeria Finucci, "La Donna di Corte: Discorso Istituzuionale e Realtà nel *Libro del Cortegiano* di B. Castiglione," *Annali d'Italianistica* 7 (1989): 90. Although she is less interested in the fictional aspects of the court, Benson notes how ambivalences about women, in *The Courtier,* seem to arise from the courtier's conceptual identification with women (*The Invention of the Renaissance Woman,* 75–77). In contrast, Greene locates the sublimatory trajectory of *The Courtier* in an attempt to contain internecine aggression and to obscure the courtier's abject dependence on his prince (*Il Cortegiano,* 8). For a similar argument, see Javitch, "*Il Cortegiano* and the Constraints of Despotism," in Hanning and Rosand, eds., *Castiglione,* 17–19. Like Greene and Javitch, Rebhorn discusses the fictionalizing tendencies of the court without elaborating on the conceptual links between fiction and femininity or effeminacy (*Courtly Performances,* 16–17, 23–26, 29–40ff.).

22. Ferguson, "A Room Not Their Own," 96–115; Stallybrass, "Patriarchal Territories," 123–42.

23. In contrast, even informal conversations between men and women are highly problematized throughout *The Courtier.* This problem is dramatized not just by the relative silence of the female participants and audience but also by the courtiers' continuous debates over how or even whether a woman should converse with a man.

24. For a more extended discussion of the artistry of Urbino's court, see Thomas M. Greene, "*Il Cortegiano,*" 6–10, and Rebhorn, *Courtly Performances,* 87–89. This retreat into fiction, femininity, and love is probably also a self-protective move on the part of Pasquier, a move that allows him to distance himself from some of the controversial interjections that his characters—particularly Philopole—utter.

25. As Valeria Finucci notes, this process of elision includes withholding names of some of the female courtiers in the circle ("La Donna di Corte," 91).

26. Benson, *The Invention of the Renaissance Woman,* 75. See also Finucci, "La Donna di Corte," 92. While most scholars have noted the influence of women on male courtiers in this text, few have discussed its problematic implications or the attempt by courtiers to circumscribe this influence. On the influence of women in *The Courtier* in general, see Burke, *The Fortunes of the "Courtier,"* 26ff.; Robert W. Hanning, "Castiglione's Verbal Portrait: Structures and Strategies," in Hanning and Rosand, eds., *Castiglione,* 136; and J. R. Woodhouse, *Baldesar Castiglione: A Reassessment of "The Courtier"* (Edinburgh: Edinburgh University Press: 1978), 109–36. On problematic implications of this influence, see Benson, *The Invention of the Renaissance Woman,* 73–90; and Thomas M. Greene, "*Il Cortegiano,*" 10–12. It is interesting that Castiglione himself circumscribed the role of women in his work, by editing out many of their speeches in later versions of *The Courtier.* On this pattern in *The Courtier* see Burke, *The Fortunes of the "Courtier,"* 36.

27. On mediation and women in *The Courtier,* see also Antonello Perli, "Le Jeu de la Société dans le *Courtisan,*" *Littératures* 34 (1996): 27. Perli sees this role as an idealization of the courtly woman.

28. I employ the term "middle-class" to describe a commoner with a background in trade, medicine, law, and related fields. While the term is somewhat anachronistic, there is no adequate Renaissance synonym for this concept.

29. Philopole is probably punning here on "queue" as a figure for "penis."

30. The concept that aristocracy depends on a system of mutual, excessive exchange, has been articulated by Britton J. Harwood ("Gawain and the Gift," *PMLA* 106 [1991]: 48).

31. Irigaray, *This Sex Which Is Not One,* 108.

32. Ibid.

33. See also Finucci, who argues that "L'unica cosa che alla donna rimane da fare . . . è di immaginarsi come gli altri la immaginano" ("La Donna di Corte," 92–94). For a less problematized reading of the Magnifico's representation of women, see Dain Trafton, "Politics and the Praise of Women: Political Doctrine in the *Courtier's* Third Book," in Hanning and Rosand, eds., *Castiglione,* 33.

34. On a similarly defensive move in the courtiers' jokes about women, see Valeria Finucci, "Jokes on Women: Triangular Pleasures in Castiglione and Freud," *Exemplaria* 4 (1992): 53–77.

35. Certainly the couples who are associated with Monophile's ideal of monogamous adultery are all famous for withdrawing from the social institutions of their aristocratic cultures—couples like Tristan and Isolde or Lancelot and Guinevere. While Monophile's ideal of heterosexual passion endangers male aristocratic circulations, his system is no less aristocratic in origin, recalling as it does the genres of chivalric romance and Petrarchan sonnets—both (despite the often middle class origins of their writers) deeply inspired and patronized by aristocratic cultures.

36. The Magnifico, too, shows something of this desire to keep his ideal court lady

to himself; this would explain why he keeps lapsing into silence as he is asked to artic-ulate a defense of the court lady.

37. On the chivalric model of men speaking for women in *The Courtier,* see Finucci, "La Donna di Corte," 95. For overviews of Renaissance profeminist works in which men speak for women, see Benson (*The Invention of the Renaissance Woman*) and Jordan (*Renaissance Feminism*).

38. There is, of course, the irony that a man—Pasquier—is ultimately speaking for her.

39. On such associations with amazons, see especially Montrose, *"A Midsummer Night's Dream,"* 70–79.

40. On The Magnifico's representation of women warriors and their relationship to the Duchess, see especially McLucas, "Amazon, Sorceress, and Queen," 37–38, 51–52.

41. What of course complicates this scenario is the fact that Castiglione may have made up or exaggerated his representation of Colonna as disseminator in order to suggest (with conventional modesty) that it was not his idea to publish *The Courtier.* Peter Burke, however, notes that Castiglione's irritation with Colonna's purported act of dissemination was probably serious: he did not give her a presentation copy of the printed version (*The Fortunes of the "Courtier,"* 39). On this passage, see also Korda, "Mistaken Identities," 55.

42. Ferguson, "A Room Not Their Own," 96–115.

43. It is perhaps for this reason that, in *The Courtier,* some of the positive attributes associated with the myth of Orpheus are attributed to another hero. From Horace on, Orpheus was commonly invoked as the poet whose ability to tame wild beasts symbol-ized a great poet's ability to civilize his audience by means of aureate rhetoric. In Castigli-one, however, Ottaviano associates this ability with Alexander the Great (312). Ottaviano's contention implies that it is great warriors—not articulate courtiers—who have Orphic powers of conversion; courtly speakers are, by implication, too often subjected to the demands of their unruly female audiences to produce great poetry.

44. Benson (*The Invention of the Renaissance Woman,* 79) and Rebhorn (*Courtly Performances,* 127–30) also discuss this passage as threatening to men, without examin-ing the symbolic significance of the trope of Orpheus. On impotence as a trope for the work as a whole, see also Finucci, "La Donna di Corte," 92.

45. The issue of dowries appears in a series of debates on the nature of marriage that often parallels those on the nature of women. For an overview of Italian and French treatises on this topic (with which Pasquier would most likely have been familiar), see Jordan, *Renaissance Feminism,* 40–64, 68–70, 80–81, and passim.

46. On the limited power of women within the system of dowries, see Natalie Zemon Davis, *Society and Culture in Early Modern France: Eight Essays by Natalie Zemon Davis* (Stanford: Stanford University Press, 1975), 142–51; Jordan, *Renaissance Feminism,* 41; Joan Kelly, "Did Women Have a Renaissance," in *Becoming Visible: Women in European History,* ed. Renate Bridenthal and Claudia Koonz (Boston: Houghton Mifflin, 1977), 137–64; and Lawrence Stone, *The Family, Sex, and Mar-riage in England, 1500–1800* (New York: Harper and Row, 1977), 109–41.

47. For the sake of brevity, I have left out a detailed description of Glaphire's opinion; suffice it to say that his preference for experiencing one grand passion while allowing for occasional lapses in fidelity speaks to his pragmatic personality.

48. On the androgyne as an emblem for marriage, see Jordan, *Renaissance Feminism,* 20–21, 136–140ff. See also Woodbridge, *Women and the English Renaissance,* 140–41, and Edgar Wind, *Pagan Mysteries in the Renaissance* (New York: Norton, 1968), 202, 212ff.

49. It is interesting, in this light, that Francis I was depicted as an androgyne in one painting, probably by Niccolò Bellin da Modena. The painting has been interpreted alternately as a positive rendering of a king victorious in "masculine" war and "feminine" peace, and as a painting that ridicules Francis I as a king dominated by female relatives. See Françoise Bardon, "Sur un portrait de François Ier," *L'information d'histoire de l'art* (1963): 1–7; André Chastel, *The Age of Humanism: 1480–1530,* trans. Katherine M. Delauney and E. M. Gwyer (London: Thames and Hudson, 1963), 204; and Waddington, "The Bisexual Portrait of Francis I," 99–126. On androgynous conceptualizations of Francis I, see also Philippa Berry, *Of Chastity and Power,* 40–60; and Vickers, "The Mistress in the Masterpiece," 19–41.

3. Effeminacy and the Anxiety of Originality: *Astrophil and Stella* and the *Rime Sparse*

1. Harold Bloom, *The Anxiety of Influence: A Theory of Poetry* (London: Oxford University Press, 1973), 11.

2. See Quint, *Origin and Originality,* especially 1–31. See also Thomas M. Greene, *The Light in Troy,* 98ff.; Guillory, *Poetic Authority,* 1–22ff.; Kerrigan, "The Articulation of the Ego in the English Renaissance," 267–99; and Jacqueline Miller, *Poetic License,* 3–33ff. Greene notes how the problematics of originality arises in part from the many conflicting definitions of the opposite to originality, imitation. See *The Light in Troy,* 1–27.

3. Quint, *Origin and Originality,* 20. In "The Elizabethan Laureate: Self-Presentation and the Literary System," Richard Helgerson ascribes this anxiety specifically to English "amateur poets" like Sidney (*English Literary History* 46 [1979]: 193–220). Significantly, love poetry fits nicely into this paradigm of originality, for it was commonly considered to be "morally suspect from a Christian point of view" (Arthur F. Marotti, *Manuscript, Print, and the English Renaissance Lyric* [Ithaca: Cornell University Press, 1995], 210, 225).

4. For a nice overview of this tendency in criticism of *Astrophil and Stella,* see Donald Stump, "Sidney's Astrophil, Vanishing," *Renaissance Papers* (1998): 1–3. One exception to this pattern is Jacqueline Miller, *Poetic License,* 139–75. Although she is less interested in Stella as a potential artistic rival to Astrophil, Miller does see *Astrophil and Stella* as dramatizing an agon between the authoritative source, Stella, and Astrophil's desire for poetic license.

5. Other critics have noted Astrophil's deceitful tendencies, without associating this trait with femininity. See, for instance, S. K. Heninger, Jr., *Sidney and Spenser: The*

Poet as Maker (University Park: Penn State University Press, 1989), 485; Richard Lanham, "*Astrophil and Stella:* Pure and Impure Persuasion," *English Literary Renaissance* 2 (1972): 100–15; and Alan Sinfield, "Astrophil's Self-Deception," *Essays in Criticism* 28 (1978): 1–14.

6. In presenting my argument I will not attempt to identify where Sidney is being "authentically" original; instead, my project is to map out the tension between conceptualizations of convention and originality in *Astrophil and Stella.* For discussions of where Sidney is, in fact, original, see Anne Ferry, *The "Inward" Language: Sonnets of Wyatt, Sidney, Shakespeare, Donne* (Chicago: University of Chicago Press, 1983), 128–69; Douglas Peterson, *The English Lyric from Wyatt to Donne: A History of the Plain and Eloquent Styles* (Princeton: Princeton University Press, 1967), 186–201; and Germaine Warkentin, "Sidney and the Supple Muse: Compositional Procedures in Some Sonnets of *Astrophil and Stella,*" in *Sir Philip Sidney: An Anthology of Modern Criticism,* ed. Dennis Kay (Oxford: Clarendon Press, 1987), 84. On the poet-lover as conceptually feminine, see also Wendy Wall, *The Imprint of Gender: Authorship and Publication in the English Renaissance* (Ithaca: Cornell University Press, 1994), 240ff. Wall, however, does not go on to associate this feminine position with fantasy and originality.

7. Of course, Petrarch himself simultaneously depends on and rebels against his poetic predecessors. On this pattern in Petrarch's works, see especially Thomas M. Greene, *The Light in Troy,* 41ff.; Peter Hainsworth, *Petrarch the Poet: An Introduction to the "Rerum Vulgarum Fragmenta"* (London: Routledge, 1988), 16–19; and Marguerite Waller, *Petrarch's Poetics and Literary History* (Amherst: University of Massachusetts Press, 1980), 1–25ff.

8. Astrophil's continued dependence on Petrarchan convention—despite his claims to the contrary—has been noted by a number of critics. See especially, Roland Greene, *Post Petrarchism: Origins and Innovations of the Western Lyric Sequence* (Princeton: Princeton University Press, 1991), 63–64, 80, 85ff.; Heninger, *Sidney and Spenser,* 483–86; Lisle Cecil John, *The Elizabethan Sonnet Sequence: Studies in Conventional Conceits* (New York: Columbia University Press, 1938), 3, 175; William Ringler, introduction to *The Poems of Sir Philip Sidney* (Oxford: Clarendon Press, 1962), xxxv; and Gary F. Waller, "The Rewriting of Petrarch: Sidney and the Languages of Sixteenth-Century Poetry," in *Sir Philip Sidney and the Interpretation of Renaissance Culture: The Poet in His Time and in Ours,* ed. Gary F. Waller and Michael D. Moore (London: Croon Helm, 1984), 69–82. What has not, however, been explored, is why there is this gap between an assertion of originality and a metaphorical and structural dependence on Petrarchan convention.

9. In his article on Astrophil as a product of the conflict between Petrarchism and Protestantism, Gary Waller gives a similar reading of Astrophil's fragmented selfhood ("The Rewriting of Petrarch," 69–83). For Paul Allen Miller, in contrast, the fragmented self is a symptom of changes in the construction of the aristocratic self that resulted from the breakdown of the feudal system ("Sidney, Petrarch and Ovid, or Imitation as Subversion," *English Literary History* 58 [1991]: 499–502).

10. Quint, *Origin and Originality*, 41. Virgil's story of Orpheus is found in *Georgics* 4; Ovid's is found in *Metamorphoses*, 9 and 10.

11. On this reading of Ovid's Orpheus, see especially W. S. Anderson, "The Orpheus of Virgil and Ovid: *flebile nescio quid*," in *Orpheus: the Metamorphoses of a Myth*, ed. John Warden (Toronto: University of Toronto Press, 1982), 26–48. This reading echoes Plato's own interpretation of the myth of Orpheus in *The Symposium*. For a somewhat different reading of the myth, see Charles Segal, *Orpheus: The Myth of the Poet* (Baltimore: Johns Hopkins University Press, 1989), 73–94.

12. See especially the stories of Ganymede, Apollo and Hyacinthus, Pygmalion, and Cinyras and Myrrha in Book 10 of the *Metamorphoses*—all four stories are told by Orpheus after he turns from his love for Eurydice to the love of young men. On homosexuality and narcissism in Ovid, see Leonard Barkan, *The Gods Made Flesh: Metamorphosis and the Pursuit of Paganism* (New Haven: Yale University Press, 1986), 49–50.

13. This representation of Orpheus as empowered by both rhetoric and didacticism is exemplified in Horace's *Ars Poetica*, 391–93.

14. Sewell, *The Orphic Voice*, 3–4.

15. Sir Philip Sidney, *The Countess of Pembroke's Arcadia (The Old Arcadia)*, ed. Jean Robertson (Oxford: Clarendon Press, 1973). 84. All subsequent references to *The Old Arcadia* are by page number to this edition of the text.

16. William Shakespeare, *The Merchant of Venice*, ed. Anne Barton, in Evans, ed., *The Riverside Shakespeare*, 5.1.78–81.

17. This shuttling back and forth between Orphic power and impotence is itself a reflection of the paradigm's mythical roots. The story of Orpheus is about a poet with unparalleled rhetorical power who was nonetheless unable to recover his lost wife and prevent his own murder at the hands of the Maenads. Other sixteenth-century expressions of Orphic power and impotence include Castiglione, *The Courtier*, Book 2; Garcilaso de la Vega, Soneto 15; Pierre de Ronsard, *L'Amour de Cassandre*, 12, 26; and Spenser, *The Faerie Queene*, 4.10.58.

18. Sir Philip Sidney, *Astrophil and Stella*, in *The Poems of Sir Philip Sidney*, ed. William A. Ringler, Jr. (Oxford: Clarendon Press, 1962): 1.1–4. All subsequent references to *Astrophil and Stella* are by poem and line number to this edition of the text. Although I quote, throughout, from Ringler's edition of *Astrophil and Stella*, here I have accepted Katherine Duncan-Jones's emendation of "the" in the second verse to "She" (following the 1598 folio) (pp. 117, 214). See her edition of *Astrophil and Stella*, 1.2, in *Sir Philip Sidney: Selected Poems* (1973; reprint, Oxford: Clarendon Press, 1979).

19. As some critics have noted, the *gradatio*, as a figure of ascension, implies a movement towards God. See Doherty, *The Mistress-Knowledge*, 24. On neoplatonism and the sonnet tradition, see Leonard Wilson Forster, *The Icy Fire: Five Studies in European Petrarchism* (Cambridge: Cambridge University Press, 1969), 20–21.

20. Anne Ferry presents a number of other words in this sonnet that have covert associations with deceit, namely: "love," "show," "paint," and "invent" (*The "Inward" Language*, 129–39). Astrophil's preference for seduction and deceit has been commented on by a number of critics, most of whom focus on Astrophil's immoral character

rather than on the aesthetic or gendered implications of this unexpected self-position-ing. See Duncan-Jones, "Philip Sidney's Toys," 61–82; Lanham, "*Astrophil and Stella*," 100–15; Sinfield, "Astrophil's Self-Deception," 1–14; and Gary Waller, "The Rewriting of Petrarch," 69–83.

21. On Stella as the meaning of "heart," see Ringler's notes to this poem, in *The Poems of Sir Philip Sidney*, 459. See also William Craft, *Labyrinth of Desire: Invention and Culture in the Work of Sir Philip Sidney* (Newark: University of Delaware Press, 1994), 60; Doherty, *The Mistress-Knowledge*, 24; Kalstone, *Sidney's Poetry*, 126–27; and Helgerson, *The Elizabethan Prodigals*, 144. On "heart" as referring to Astrophil's desir-ing self, see Gordon Braden, "Unspeakable Love: Petrarch to Herbert," in *Soliciting Interpretation: Literary Theory and Seventeenth-Century English Poetry*, ed. Elizabeth D. Harvey and Katharine Eisaman Maus (Chicago: University of Chicago Press, 1990), 258; see also Lanham, *Motives of Eloquence*, 100–115. On the ambiguities over whether it is Stella or his own passion that inspires Astrophil's poetry, see Levao, *Renaissance Minds and their Fictions*, 157. Heather Dubrow makes the interesting point that "heart" is a homonym for "art" in this line, given that the "h" was often silent during the Elizabethan period. See her *Echoes of Desire: English Petrarchism and Its Counterdis-courses* (Ithaca: Cornell University Press, 1995), 103.

22. Petrarch, *Rime Sparse*, 1.1–4, in *Petrarch's Lyric Poems: The "Rime Sparse" and Other Lyrics*, ed. and trans. Robert Durling (Cambridge: Harvard University Press, 1973). All subsequent references to the *Rime Sparse* are by poem and line number to Durling's edition of the text. Robert Durling, trans., the *Rime Sparse*, 1.13, in *Petrarch's Lyric Poems*. All translations of the *Rime Sparse* are from this translation of the text.

23. On transgressive speech in the *Rime Sparse*, see Gordon Braden, "Love and Fame: The Petrarchan Career," in *Pragmatism's Freud: The Moral Disposition of Psycho-analysis*, ed. Joseph H. Smith and William Kerrigan (Baltimore: Johns Hopkins Uni-versity Press, 1986), 135–36; Durling's introduction to *Petrarch's Lyric Poems*, 29–30; and Nancy Vickers, "Diana Described," 99–100, 108–9. Dubrow discusses references to Orpheus in the *Rime Sparse*, without pursuing their significance to the thematics of gender and fragmentation in the sequence. See *Echoes of Desire*, 22. A number of re-marks by Dubrow parallel those expressed in my article, "The Unauthorized Orpheus of *Astrophil and Stella*"; because her book and my article on *Astrophil and Stella* (on which this chapter is based) were published in the same year, we did not consult each other's publications.

24. On the first sonnet as an expression of writer's block, see Braden, "Unspeakable Love," 258–59.

25. Durling, intro., *Petrarch's Lyric Poems*, 10–11.

26. On fragmentation as an enabling as well as problematic discourse in Petrarch, see Vickers, "Diana Described," 103–9. On Petrarch as displacing the authority of God, see especially William J. Kennedy, *Authorizing Petrarch* (Ithaca: Cornell Universi-ty Press, 1994), 207–8; and Marguerite Waller, *Petrarch's Poetics and Literary History*, 1–26. Marjorie O'Rourke Boyle (*Petrarch's Genius: Pentimento and Prophecy* [Berkeley:

University of California Press, 1991], 1–10), gives an interesting critique of this notion as somewhat simplistic.

27. On this poetics of "perversion" as "the appropriate subject and discourse for poetry" in the *Rime Sparse*, see Waller, *Petrarch's Poetics and Literary History*, 42.

28. John Freccero, "The Fig Tree and the Laurel: Petrarch's Poetics," in *Literary Theory / Renaissance Texts*, ed. Patricia Parker and David Quint (Baltimore: Johns Hopkins University Press, 1986), 20–32. On this concept, see also Braden, "Love and Fame," 133–55; Thomas M. Greene, *The Light in Troy*, 114; Marguerite Waller, *Petrarch's Poetics and Literary History*, 8–26; and Naomi Yavneh, "The Ambiguity of Beauty in Tasso and Petrarch," in *Sexuality and Gender in Early Modern Europe*, ed. James Grantham Turner, 136–37. Boyle (*Petrarch's Genius: Pentimento and Prophecy*, 1–10) presents an interesting critique of this position.

29. On idolatry in the *Rime Sparse*, see Freccero, "The Fig Tree and the Laurel," 34–39. See also Robert M. Durling, *The Figure of the Poet in Renaissance Epic* (Cambridge: Harvard University Press, 1965), 67–86, as well as Durling's introduction to *Petrarch's Lyric Poems*, 29–33. A more recent elaboration of the idolatry of Laura is given by Dubrow, in *Echoes of Desire*, 40. For a reading of this process in Sidney's poetry, see Braden, "Unspeakable Love," 253–74.

30. Harry Berger, Jr., "Orpheus, Pan, and the Poetics of Misogyny: Spenser's Critique of Pastoral Love and Art," *English Literary History* 50 (1983): 32.

31. The distinctions between Petrarch's poetry and the Petrarchan poetics that followed it have been charted by a number of critics; see especially Dubrow, *Echoes of Desire*, 6ff.; Forster, *The Icy Fire*, 4ff.; and Kennedy, *Authorizing Petrarch*, 1–24.

32. On this notion of originality, see especially Quint, *Origin and Originality*, 1–31. This project has clear resonances with Protestant claims that, by looking past Roman Catholic doctrine and back to St. Paul's writings, they were grounding their theology within the origins of Christianity.

33. See especially Sonnets 5, 15, 16, 21, and 23.

34. Quint, *Origin and Originality*, 41. Murray Krieger discusses the significance of naming as an attempt to invoke Stella's presence in *Astrophil and Stella*, in "Presentation and Representation in the Renaissance Lyric: The Net of Words and the Escape of the Gods," in *Mimesis: From Mirror to Method*, ed. John D. Lyons and Stephen G. Nichols, Jr. (Hanover: University Press of New England, 1982), 110–31. For Daniel Javitch, in contrast, Astrophil's repeated naming of Stella reveals how Astrophil claims to ground his sequence in his desire for the beloved, rather than in a desire for courtly advancement. See "The Impure Motives of Elizabethan Poetry," *Genre* 15 (1982): 225–38.

35. In *Astrophil and Stella* Nature as creatrix appears primarily as a figure of fertility, whose fecundity brings forth a spontaneous, natural birth. Her procreation thus stands in opposition to the poet's artificial and conscious reshaping of his source.

36. On Stella's moral power, see especially Robert Mongtomery, "Astrophil's Stella and Stella's Astrophil," in Waller and Moore, eds., *Sir Philip Sidney*, 44–55.

37. Plato, *Symposium*, in Hamilton and Cairns, eds., *The Collected Dialogues of*

Plato, 181c. Like most heroines of sonnets, Stella is in the position of control not only because she represents a more exalted manifestation of love than does her lover, nor because she is naturally a greater creator than he is, but simply because she is chaste. It is because of the association between female chastity and a masculine mode of power that Renaissance debates, including *Monophile,* often debate how a young woman can make the difficult transition from her position of superiority as a virgin to her position of inferiority within marriage.

38. A number of critics have noted how *Astrophil and Stella* unfolds as a power struggle between the two protagonists. See especially Clark Hulse, "Stella's Wit: Penelope Rich as Reader of Sidney's Sonnets," in Ferguson et al., eds., *Rewriting the Renaissance,* 272–86; Ann Rosalind Jones and Peter Stallybrass, "The Politics of *Astrophil and Stella,*" *Studies in English Literature* 24 (1984): 53–68; William Kerrigan and Gordon Braden, *The Idea of the Renaissance* (Baltimore: Johns Hopkins University Press, 1989), 172; and Jacqueline T. Miller, "'Love Doth Hold my Hand': Writing and Wooing in the Sonnets of Sidney and Spenser," *English Literary History* 46 (1979): 541–48. They have not, however, discussed Stella as a rival poet to Astrophil.

39. See, for example, Sonnets 36, 42, 48, 52, 59, and 61. On Astrophil's lust for Stella, see also Lanham, *"Astrophil and Stella,"* 100–115; McCoy, *Sir Philip Sidney,* 84–96; and Sinfield, "Astrophil's Self-Deception," 1–14. On the coterie poet's feminized position vis à vis the beloved, see especially Wall, *The Imprint of Gender,* 240–41.

40. As such, Sidney may be capitalizing on the tendency to associate sonnet writing with femininity. On this symbology, see Wall, *The Imprint of Gender,* 241–43.

41. See also Sonnet 50.

42. This, of course, is the opposite of Renaissance biological theory, in which, for the most part, the sperm was considered to actively create the child within the passive womb of the mother. On this theory, see Laqueur, *Making Sex,* 35–42.

43. See Cropper, "The Beauty of Woman," 175–90.

44. Levao gives a pessimistic reading of this sonnet (*Renaissance Minds and Their Fictions,* 167–68); as I show later on, I read this undoing of the self as a potentially constructive strategy on Astrophil's part. Ferry (*The "Inward" Language,* 134–35) presents an alternative reading of "I am not I"; she interprets this negation of the self as a means by which Astrophil may paradoxically affirm his selfhood. For Elizabeth M. Hull, "I am not I" suggests that the identities of Astrophil and Stella have merged with each other ("'All My Deed But Copying Is': The Erotics of Identity in *Astrophil and Stella,*" *Texas Studies in Literature and Language* 38 [1996]: 187).

45. For a historical account of Sidney's identification with the feminine, see Nona Fienberg, "The Emergence of Stella in *Astrophil and Stella,*" *Studies in English Literature* 25 (1985): 5–19.

46. Wyatt, "Who hath heard of such cruelty before?"; and Gascoigne, "The Lullaby of a Lover." The other expression of female artistry in the English Renaissance is that of playing a lute or a spinet. See Giles Fletcher's *Parthenophil,* Sonnet 31, and Shakespeare's *Sonnets,* Sonnet 128. On this tradition, see also Forster, *The Icy Fire,* 12.

47. Edmund Spenser, *Amoretti: The Yale Edition of the Shorter Poems of Edmund Spenser,* ed. William Oram, Einar Bjorvand, Ronald Bond, Cain Thomas, Alexander Dunlop, and Richard Schell (New Haven: Yale University Press, 1989). All subsequent references to the *Amoretti* are by poem and line number to this edition of the text.

48. On this conceptualization of the *Amoretti,* see also Kennedy, *Authorizing Petrarch,* 232–80.

49. On Elizabeth Boyle and other beloveds in the English sonnet tradition, see Dubrow, *Echoes of Desire,* 87–94; and Wall, *The Imprint of Gender,* 34–50.

50. There is, however, a certain amount of controversy over whether it is Elizabeth Boyle or Spenser's persona who speaks in this sonnet. For an overview of this controversy, see Kennedy, *Authorizing Petrarch,* 244–47.

51. On the ways that Laura is at once an idolatrous object and speaking subject, see also Dubrow, *Echoes of Desire,* 11ff.; and Barbara L. Estrin, *Laura: Uncovering Gender and Genre in Wyatt, Donne, and Marvell* (Durham: Duke University Press, 1994), 13–19, and passim.

52. Suggestively, when Laura does speak earlier in the sequence (poem 33), it is to silence Petrarch.

53. On this point, see also Jacqueline T. Miller, "'Love Doth Hold my Hand,'" 554.

54. I discuss this pattern of self-presentation in chapter 1.

55. Similarly, in Sonnet 99 he tells love: "Frate, tu vai / mostrando altrui la via dove sovente / foste smarrito et or se' più che mai" (ll. 12–14). On Petrarch's ambivalent responses to Laura, see also Forster, *The Icy Fire,* 3–8; and Marguerite Waller, *Petrarch's Poetics and Literary History,* 56–57.

56. On the unconventional nature of ending a sonnet sequence without closure, see A. C. Hamilton, *Sir Philip Sidney: A Study of his Life and Works* (Cambridge: Cambridge University Press, 1977), 79. Anthony Low presents a more pessimistic reading of this ending in *The Reinvention of Love: Poetry, Politics, and Culture from Sidney to Milton* (Cambridge: Cambridge University Press, 1993), 12–14.

57. The concept of "fall," of course, has religious implications. I do not cover this issue here, but see, for instance, Doherty, *The Mistress-Knowledge,* xii, 135; and A. C. Hamilton, "Sidney's Humanism," 113–16.

58. As such his "experience" prefigures Lacan's statement that the subject becomes "engaged in an ever-growing dispossession of that being of his, concerning which—by dint of sincere portraits which leave its idea no less incoherent, . . . and defences that do not prevent his statue from tottering, of narcissistic embraces that become like a puff of air in animating it—he ends up by recognizing that this being has never been anything more than his construct in the imaginary" (Jacques Lacan, "Function and Field of Speech and Language," in *Écrits,* 42).

59. The alternative title to *A Defence of Poetry* is, of course, *An Apology for Poetry.* On *A Defence of Poetry* as itself an apologue, see Ferguson, *Trials of Desire,* 152–62. Although she is less interested in the ways that the sonnet sequence as a whole may be read as an apologue, Warkentin notes that some of the sonnets may be classified as

apologues. See "Sidney and the Supple Muse," 175. I am grateful to Dan Kinney for calling my attention to the string of etymological associations between apology, *apologue,* and apologist.

4. Prose, Femininity, and the Prodigal Triangle in the *Decameron* and *The Old Arcadia*

1. I discuss this paradigm in more detail in the introduction. See also my article, "Engendering *Pericles," Literature and Psychology* 32 (1996): 53–72. For a somewhat different discussion of the oedipal paradigm in the *Decameron,* see Suzuki, "Gender, Power, and the Female Reader," 238.

2. Indeed, in some of Boccaccio's stories, even this complicity is irrelevant. In the story of King Agiluf (3.2), for instance, the queen does not even know that she has been seduced by the prodigal claimant, as the claimant, pretending to be the king, slips into her bed in the dark, then disappears. What *is,* apparently, significant is that Boccaccio represents the prodigal youth as deserving the female object of desire. On stories in which the woman is unwittingly liberated, or even compelled to be liberated, see Donaldson-Evans, "The Narrative of Desire," 542–44.

3. Jean Robertson discusses the influence of these works on *The Old Arcadia* in her edition of *The Countess of Pembroke's Arcadia (The Old Arcadia)* (Oxford: Clarendon Press, 1973), xix–xxix. Sidney would certainly have had access to the *Decameron* or one of its many English translations. On the dissemination of the *Decameron* in England, see especially Peter Stallybrass, "Dismemberments and Re-memberments: Rewriting the *Decameron,* 4.1, in the English Renaissance," *Studi Sul Boccaccio* 20 (1991–92): 299–324.

4. William Nelson, "From 'Listen Lordings,' to 'Dear Reader,'" *University of Toronto Quarterly* 46 (1976–77): 110–24.

5. See the introduction, where I discuss this passage in more detail.

6. This chapter will not dwell on in-between or heterogenous modes of narrative in the work—forms that mediate between idolatrous poetry and supple prose. Such utterances as inset epistolary narrations, poems expressed outside of the eclogues, or the story of Plangus told within the eclogue sections are most often placed on the margins of the prose and eclogue sections. Although these are also significant to a study of the structures of femininity in the work, I can only touch on the major oppositions between prose and poetry here, while suggesting that the opposition is not always antipodal.

7. On the ways in which Boccaccio employs prose differently from his predecessors, see Millicent Marcus, *An Allegory of Form,* 11–12. In contrast to most critics, like myself, Robert Hollander argues that in the *Decameron* Boccaccio is demystifying, rather than celebrating, sexual proclivities. See *Boccaccio's Two Venuses* (New York: Columbia University Press, 1977), especially 92–116. Pier Massimo Forni presents a middle ground to these two perspectives by arguing that the *Decameron* is both an *ars amatoria* and a *remedium amoris.* See his *Adventures in Speech: Rhetoric and Narration in Boccaccio's Decameron* (Philadelphia: University of Pennsylvania Press, 1996), 6–7. A number

of arguments about Sidney's *The Old Arcadia* come from my article "Philoclea Parsed: Prose, Verse, and Femininity in Sidney's *Old Arcadia*," in *Framing Elizabethan Fictions: Contemporary Approaches to Early Modern Narrative Prose,* ed. Constance C. Relihan (Kent, Ohio: Kent State University Press, 1996), 99–116.

8. Linked to this displacement of verse by "feminine" prose is the strong association between prose fiction and writing in the vernacular; for, as McLeod has noted, writing in the vernacular was strongly associated with a female readership (*Virtue and Venom,* 63).

My discussion of triangulation in the *Decameron* will not attempt to encompass all of Boccaccio's stories: the *Decameron* is nothing if not a heterogenous work, whose stories consistently exceed any attempt to locate one critical paradigm that will explain them all. But the prominence of the triangulated structure throughout this collection of novellas suggests that this is a crucial element for understanding Boccaccio's aesthetics of prodigality.

9. On the type of audience and characters—at once of merchant background and with aristocratic aspirations—that Boccaccio seems to privilege, see Norbert Jonard, "Le *Decameron* et 'La Légende de la Bourgeoisie,'" *Studi sul Boccaccio* 18 (1989): 351–68.

10. Musidorus's derision of poets clearly includes writers in prose as well as in verse. As Sidney himself made clear in his *Defence of Poetry* a few years later, "verse being but an ornament and no cause to poetry, since there have been many most excellent poets that never versified" (27). "Poetry," for Sidney, in other words, is closer to what we term "fiction."

11. Sidney's characterization of the other female protagonist, Pamela, is analogous to his characterization of Philoclea: the description of Pamela in poetry is so conventional as to be easily interchangeable with that of Philoclea, while, in prose descriptions, she emerges with a personality that is clearly distinct from that of Philoclea.

12. See Renato Poggioli, *The Oaten Flute: Essays on Pastoral Poetry and the Pastoral Ideal* (Cambridge: Harvard University Press, 1975), especially 22.

13. My translation. The French original is in Roland Barthes, *S/Z* (Paris: Editions du Seuil, 1970), 118–19.

14. Similarly, Pyrocles's first eclogue reveals how his love for Philoclea will make him immortal; the second is about his inability to communicate with Philoclea; while the third is a kind of blazon of himself, in which Pyrocles enumerates the many agonies that he has experienced since he fell in love. There is another extended blazon about Philoclea, which begins with the phrase, "What words may her perfection tell" (238–42). The poem, which exists on the threshold between the prose and eclogue sections of *The Old Arcadia,* participates in elements of both.

15. On debates about the merit of Sidney's eclogues, or lack thereof, see especially Ringler's introduction to *The Poems of Sir Philip Sidney,* xxxviii–xl. See also Duncan-Jones, *Sir Philip Sidney: Courtier Poet,* 82, 99; Neil L. Rudenstine, *Sidney's Poetic Development* (Cambridge: Harvard University Press, 1967), 75–105; and Hallett Smith, *Elizabethan Poetry* (Cambridge: Harvard University Press, 1952), 52. The one eclogue most critics seem to like is "Ye Goatherd Gods" (see, for instance, William Empson, *Seven Types of Ambiguity* [1930; reprint, Norfolk, Conn.: New Directions, 1953]; and

C. S. Lewis, *English Literature in the Sixteenth-Century, Excluding Drama* [London: Oxford University Press, 1954], 325–26). Andrew D. Weiner does present an eloquent defense of the eclogues, although he does so by focusing on their content and, essentially, ignoring their form (*Sir Philip Sidney and the Poetics of Protestantism: A Study of Contexts* [Minneapolis: University of Minnesota Press, 1978], 101–46).

16. Jeffrey Kittay and Wlad Godzich, *The Emergence of Prose: An Essay on Prosaics* (Minneapolis: The University of Minnesota Press, 1987), 203.

17. On the reasons for the growing popularity of prose fiction, see H. J. Chaytor, *From Script to Print: An Introduction to Medieval Vernacular Literature* (Cambridge: W. Heffer and Sons, 1945), 83–113. See also Kittay and Godzich, *The Emergence of Prose,* xiii–xix. On the problems of shifting from verse to prose in the English literary tradition, see Hildegard L. C. Tristram, "Aggregating Versus Integrating Narrative: Original Prose in England from the Seventh to the Fifteenth Century," in *Mündlichkeit und Schriflichkeit im Englischen Mittelalter* (Tübingen: Gunter Narr Verlag, 1988), 53–64.

18. On the minstrel's loss of status in sixteenth-century England, see also Tessa Watt, *Cheap Print and Popular Piety, 1550–1640* (Cambridge: Cambridge University Press, 1991), 14–15.

19. Clearly these poems are symbolically, not actually, oral in origin; their intricate metrical and rhetorical patterns reveal their grounding in the subordinative, analytical and abstract hermeneutics of written fiction, not in the additive, aggregative, paratactic nature of oral poetry. In fact, as Walter Ong tells us, it is the permanent, iconic discourse of the written word that is associated with the attempt to master the elusiveness of the spoken word; see *Orality and Literacy: The Technologizing of the Word* (London: Methuen, 1982), 78, 91, 132.

20. Claude Lévi-Strauss, *The Elementary Structures of Kinship,* trans. James Harle Bell and John Richard von Strumer, ed. Rodney Needham (Boston: Beacon Press, 1969), 494.

21. Ibid., 494, 496.

22. My reading of Alatiel has been strongly influenced by Millicent Marcus's analysis of this narrative. See her *Allegory of Form,* 35–44.

23. Boccaccio prepares us for this shift in narrative focus with his fourth story—about Landolfo Rufolo. Here, the ultimate object of desire is, literally, an object—the treasure which Landolfo steals. This separation of speech from desire yields not only a less than significant female protagonist—as it does in this story, but also, at times, female rapaciousness. The stories of Andreuccio and Gualtieri which follow this one represent the articulate female as a nefarious creature who misappropriates her powers of articulation in order to subdue and silence the desired youth.

24. In the Italian, Alatiel's betrothed is called the "re del Garbo," but I follow McWilliam's modernization of his name.

25. For a more thorough discussion of Alatiel as sexual object, see Millicent Marcus, *An Allegory of Form,* 40–41.

26. On the loss of Alatiel's human identity, see especially *Decameron,* 130.

27. My translation, since McWilliam's version does not translate "cosa."

28. On Alatiel's inability to communicate and her objectification, see also Laura Benedetti, "I silenzi di Alatiel," *Quaderni d'italianistica* 13 (1992): 246–51; Joan M. Ferrante, "Politics, Finance and Feminism in *Decameron*, II, 7," *Studi sul Boccaccio* 21 (1993): 151, 165–74; Joy Potter, "Woman in the *Decameron*," in *Studies in the Italian Renaissance: Essays in Memory of Arnolfo B. Ferruolo,* ed. Gian Paolo Biasin, Albert N. Mancini, and Nicolas J. Perella (Naples: Società Editrice Napoletana, 1985), 100; and L. Di Sisto, "Boccaccio, Friend or Foe? An Examination of the Role of Women in the *Decameron*," *Spunti e Ricerche* 10 (1994): 68.

29. On the destruction of homosocial bonds in the story, see also Potter, "Woman in the *Decameron*," 97.

30. Millicent Marcus, *An Allegory of Form,* 41. As Benedetti notes, Antigono—the first to speak to Alatiel, and therefore the first to avoid objectifying her—is the first of Alatiel's lovers who does not die violently ("I silenzi di Alatiel," 251).

31. The iterative nature of this narrative has been commented on by a number of critics, though not from the perspective of repetition compulsion. For a discussion of different perspectives on repetition in Alatiel, see Manuela Marchesini, "Le Ragioni di Alatiel (*Decameron* II.7)," *Studi sul Boccaccio* 22 (1994): 257–76.

32. Most critics, including myself, consider this description of Philoclea as positive in intention. For a contrasting perspective, see Heninger, *Sidney and Spenser: The Poet as Maker,* 419. On the problematics of erotically charged descriptions of women in Sidney's works, see Clare Kinney, "The Masks of Love: Desire and Metamorphosis in Sidney's *New Arcadia*," *Criticism* 33 (1991): 462–65, and Mary Ellen Lamb, *Gender and Authorship in the Sidney Circle* (Madison: University of Wisconsin Press, 1990), 6.

33. Given the more complex rendering of Philoclea in prose, it is not surprising that critics who evaluate this character base their readings on the prose passages of the work, rather than the eclogues. Most evaluations are positive: Duncan-Jones dwells on the complexity of her characterization (*Sir Philip Sidney: Courtier Poet*, 82–84); C. S. Lewis showers nothing but praise on Philoclea (*English Literature in the Sixteenth Century,* 338–39); just as Joan Rees writes that "Sidney's success in creating her is a triumph" (*Sir Philip Sidney and Arcadia* [Rutherford: Farleigh Dickinson Press, 1991], 65). In contrast, Katherine J. Roberts sees Philoclea and Pamela as "collections of various stereotypes" (*Fair Ladies,* 29). For a discussion of Philoclea that involves the more problematic aspects of Sidney's characterization of female characters, see the introduction and chapter 2 of Lamb, *Gender and Authorship in the Sidney Circle.*

34. Despite such conventional attributes, the prose Philoclea often appears as complex, even unpredictable. One such moment occurs when, after Philoclea discovers that Pyrocles has been flirting with her mother, she wittily scolds him by shaping an analogy between his disguise as an amazon and the deceptive nature of his love for her (234.27–30, 235.1).

35. As such, Philoclea partakes not just of the tradition of heroines like Hero and Griselda, but also of a more unconventional lineage of articulate and aggressive heroines

like the women of Ovid's love elegies, Shakespeare's Beatrice, or the women addressed in Donne's elegies. Perhaps because she is expressed as at once chaste and sexually awakened, Philoclea resembles both Hero and Beatrice.

36. Richard Brathwait, *The English Gentlewoman*, 6.

37. Issues of gazing in *The Old Arcadia* are too complex to discuss adequately within the scope of this chapter. Less interested in female characters as consistently victims of the male gaze (as in Ovid's *Metamorphoses*) or as shamed by the gaze (as in Spenser's *The Faerie Queene*), Sidney seems to be exploring different manifestations of the gaze—as at once transgressive and interactive, disabling and enabling—by men, women (though usually by men), and by readers as well. It is in *The New Arcadia*, as Clare Kinney has shown, that Sidney becomes more interested in the gaze as a purely transgressive act ("The Masks of Love," 461–90).

38. Philoclea composes poems about chastity and its loss in the second book; in the third book she utters three poems about her passion for Pyrocles; while in the last book she turns from poetry to prose as she writes an extended letter to the Arcadian court. But perhaps the moment that Sidney comes closest to disrupting convention is when he has Philoclea sleep with Pyrocles before they are married. For a more extended discussion of how Sidney at once questions and limits conventional representations of female characters, see Louise Schleiner, "Ladies and Gentlemen in Two Genres of Elizabethan Fiction," *Studies in English Literature, 1500–1900* 29 (1989): 1–19; see also Lamb, *Gender and Authorship in the Sidney Circle*, 72–114. Although I concur on the whole with Lamb's analysis of Philoclea, I disagree with her contention that "Philoclea's words are pervaded with an overwhelming sexuality which precludes any sustained role for her as an author" (3). In *The Old Arcadia*, at least, awakening sexuality is the necessary prerequisite for creating poetry.

39. Barkan, *The Gods Made Flesh*, 8.

40. For an opposing interpretation of the Pygmalion and Galatea myth, see Susan Gubar, "'The Blank Page' and the Issues of Female Creativity," in Abel, ed., *Writing and Sexual Difference*, 73–94. Gubar argues that Pygmalion symbolizes the male artist who rejects flesh and blood women, replacing them with his own imaginative and narcissistic fantasy of womankind.

41. As I discussed in chapter 3, Petrarchan poetry does not so much describe Petrarch's *Rime Sparse* per se, as it describes the tradition of love poetry that was influenced by it.

42. The shift, during the Renaissance, from a Petrarchan to an Ovidian perspective in love poetry is charted by Gordon Braden, in "Beyond Frustration: Petrarchan Laurels in the Seventeenth Century," *Studies in English Literature, 1500–1900*, 26 (1986): 5–23, although he focuses more on differences between these two perspectives within the lyric tradition.

43. The influence of Ovid upon Boccaccio has been noted by a number of critics. See especially Hollander, *Boccaccio's Two Venuses*, 112–16 (Hollander, however, sees Boccaccio as strongly critiquing the often salacious content of Ovidian verse); see also Forni, *Adventures in Speech*, 6–7, 82–88, 120–27; Mazzotta, *The World at Play*, 39; and

Janet Levarie Smarr, "Ovid and Boccaccio: A Note on Self-Defense," *Mediaevalia* 13 (1987): 247–53.

44. As Glenda McLeod has noted, Boccaccio is unusual, for his time, in his affirmation of female artistry. See *Virtue and Venom,* 69.

45. In particular Dioneo tends to affirm the prodigal triangle and a literature of pleasure. On Dioneo's narrative perspective, see also Suzuki, "Gender, Power, and the Female Reader," 233; and Hollander, *Boccaccio's Two Venuses,* 91. As a version of Boccaccio's prodigal narrator, Dioneo expresses two contrasting views of women. Michael Sherberg has noted how he is represented as speaking for women, particularly in his affirmation of a female comic spirit and in his antipatriarchal stance ("The Patriarch's Tale and the Frametale Crisis: *Decameron* IV–V," *Romance Quarterly* 38 [1991]: 229, 236). In contrast, Suzuki has dwelt on the misogynistic implications of Dioneo's sexual plots— particularly his narration of the story of Ginevra.

46. On this passage, see also Mazzotta, *The Word at Play in Boccaccio's Decameron,* 37. Mazzotta stresses analogies between speech and life in this passage.

47. On fiction as unsuitable for women, see Lamb, "The Cooke Sisters," 113.

48. In the introduction I more thoroughly discuss Boccaccio's claim to write for a female audience.

49. On the homosocial nature of these verse exchanges, see also Wall, *The Imprint of Gender,* 39.

50. This concept of reading the body carefully is suggested as Boccaccio writes: "E quinci cominciò a distinguer le parti di lei, lodando i capelli, li quali d'oro estimava, le fronte, il naso e la bocca, la gola e le braccia, e sommamente il peto" (355).

51. Michael Sherberg, "The Patriarch's Tale and the Frametale Crisis," 227–38.

52. The association between imagination and sensuality is expressed somewhat differently by Dorothy Connell, who says about Philoclea: "She draws the lover into a 'contemplation' (p. 38) of her beauty which ends . . . in a bed of earthly sexual joy." See *Sir Philip Sidney: The Maker's Mind,* 24.

53. On the female coterie audience of the old and new *Arcadia,* see Alan Hager, "Dazzling Images," 28, 157–66. See also Duncan-Jones, *Sir Philip Sidney: Courtier Poet,* 16. Where Duncan-Jones identifies Sidney's audience of "fair ladies," as, literally, the Countess of Pembroke and "her entourage of 'fair ladies' at Wilton," I am somewhat uncomfortable with this literal identification (16). Although it may well be these historical women whom Sidney's narrator repeatedly addresses, they may also be the same generalized and partly fictional female courtly audience that Boccaccio, Boiardo, and Ariosto address in the framing narratives of their fictions. What is significant is that Sidney claims this audience as his readership.

54. For the most part the narrator's asides to his "ladies" are notable for their playful, engaging tone, a tone that may also at times be condescending. It is difficult, for instance, to interpret the speaker's tone as he prepares the ladies for the first eclogues by stating that, "I hope your ears, fair ladies, be not so full of great matter that you will disdain to hear" (243.9–10). The overblown diction suggests that the ladies are considering anything but

complex philosophical problems; yet the irony of the remark also implies that the audience must be witty enough to catch its subtle turns of phrase. Apparently the narrator hopes for listeners who are perceptive enough to catch his double entendres, but not so educated as to threaten his authoritative position. For a more detailed discussion of Sidney's construction of the female audience in *The Old Arcadia,* see my "Ruptured Closure," 233–303. On Sidney's assumption that his female audience is intelligent and subtle, see also Roberts, *Fair Ladies,* 30–31.

55. On the feminine nature of the *brigata,* see also Sherberg, "The Patriarch's Tale and the Frametale Crisis," especially 227–28. On the *brigata* as characterizing the space of fantasy, see Cottino-Jones, "Desire and the Fantastic in the *Decameron,*" 1–18; and Millicent Marcus, *An Allegory of Form,* 7. As such, this space even interrogates Boccaccio's threshold paradigm, in which the female audience is primarily represented as silent and passive. By situating female narration one frame away from his threshold narrative, Boccaccio at once reveals how difficult it is to envision empowered female narrators outside of fantasy and protects himself from being displaced by his female audience.

56. Such symbolism may have inspired John Aubrey's piece of gossip about Sidney that "there was so great love between him and his faire sister that I have heard old Gentlemen say that they lay together." In *Aubrey's Brief Lives,* ed. Oliver Lawson Dick (1949; reprint, London: Penguin Books, 1987), 220. On the intimate tone of this dedication, see also Lucas, *Writing for Women,* 119.

57. On the story of Masetto as a kind of mirror image to that of Alatiel, see Di Sisto, "Boccaccio, Friend or Foe?" 66–70.

58. On this passage, see also Cottino-Jones, "Desire and the Fantastic in the *Decameron,*" 5.

59. The analogy between the nuns' desires to be seduced by Masetto and the narrator's textual seduction of his fair ladies is reinforced as Filostrato adds that the "gran forze dell'ozio e della sollicitudine" are powerful stimuli for sexual pleasure (188). The passage echoes Boccaccio's contention that women, cooped up by authority figures, can only sit, "quasi oziose" (4).

60. See Susanne Wofford, "The Social Aesthetics of Rape: Closural Violence in Boccaccio and Botticelli," in *Creative Imitation: New Essays on Renaissance Literature in Honor of Thomas M. Green,* ed. David Quint, Margaret W. Ferguson, G. W. Pigman III, and Wayne A. Rebhorn (Binghamton: Medieval and Renaissance Texts and Studies, 1992), 189–238.

61. For other readings of misogyny in the *Decameron,* see Di Sisto, "Boccaccio, Friend or Foe," 63–76; Ray Fleming, "Happy Endings? Resisting Women and the Economy of Love in Day Five of Boccaccio's *Decameron,*" *Italica* 70 (1993): 30–43; and Potter, "Woman in the *Decameron,*" 87–101. Wofford does, however, argue for a complex representation in the work that is at once misogynistic and sympathetic to victimized women ("The Social Aesthetic of Rape," 189–238).

62. On this novella as anti-chastity, see also Giovanni Sinicropi, "Chastity and Love in the *Decameron,*" in *The Olde Daunce: Love, Friendship, Sex, and Marriage in the*

Medieval World, ed. Robert R. Edwards and Stephen Spector (Albany: State University of New York Press, 1991), 104–20.

63. On paradigms of castration in the *Decameron,* see also Suzuki, "Gender, Power, and the Female Reader," 237–38.

64. Erich Auerbach also notes how Alberto's exploitation of Lisetta transgresses Boccaccio's ethics of sexual service for the female object of desire (*Mimesis: The Representation of Reality in Western Literature,* trans. Willard R. Trask [Princeton: Princeton University Press, 1953], 227). On Monna Lisetta as a bad reader, see also Millicent Marcus, *An Allegory of Form,* 79.

65. Aldo D. Scaglione makes a similar point in *Nature and Love in the Late Middle Ages: An Essay on the Cultural Context of the "Decameron"* (Berkeley: University of California Press, 1963), 70–71.

66. On Guismonda's inability to save Guiscardo, see also Millicent Marcus, *An Allegory of Form,* 54.

67. On this story as reflecting the perversely incestuous desires of Tancredi, see especially Guido Almansi, *The Writer as Liar: Narrative Technique in the Decameron* (London: Routledge, 1975), 133–57; and Mazzotta, *The World at Play in Boccaccio's Decameron,* 134–36.

68. On Boccaccio's aristocratic and commoner readership, see especially Auberach, who defines Boccaccio's ideal audience as urban aristocratic and what he calls "patrician burgher" (*Mimesis,* 206–7, 217–19). On class implications in the *Decameron,* see Vittore Branca, introduction to *Decameron: Edizione critica secondo l'autografo hamiltoniano* (Florence: Presso L'Accademia della Crusca, 1976), 34; Scaglione, *Nature and Love in the Late Middle Ages,* 69–77; and Suzuki, "Gender, Power, and the Female Reader," 238–39.

69. On "loose sheets" as a term for manuscript writing, see Marotti, *Manuscript, Print, and the English Renaissance Lyric,* 2; and Wall, *The Imprint of Gender,* 57. Marotti discusses, as well, how manuscripts were associated with an elite aristocratic or university culture (see especially page 42).

70. On verse as a form associated with an aristocratic audience, see Constance Relihan, *Fashioning Authority: The Development of Elizabethan Novelistic Discourse* (Kent, Ohio: Kent State University Press, 1994), 17–20; and Wall, *The Imprint of Gender,* 28–31.

71. M. M. Bakhtin, *The Dialogic Imagination: Four Essays,* ed. Michael Holquist, trans. Caryl Emerson and Michael Holquist (Austin: University of Texas Press, 1981).

72. Sidney's attempt to dissociate himself from print culture is evident in his decision not to publish any of his works. It may also have influenced his desire to have his works burnt upon his death. On the reluctance of aristocrats to publish their works, see especially J. W. Saunders, "The Stigma of Print: A Note on the Social Bases of Tudor Poetry," *Essays in Criticism* 9 (April 1951): 139–64. See also Marotti, *Manuscript, Print, and the Renaissance Lyric,* 222–90; Wall, *The Imprint of Gender,* 12–14, 25–31, 41–50ff.; and Whigham, "Interpretation at Court," 624–27. Jean Brink, in contrast, has questioned the very notion of this "stigma," in her paper, "The Stigma of Print: Sidney and Shakespeare" (presented at the annual meeting of the Shakespeare Association of

America, Albuquerque, New Mexico, April 1994). On the notion that the medium of print symbolically emasculates writers—whatever their background, see Susan C. Staub, "The Lady Francis Did Watch: Gascoigne's Voyeuristic Narrative," in Relihan, ed. *Framing Elizabethan Fictions*, 44–45.

For a more extensive discussion of the transition from chirographic to print culture, see Chaytor, *From Script to Print*, 48–113; David Margolies, *Novel and Society in Elizabethan England* (Totowa, N.J.: Barnes and Noble Books, 1985), 22–45; Arthur F. Marotti, "The Transmission of Lyric Poetry and the Institutionalizing of Literature in the English Renaissance," in *Contending Kingdoms: Historical, Psychological, and Feminist Approaches to the Literature of Sixteenth-Century England and France*, ed. Marie-Rose Logan and Peter L. Rudnytsky (Detroit: Wayne State University Press, 1991), 21–41; William Nelson, "From 'Listen Lordings' to 'Dear Readers'," *University of Toronto Quarterly* 46 (1976–77): 110–24; and Ong, *Orality and Literacy*, 117–38. On the associations between print and non-courtly or middle-class readers, see Elizabeth L. Eisenstein, *The Printing Revolution in Early Modern Europe* (Cambridge: Cambridge University Press: 1983), 24–41, 92–107; Relihan, *Fashioning Authority*, 58–61; and Spufford, *Small Books and Pleasant Histories*, 1–18. The associations between prose fiction in print and a growing nonaristocratic readership also underlie Bakhtin's *The Dialogic Imagination: Four Essays*.

5. "THE TRUEST POETRY": GENDER, GENRE, AND CLASS IN *AS YOU LIKE IT* AND *A DEFENCE OF POETRY*

1. Albert Gilman, introduction to *As You Like It*, ed. Albert Gilman (New York: New American Library, 1986), xxii. This aspect of the play has been commented on by a number of critics. See also Anne Barton, "*As You Like It* and *Twelfth Night*: Shakespeare's Sense of an Ending," in *Shakespearian Comedy*, ed. David Palmer and Malcolm Bradbury, vol. 14 of *Stratford-upon-Avon Studies* (London: Edward Arnold, 1972), 162; J. A. Bryant, *Shakespeare and the Uses of Comedy* (Lexington: University Press of Kentucky, 1986), 152; and Raymond B. Waddington, "Moralizing the Spectacle: Dramatic Emblems in *As You Like It*," *Shakespeare Quarterly* 33 (1982): 157.

2. These debates take place, respectively, in 2.1, 2.4, and 2.5.

3. On the influence of debate structure on English drama, see especially Joel Altman, *The Tudor Play of Mind: Rhetorical Inquiry and the Development of Elizabethan Drama* (Berkeley: University of California Press, 1978), 3–4, 6–10, 34ff. Altman is more interested in pedagogical practices of debate than in the influence of debate treatises themselves. Grace Tiffany suggests that yet another debate lies behind *As You Like It*, the "theater wars" of the late fifteenth/early sixteenth centuries. See "'That Reason Wonder May Diminish': *As You Like It*, Androgyny, and the Theater Wars," *The Huntington Library Quarterly* 57 (1994): 213–40.

4. Shakespeare, *As You Like It*, ed. Anne Barton, in Evans, ed., *The Riverside Shakespeare*, 2.1.16–17. All subsequent references to *As You Like It* are by act, scene, and line

number to this edition of the text. On self-conscious references to fiction in this passage, see also William Kerrigan, "Female Friends and Fraternal Enemies in *As You Like It*," in Finucci and Schwartz, eds., *Desire in the Renaissance*, 194–95.

5. I am grateful to Dan Kinney for pointing out to me resonances between *A Defence of Poetry* and *As You Like It*. My discussions of the dialogue between Touchstone and Audrey and of Sidney's critique of drama are particularly influenced by his comments.

6. For a detailed list of language in *As You Like It* that resonates with passages from *A Defence of Poetry*, see the appendix.

7. While Renaissance spectators might not necessarily have recognized the voice of Sidney behind Shakespeare, it seems likely that a good number of late Elizabethan university and courtly playgoers would have recognized these verbal echoes, given the popularity of *A Defence* in this period (a popularity enhanced by Sidney's dramatic and heroic death a decade earlier). *A Defence of Poetry* was first published in 1595. *As You Like It* is commonly considered to have been written and performed around 1599.

8. See, for example, Anne Barton's introduction to *As You Like It*, in Evans, ed., *The Riverside Shakespeare*; and Ferguson, *Trials of Desire*, 84.

9. Touchstone also builds his defense of fantasy around one of Sidney's favorite terms, "feigning," with its implied pun on "faining"—a pun that invokes the close associations between fantasy, seduction, and deception. It is (as I noted in chapter 3) in the opening lines of *Astrophil and Stella* that Sidney most ingeniously plays on the "feign"/"fain" pun, but it also crops up in *A Defence of Poetry*, 36–37. Touchstone's lines here recall as well Sidney's contention that a poet will never "conjure you to believe for true what he writes" (53).

10. Sidney's ironic and playful repetition of the term "truly" occurs as well on pages 18–20, 22, 31, 34, and passim. Almost each time the term appears it is associated, ironically, with poetical feigning.

11. Boccaccio, *Boccaccio on Poetry*, 39.

12. Girolamo Fracastoro, *Naugerius, Sive de Poetica Dialogus*, trans. Ruth Kelso, *University of Illinois Studies in Language and Literature*, vol. 9 (Urbana: University of Illinois Press, 1924), 70; Castelvetro, *Castelvetro on the Art of Poetry*, 6.1–6.

13. The quotation is from Ferguson, *Trials of Desire*, 184.

14. While this debate, expressed as it is by a fool and a "foul" woman, seems to call attention to Sidney's defense of poetry in order to diminish it, it is worth noting that Shakespeare's fools are often keepers of wisdom.

15. Shakespeare's fullest critique of such audiences is, of course, in *A Midsummer Night's Dream*, especially 1.2.66–82 and 3.1.8–69.

16. This is why, I suspect, most audiences (like many actors, directors, and critics) tend to overlook the theories of poetical feigning in Touchstone's dialogue: they are often too busy reacting to Touchstone's humorous attempts to seduce a woman who cannot understand his witty repartee.

17. Sidney's strong emphasis on characterization as the primary means by which poets seduce readers to virtue is also dramatic; for, as Sidney tells us, poetry excels in its

ability to bring forth "so true a lover as Theagenes, so constant a friend as Pylades, so valiant a man as Orlando, so right a prince as Xenophon's Cyrus" (24). Behind these assertions lies one of the few consistent points that Sidney makes about poetry—that its power inheres in its ability to animate abstract concepts by "figuring forth . . . a speaking picture" (25).

18. See pages 19, 25, 27, 39, 41ff.

19. Sidney, of course, shows little sympathy for the work of most English writers. I suggest reasons for this contempt in chapter 1.

20. On the apparent contradictions in this statement, see especially Hardison, "The Two Voices of Sidney's *Apology for Poetry*," 83–99.

21. I stress this point because Sidney, despite his Calvinist sympathies, seems to have no problems with the aspect of drama that most often disturbed Puritan polemicists— the fact that drama does not simply refer to lies and seductions but actually has actors lying and seducing on stage. On Calvinist attacks on acting, see especially Lisa Jardine, *Still Harping on Daughters: Women and Drama in the Age of Shakespeare* (New York: Columbia University Press, 1983), 9–32.

22. For a more extended discussion of the Elizabethan theatrical space, see Robert Weimann, *Shakespeare and the Popular Tradition in the Theater: Studies in the Social Dimension of Dramatic Form and Function*, ed. Robert Schwartz (Baltimore: Johns Hopkins University Press, 1978), 208–37. I discuss the coterie enclosure in chapter 4.

23. Peter C. Herman makes a similar point in *Squitter-wits and Muse-haters*, 89–90. See also Gary Waller, *The Sidney Family Romance: Mary Wroth, William Herbert, and the Early Modern Construction of Gender* (Detroit: Wayne State University Press, 1993), 223. On the forest of *As You Like It* as a space of social equality, see Bruce Smith, *Homosexual Desire*, 82–83. For a broader discussion of the heterogenous nature of the stage (as opposed to courtly or university experiences of fiction), see Louis Adrian Montrose, "The Purpose of Playing: Reflections on a Shakespearean Anthropology," *Helios* 7 (1980): 55–62; and Mary Beth Rose, *The Expense of Spirit: Love and Sexuality in English Renaissance Drama* (Ithaca: Cornell University Press, 1988), 1–2.

24. On this conceptualization of the pastoral, see especially Louis Adrian Montrose, "Of Gentlemen and Shepherds: The Politics of Elizabethan Pastoral Form," *English Literary History* 50 (1983): 415–59.

25. This representation of a clownish rural person may also be a way to engage the predominantly urban, anti-rural audiences who would have seen the play. On the notion that Shakespeare wrote his dramas for certain audiences see especially Leah S. Marcus, *Puzzling Shakespeare: Local Reading and its Discontents* (Berkeley: University of California Press, 1988), 1–50.

26. As I mentioned in the introduction, the issue of whether Sidney was or was not an aristocrat is somewhat vexed—while not technically an aristocrat, he was the heir apparent to an earlship and he had been named the "Baron de Sidenay" in France; whether or not this constituted him as an aristocrat, it is clear that he identified, to a large extent, with the aristocratic literary perspective. I discuss Sidney's poetics more thoroughly in chapter 1.

27. On Shakespeare as sympathetic to female characters, see Carol Rutter (interview with Juliet Stevenson), *Clamorous Voices: Shakespeare's Women Today,* ed. Faith Evans (London: Routledge, 1989), 97–121. On Shakespeare as ultimately patriarchal, see especially, see especially Peter Erickson, *Patriarchal Structures in Shakespeare's Drama* (Berkeley: University of California Press, 1985). On Shakespeare's partial feminism, see Paula S. Berggren, "The Woman's Part: Female Sexuality as Power in Shakespeare's Plays," in *The Woman's Part: Feminist Criticism of Shakespeare,* ed. Carolyn Ruth Swift Lenz, Gayle Greene, and Carol Thomas Neely (Urbana: University of Illinois Press, 1983), 23–31; Clara Clairborne Park, "As We Like It: How a Girl Can Be Smart and Still Popular," in Lanz, et al., eds., *The Woman's Part,* 102–14; and Rose, *The Expense of Spirit,* 39–40. More recently, critics, focusing on the boy actor behind Rosalind, have set aside Shakespeare's sympathy (or lack of it) with Rosalind as female character. See, for instance, Garber, *Vested Interests,* 74–76; Jan Kott, "The Gender of Rosalind," *New Theatre Quarterly* 7 (1991): 113–25; and Lesley Anne Soule, "Subverting Rosalind: Cocky Ros in the Forest of Arden," *New Theatre Quarterly* 7 (1991): 126–36.

28. On the boy actor behind Rosalind, see especially, Penny Gay, *As She Likes It: Shakespeare's Unruly Women* (London: Routledge, 1994), 48–85; Jardine, *Still Harping on Daughters,* 19, 20, 24; Kott, "The Gender of Rosalind," 113–25; and Michael Shapiro, *Gender in Play on the Shakespearean Stage: Boy Heroines and Female Pages* (Ann Arbor: University of Michigan Press, 1996), 119–42.

29. For a quite different reading of the gendered poetics of *As You Like It,* see Juliet Dusinberre, "As Who Liked It?" *Shakespeare and Sexuality,* vol. 46 of *Shakespeare Survey,* ed. Stanley Wells (Cambridge: Cambridge University Press, 1993), 9–21. Dusinberre argues that Rosalind "finds herself in a script supplied by men which she rewrites as the play progresses."

30. On this rivalry with Orlando-as-poet, see also Rutter, *Clamorous Voices,* 105–13.

31. See *A Defence,* 17–18; and *As You Like It,* 1.1.33.

32. On associations between Rosalind and Touchstone, see Bamber, *Comic Women, Tragic Men,* 231.

33. I quote here from Albert Gilman's edition of *As You Like It,* which brings out more clearly the clerical references in this line. (Barton substitutes "Jupiter" for "pulpiter.")

34. On Rosalind's devaluation of courtly lyric, see also Dusinberre, who sees it as a critique of patriarchy ("As Who Liked It?" 11). In contrast, Erickson sees it as an indirect affirmation of patriarchy (21). Tiffany examines this devaluation from the perspective of the late Elizabethan theater wars ("'That Reason Wonder May Diminish,'" 213–40). Susanne Wofford looks at its implications for performative utterances ("'To You I Give Myself, for I Am Yours': Erotic Performance and Theatrical Performatives in *As You Like it,*" in *Shakespeare Reread: The Texts in New Contexts,* ed. Russ McDonald [Ithaca: Cornell University Press: 1994], 154–55). Clare Kinney presents this defense of dramatic dialog as a kind of rebellion against Thomas Lodge's prose style in *Rosalynde.* See her "Feigning Female Faining: Spenser, Lodge, Shakespeare and Rosalind," *Modern Philology* 95 (1998): 291–315.

35. *Astrophil and Stella,* most scholars agree, was composed shortly after *A Defence of Poetry.*

36. At least one production of *As You Like It,* Peter Stein's production, projects a second, female, homoerotic relationship in the play—that between Rosalind and Celia. For a discussion of this production, see Kott, "The Gender of Rosalind," 117.

37. The notion that boy actors problematize heterosexuality is broached by most critics who have recently discussed the performative experience of boy actors. See especially Jardine, *Still Harping on Daughters,* 9–36; Kott, "The Gender of Rosalind," 113–25; Smith, *Homosexual Desire in Shakespeare's England,* 146–57; Shapiro, *Gender in Play on the Shakespearean Stage,* 199–204; and Traub, *Desire and Anxiety,* 117–44.

38. Stephen Orgel, "Nobody's Perfect: Or Why did the English Stage Take Boys for Women?" *South Atlantic Quarterly* 88 (1989): 7–29. See also Peter Stallybrass, "Transvestism and the 'Body Beneath': Speculating on the Boy Actor," in Zimmerman, ed., *Erotic Politics,* 64–83.

39. For a more extended discussion of this notion, see especially Garber, *Vested Interests,* 10. See also Jardine, who discusses how the liminal identity of transvestite players hovers "somewhere between the heterosexual and the homosexual" (*Still Harping on Daughters,* 11). Garber and Jardine are, however, less interested in how this concept is associated with the poetics of *As You Like It.*

40. On confusions of desire in *As You Like It,* see also Gay, *As She Likes It,* 15, 16ff., and Traub, *Desire and Anxiety,* 116–44.

41. This representation of the chaste female heroine as a site of strong heterosexual and homosexual attraction is often the measure by which productions of *As You Like It* are judged. Peter Holland, for instance, complained that the lack of onstage eroticism is what weakened the 1992 production of *As You Like It* at Stratford ("Shakespeare Performances in England, 1992," in Wells, ed., *Shakespeare and Sexuality,* vol. 46, 178). Such expectations, deeply tied to androgynous representations of Rosalind, may be traced at least as far back as the 1952 production of *As You Like It.* The *Western Daily Press* focused on Margaret Leighton's performance of Rosalind as "boyish and girlish together" (qtd. Gay, *As She Likes It,* 50). Leighton's androgynous Rosalind was enhanced by Vanessa Redgrave's quite liberated and libidinous Rosalind (1961). Given the greater acceptance of sexual ambiguity in portrayals of Rosalind, it is not surprising that *As You Like It* should be one of the first plays of the postwar period to experiment with an all male cast, as did Clifford Williams in his 1967 production of the play; on this production, see Gay, *As She Likes It,* 62). But more characteristic of recent performances is Juliet Stevenson's portrayal of Rosalind as "an exploration of gender, the male and the female within us all" (*Plays and Players,* May 1985; qtd. ibid., 76). On this production, see Yu-Jin Ko, "Straining Sexual Identity: Cheek by Jowl's All-Male *As You Like It,*" *Shakespeare Bulletin* 13 (1995): 16–17. For an invaluable overview of postwar productions of *As You Like It,* see Gay, *As She Likes It,* chapter 4.

42. On the problematics of moving from all male to male and female actors, see also Garber, *Vested Interests,* 126. This problematics is implied as well by Traub in *Desire and Anxiety,* 117.

43. Anthony B. Dawson, "Performance and Participation: Desdemona, Foucault, and the Actor's Body," in *Shakespeare, Theory, and Performance,* ed. James C. Bulman (London: Routledge, 1996), 43.

44. Stubbs, *The Anatomy of Abuses* (New York: Johnson Reprint Company Limited, 1972), L7r–v (facsimile).

45. Rackin, "Androgyny, Mimesis, and the Marriage of the Boy Heroine," 33–34. Without calling attention specifically to Rosalind's gender, John Russell Brown makes a similar, though less constructively posited, point: "she triumphs only in fancy, when she is almost alone in excitement and danger. Faced with unambiguous reality, she may faint or cry out in pain and hunger" (*Discovering Shakespeare: A New Guide to the Plays* [New York: Columbia University Press, 1981], 148).

46. Wofford has argued that this movement toward marriage is prepared for throughout the play, a play which gestures to homoerotic desire in order, apotropaically, to ward off this very threat to heterosexual marriage ("To You I Give Myself," 147–69).

47. Sidney most dramatically illustrates the contingent power of poetical feigning with the story of the tyrant Pheraeus, "from whose eyes a tragedy, well made and represented, drew abundance of tears" (45). Despite being moved by the eloquence of tragedy, Pheraeus never changes his ways.

48. See, for example, Bulman's introduction to *Shakespeare, Theory, and Performance,* 4; see also Dawson, "Performance and Participation," 30.

49. The significance of Rosalind's/the boy actor's ability to awaken the erotic interest of the audience has been commented on by a number of critics, from different perspectives. See especially Kerrigan, "Female Friends and Fraternal Enemies in *As You Like It,"* 198–99; and Tiffany, "That Reason Wonder May Diminish," 219, 233–35.

50. For a different perspective on this passage, see Erickson, *Patriarchal Structures in Shakespeare's Drama,* 35.

Bibliography

Abel, Elizabeth, ed. *Writing and Sexual Difference*. Chicago: University of Chicago Press, 1982.

Agrippa, Henricus Cornelius. *Declamation on the Nobility and Preeminence of the Female Sex*. Trans. and ed. Albert Rabil, Jr. Chicago: University of Chicago Press, 1996.

Allen, M. J. B. "Sidney's *Defence* and the Image Making of Plato's *Sophist*." Allen, et. al. eds., *Sir Philip Sidney's Achievements*.

Allen, M. J. B., Dominick Baker-Smith, and Arthur Kinney, eds., *Sir Philip Sidney's Achievements*. New York: AMS Press, 1990.

Almansi, Guido. *The Writer as Liar: Narrative Technique in the Decameron*. London: Routledge, 1975.

Altman, Joel B. *The Tudor Play of Mind: Rhetorical Inquiry and the Development of Elizabethan Drama*. Berkeley: University of California Press, 1978.

Anderson, W. S. "The Orpheus of Virgil and Ovid: *flebile nescio quid*." *Orpheus: The Metamorphoses of a Myth*. Ed. John Warden. Toronto: University of Toronto Press, 1982.

Anger, Jane. *Jane Anger, Her Protection for Women. . . . The Women's Sharp Revenge: Five Women's Pamphlets from the Renaissance*. Ed. Simon Shepherd. New York: St. Martin's Press, 1985.

Aristotle. *Historia Animalium (History of Animals)*. Trans. D'Arcy Wentworth Thompson. In *The Basic Works of Aristotle*. Ed. Richard McKeon. New York: Random House, 1941.

Asch, Ronald G. "Introduction: Court and Household from the Fifteenth to the Seventeenth Centuries." Asch and Birke, eds., *Princes, Patronage and the Nobility*.

Asch, Ronald G., and Adolf M. Birke, eds. *Princes, Patronage, and the Nobility: The Court at the Beginning of the Modern Age, c.* 1450–1650. London: Oxford University Press, 1991.

Ascham, Roger. *The Scholemaster.* Ed. Edward Arber. *English Reprints.* Vol. 10. Birmingham, England: 1870.

Attebery, Brian. *Strategies of Fantasy.* Bloomington: Indiana University Press, 1992.

Aubrey, John. *Aubrey's Brief Lives.* Ed. Oliver Lawson Dick. 1949. Reprint. London: Penguin Books, 1987.

Auerbach, Erich. *Mimesis: The Representation of Reality in Western Literature.* Trans. Willard R. Trask. Princeton: Princeton University Press, 1953.

Aughterson, Kate, ed. *Renaissance Woman: A Sourcebook, Constructions of Femininity in England.* London: Routledge, 1995.

Axton, Marie. *The Queen's Two Bodies: Drama and the Elizabethan Succession.* London: Royal Historical Society, 1977.

Bakhtin, M. M. *The Dialogic Imagination: Four Essays.* Ed. Michael Holquist. Trans. Cary Emerson and Michael Holquist. Austin: University of Texas Press, 1981.

Bamber, Linda. *Comic Women, Tragic Men: A Study of Gender and Genre in Shakespeare.* Stanford: Stanford University Press, 1982.

Barbaro, Francesco. *Directions for Love and Marriage.* Anonymous translation. London: 1676.

Bardon, Françoise. "Sur un portrait de François Ier." *L'information d'histoire de l'art* 8 (1963): 1–7.

Barkan, Leonard. *The Gods Made Flesh: Metamorphosis and the Pursuit of Paganism.* New Haven: Yale University Press, 1986.

Barthes, Roland. *S/Z.* Paris: Éditions du Seuil, 1970.

Barton, Anne. "*As You Like It* and *Twelfth Night:* Shakespeare's Sense of an Ending." *Shakespearean Comedy.* Ed. David Palmer and Malcolm Bradbury. Vol. 14 of *Stratford-upon-Avon Studies.* London: Edward Arnold, 1972.

———. Introduction to *As You Like It. The Riverside Shakespeare.* Ed. G. Blakemore Evans. Boston: Houghton Mifflin, 1974.

Bassanese, Fiora A. "Gaspara Stampa's Poetics of Negativity." *Italica* 61 (1984): 335–46.

Beilin, Elaine V. *Redeeming Eve: Women Writers of the English Renaissance.* Princeton: Princeton University Press, 1987.

Belsey, Catherine. "Alice Arden's Crime: *Arden of Faversham* (c. 1590)." *Staging the Renaissance: Reinterpretations of Elizabethan and Jacobean Drama.* Ed. David Scott Kastan and Peter Stallybrass. New York: Routledge, 1991.

Benedetti, Laura. "I silenzi di Alatiel." *Quaderni d'italianistica* 13 (1992): 245–55.

Benson, Pamela Joseph. *The Invention of the Renaissance Woman: The Challenge of Female Independence in the Literature and Thought of Italy and England.* University Park: Penn State University Press, 1992.

Berger, Harry, Jr. "Orpheus, Pan, and the Poetics of Misogyny: Spenser's Critique of Pastoral Love and Art." *English Literary History* 50 (1983): 27–60.

Berggren, Paula S. "The Woman's Part: Female Sexuality as Power in Shakespeare's Plays." In *The Woman's Part,* Lenz et al., eds.

Berry, Edward. "The Poet as Warrior in Sidney's *Defence of Poetry.*" *Studies in English Literature 1500–1900* 29 (1989): 21–34.

Berry, Philippa. *Of Chastity and Power: Elizabethan Literature and the Unmarried Queen.* London: Routledge, 1989.

Bloom, Harold. *The Anxiety of Influence: A Theory of Poetry.* London: Oxford University Press, 1973.

Boccaccio, Giovanni. *Boccaccio on Poetry: Being the Preface and the Fourteenth and Fifteenth Books of Boccaccio's "Genealogia Deorum Gentilium."* Ed. and trans. Charles G. Osgood. 1930. Reprint. Indianapolis: The Liberal Arts Press, 1956.

———. *Decameron.* Ed. Enrico Bianchi. *Giovanni Boccaccio: Decameron, Filocolo, Ameto, Fiammetta.* Vol. 8 of *La Letterature Italiana: Storia e Testi.* Ed. Rafaele Mattioli, Pietro Pancrazi, and Alfredo Schiaffini. Milan: Riccardo Ricciardi Editore, 1969.

———. *The Decameron.* Trans. G. H. McWilliam. London: Penguin Books, 1972.

Boyle, Marjorie O'Rourke. *Petrarch's Genius: Pentimento and Prophecy.* Berkeley: University of California Press, 1991.

Braden, Gordon. "Beyond Frustration: Petrarchan Laurels in the Seventeenth Century." *Studies in English Literature, 1500–1900* 26 (1986): 5–23.

———. "Love and Fame: The Petrarchan Career." *Pragmatism's Freud: The Moral Disposition of Psychoanalysis.* Ed. Joseph H. Smith and William Kerrigan. Baltimore: Johns Hopkins University Press, 1986.

———. "Unspeakable Love: Petrarch to Herbert." *Soliciting Interpretation: Literary Theory and Seventeenth-Century English Poetry.* Ed. Elizabeth D. Harvey and Katharine Eisaman Maus. Chicago: University of Chicago Press, 1990.

Branca, Vittore. Introduction. *Decameron: Edizione critica secondo l'autografo hamiltoniano.* By Giovanni Boccaccio. Florence: Presso l'Accademia della Crusca, 1976.

Brathwait, Richard. *The English Gentlewoman.* New York: Da Capo Press, 1970.

Bray, Alan. *Homosexuality in Renaissance England.* 1982. Reprint. New York: Columbia University Press, 1985.

Bredbeck, Gregory W. *Sodomy and Interpretation: Marlowe to Milton.* Ithaca: Cornell University Press, 1991.

Brennan, Michael G. *Literary Patronage in the English Renaissance: The Pembroke Family.* London: Routledge, 1988.

Brink, Jean. "The Stigma of Print: Sidney and Shakespeare." Paper presented at the annual meeting of the Shakespeare Association of America, Albequerque, New Mexico, April 1994.

Brown, John Russell. *Discovering Shakespeare: A New Guide to the Plays.* New York: Columbia University Press, 1981.

Bryant, J. A. *Shakespeare and the Uses of Comedy.* Lexington: University of Kentucky Press, 1986.

Bundy, Murray Wright. "'Invention' and 'Imagination' in the Renaissance." *Journal of English and Germanic Philology* 29 (1930): 535–45.

———. *The Theory of Imagination in Classical and Mediaeval Thought.* 1927. Reprint. N.p.: Norwood Editions, 1976.

Burke, Peter. *The Fortunes of the "Courtier": The European Reception of Castiglione's "Cortegiano."* 1995. Reprint. University Park: Penn State University Press, 1996.

Castelvetro, Lodovico. *Castelvetro on the Art of Poetry: An Abridged Translation of Lodovico Castelvetro's Poetica d'Aristotele Vulgarizzata et Sposta.* Trans. Andrew Bongiorno. Binghamton: Medieval and Renaissance Texts and Studies, 1984.

Castiglione, Baldesar. *The Book of the Courtier.* Trans. George Bull. Harmondsworth: Penguin Books, 1967.

———. *Il Libro del Cortegiano.* Ed. Bruno Maier. Turin: Unione Tipografico-Editrice Torinese, 1964.

Cavendish, Margaret. *Poems, and Fancies.* Providence: Brown University Women Writers Project, Version 0.1, 1991.

Chastel, André. *The Age of Humanism: Europe 1480–1530.* Trans. Katherine M. Delavenay and E. M. Gwyer. London: Thames and Hudson, 1963.

Chaytor, H. J. *From Script to Print: An Introduction to Medieval Vernacular Literature.* Cambridge: W. Heffer and Sons, Ltd., 1945.

Connell, Dorothy. *Sir Philip Sidney: The Maker's Mind.* Oxford: Clarendon Press, 1977.

Cottino-Jones, Marga. "Desire and the Fantastic in the *Decameron:* The Third Day." *Italica* 70 (1993): 1–18.

Couton, Marie. "*The Anatomie of Absurditie:* Portrait of the Satirist as a Compiler." *Cahiers Élisabéthains* 37 (1990): 17–26.

Cox, Virginia. *The Renaissance Dialogue: Literary Dialogue in its Social and Political Contexts, Castiglione to Galileo.* Cambridge: Cambridge University Press, 1992.

Craft, William. *Labyrinth of Desire: Invention and Culture in the Work of Sir Philip Sidney.* Newark: University of Delaware Press, 1994.

Crewe, Jonathan V. *Unredeemed Rhetoric: Thomas Nashe and the Scandal of Authorship.* Baltimore: The Johns Hopkins University Press, 1982.

Cropper, Elizabeth. "The Beauty of Woman: Problems in the Rhetoric of Renaissance Portraiture." Ferguson et al., eds., *Rewriting the Renaissance.*

Davis, Natalie Zemon. *Society and Culture in Early Modern France: Eight Essays by Natalie Zemon Davis.* Stanford: Stanford University Press, 1975.

Davis, Robert Con. "The Discourse of the Father." Introduction to *The Fictional Father: Lacanian Readings of the Text.* Ed. Robert Con Davis. Amherst: The University of Massachusetts Press, 1981.

Dawson, Anthony B. "Performance and Participation: Desdemona, Foucault, and the Actor's Body." *Shakespeare, Theory and Performance.* Ed. James C. Bulman. London: Routledge, 1996.

Demadre, Antoine. *Essais sur Thomas Nashe.* Salzburg: University of Salzburg Press, 1986.

Dickson, Lynne. "Sidney's Grotesque Muse: Fictional Excess and the Feminine in the Arcadias." *Renaissance Papers* (1992): 41–55.

DiGangi, Mario. *The Homoerotics of Early Modern Drama.* Cambridge: Cambridge University Press, 1997.

Di Sisto, L. "Boccaccio, Friend or Foe? An Examination of the Role of Women in the *Decameron.*" *Spunti e Ricerche: Rivista d'Italianistica* 10 (1994): 63–75.

Doherty, M. J. *The Mistress-Knowledge: Sir Philip Sidney's "Defence of Poesie" and Literary Architectonics in the English Renaissance.* Nashville: Vanderbilt University Press, 1991.

Dolan, Frances E. "Taking the Pencil Out of God's Hand: Art, Nature, and the Face-Painting Debate in Early Modern England." *PMLA* 108 (1993): 224–39.

Donaldson-Evans, Lance. "The Narrative of Desire: Boccaccio and the French *Decamerons* of the Fifteenth and Sixteenth Centuries." *Neophilologus* 77 (1993): 541–52.

Dubrow, Heather. *Echoes of Desire: English Petrarchism and Its Counterdiscourses.* Ithaca: Cornell University Press, 1995.

Duncan-Jones, Katherine. "Philip Sidney's Toys." Kay, ed., *Sir Philip Sidney.*

———. *Sir Philip Sidney: Courtier Poet.* New Haven: Yale University Press, 1991.

———, ed. *Sir Philip Sidney: Selected Poems.* 1973. Reprint. Oxford: Oxford University Press, 1979.

Dunn, Catherine M. "The Changing Image of Woman in Renaissance Society and Literature." *What Manner of Woman: Essays on English and American Life and Literature.* Ed. Marlene Springer. New York: New York University Press, 1977.

Durling, Robert M. *The Figure of the Poet in Renaissance Epic.* Cambridge: Harvard University Press, 1965.

———, ed. and trans. *Petrarch's Lyric Poems: The "Rime Sparse" and Other Lyrics.* Cambridge: Harvard University Press, 1976.

Dusinberre, Juliet. "As Who Liked It?" *Shakespeare and Sexuality.* Vol. 46 of *Shakespeare Survey.* Ed. Stanley Wells. Cambridge: Cambridge University Press, 1993.

Edelman, Lee. *Homographesis: Essays in Gay Literary and Cultural Theory.* New York: Routledge, 1994.

Eisenstein, Elizabeth L. *The Printing Revolution in Early Modern Europe.* Cambridge: Cambridge University Press, 1983.

Elyot, Sir Thomas. *The Defence of Good Women.* Ed. Edwin Johnston Howard. Oxford, Ohio: Anchor Press, 1940.

Empson, William. *Seven Types of Ambiguity.* 1930. Reprint. Norfolk, Conn.: New Directions, 1953.

Erickson, Peter. *Patriarchal Structures in Shakespeare's Drama.* Berkeley: The University of California Press, 1985.

Estrin, Barbara L. *Laura: Uncovering Gender and Genre in Wyatt, Donne, and Marvell.* Durham: Duke University Press, 1994.

Evans, G. Blakemore, ed. *The Riverside Shakespeare.* Boston: Houghton Mifflin, 1974.

Ferguson, Margaret W. "A Room Not Their Own: Renaissance Women as Readers and Writers." *The Comparative Perspective on Literature: Approaches to Theory and Practice.* Ed. Clayton Koelb and Susan Noakes. Ithaca: Cornell University Press, 1988.

———. *Trials of Desire: Renaissance Defenses of Poetry.* New Haven: Yale University Press, 1983.

Ferguson, Margaret W., Maureen Quilligan, and Nancy J. Vickers, eds. *Rewriting the Renaissance: The Discourses of Sexual Difference in Early Modern Europe.* Chicago: The University of Chicago Press, 1986.

Ferrante, Joan M. "Politics, Finance and Feminism in *Decameron*, II, 7." *Studi sul Boccaccio* 21 (1993): 151–74.

Ferry, Anne. *The "Inward" Language: Sonnets of Wyatt, Sidney, Shakespeare, Donne.* Chicago: University of Chicago Press, 1983.

Fienberg, Nora. "The Emergence of Stella in *Astrophil and Stella*," *Studies in English Literature* 25 (1985): 5–19.

Fineman, Joel. "Fratricide and Cuckoldry: Shakespeare's Doubles." In *Representing Shakespeare: New Psychoanalytic Essays*. Ed. Murray M. Schwartz and Coppélia Kahn. Baltimore: Johns Hopkins University Press, 1980.

Finucci, Valeria. "Jokes on Women: Triangular Pleasures in Castiglione and Freud." *Exemplaria* 4 (1992): 51–77.

———. "La Donna di Corte: Discorso Istituzuionale e Realtà nel *Libro del Cortegiano* di B. Castiglione." *Annali d'Italianistica* 7 (1989): 88–103.

Finucci, Valeria, and Regina Schwartz, eds. *Desire in the Renaissance: Psychoanalysis in Literature*. Princeton: Princeton University Press, 1994.

Firenzuola, Agnolo. *On the Beauty of Women*. Ed. and trans. Konrad Eisenbichler and Jacqueline Murray. Philadelphia: University of Pennsylvania Press, 1992.

Fleming, Ray. "Happy Endings? Resisting Women and the Economy of Love in Day Five of Boccaccio's *Decameron*." *Italica* 70 (1993): 30–45.

Forni, Pier Massimo. *Adventures in Speech: Rhetoric and Narration in Boccaccio's Decameron*. Philadelphia: University of Pennsylvania Press, 1996.

Forster, Leonard Wilson. *The Icy Fire: Five Studies in European Petrarchism*. Cambridge: Cambridge University Press, 1969.

Fracastoro, Girolamo. *Naugerius, Sive de Poetica Dialogus*. Trans. Ruth Kelso. Intro. Murray W. Bundy. *University of Illinois Studies in Language and Literature*. Vol. 9. Urbana: University of Illinois Press, 1924.

Freccero, John. "The Fig Tree and the Laurel: Petrarch's Poetics." *Literary Theory / Renaissance Texts*. Ed. Patricia Parker and David Quint. Baltimore: Johns Hopkins University Press, 1986.

Freud, Sigmund. "Medusa's Head." Vol. 5 *Collected Papers*. Trans. Joan Rivière. Ed. James Strachey. London: Hogarth Press, 1950.

Garber, Marjorie. *Vested Interests: Cross-Dressing and Cultural Anxiety*. 1992. Reprint. New York: HarperPerennial, 1993.

———. *Vice Versa: Bisexuality and the Eroticism of Everyday Life*. New York: Simon and Schuster, 1996.

Gay, Penny. *As She Likes It: Shakespeare's Unruly Women*. London: Routledge, 1994.

Gilman, Albert, ed. *As You Like It*. New York: New American Library, 1986.

Girard, René. *Deceit, Desire, and the Novel: Self and Other in Literary Structure*. Trans. Yvonne Freccero. Baltimore: The Johns Hopkins University Press, 1965.

Goldberg, Jonathan. *Sodometries: Renaissance Texts, Modern Sexualities*. Stanford: Stanford University Press, 1992.

Gosson, Stephen. *The School of Abuse: Containing a Pleasant Invective against Poets, Pipers, Players, Jesters, &c.* 1841. Reprint. New York: AMS Press, 1970.

Gosynhill, Edmund. *Mulierum Paean*. Henderson and McManus, eds., *Half Humankind*.

[———?]. *The Schoolhouse of Women*. Henderson and McManus, eds., *Half Humankind*.

Gough, Melinda. "'Effeminate Wantonness' or 'the Companion of Camps'?" Paper presented at the annual meeting of the Shakespeare Association of America, Albuquerque, New Mexico, April 1994.

Greenblatt, Stephen. *Shakespearean Negotiations: The Circulation of Social Energy in Renaissance England.* Berkeley: University of California Press, 1988.

Greene, Roland. *Post-Petrarchism: Origins and Innovations of the Western Lyric Sequence.* Princeton: Princeton University Press, 1991.

Greene, Thomas M. "*Il Cortegiano* and the Choice of a Game." Hanning and Rosand, ed., *Castiglione.*

———. *The Light in Troy: Imitation and Discovery in Renaissance Poetry.* Vol. 7 of *The Elizabethan Club Series.* New Haven: Yale University Press, 1982.

Gubar, Susan. "'The Blank Page' and the Issues of Female Creativity." Abel, ed., *Writing and Sexual Difference.*

Guillory, John. *Poetic Authority: Spenser, Milton, and Literary History.* New York: Columbia University Press, 1983.

Hager, Alan. *Dazzling Images: The Masks of Sir Philip Sidney.* Newark: University of Delaware Press, 1991.

Hainsworth, Peter. *Petrarch the Poet: An Introduction to the Rerum Vulgarium Fragmenta.* London: Routledge, 1988.

Hamilton, A. C. *Sir Philip Sidney: A Study of his Life and Works.* Cambridge: Cambridge University Press, 1977.

———. "Sidney's Humanism." Allen et al., eds., *Sir Philip Sidney's Achievements.*

Hamilton, Edith, and Huntington Cairns, eds. *Plato: The Collected Dialogues, Including the Letters.* Bollingen Series, vol. 71. Princeton: Princeton University Press, 1961.

Hannay, Margaret Patterson, ed. *Silent but for the Word: Tudor Women as Patrons, Translators, and Writers of Religious Works,* Kent, Ohio: Kent State University Press, 1985.

Hanning, Robert W. "Castiglione's Verbal Portrait: Structures and Strategies." Hanning and Rosand, eds. *Castiglione.*

Hanning, Robert W., and David Rosand, eds. *Castiglione: the Ideal and the Real in Renaissance Culture.* New Haven: Yale University Press, 1983.

Harbage, Alfred, ed. *William Shakespeare: The Complete Works.* Baltimore: Penguin Books, 1969.

Hardison, O. B., Jr. "The Two Voices of Sidney's *Apology for Poetry.*" *English Literary Renaissance* 2 (1972): 83–99.

Harwood, Britton J. "Gawain and the Gift." *PMLA* 106 (1991): 483–99.

Hathaway, Baxter. *The Age of Criticism: The Late Renaissance in Italy.* Ithaca: Cornell University Press, 1962.

Helgerson, Richard. "The Elizabethan Laureate: Self-Presentation and the Literary System." *English Literary History* 46 (1979): 193–220.

———. *The Elizabethan Prodigals.* Berkeley: University of California Press, 1976.

Henderson, Katherine Usher, and Barbara F. McManus. *Half Humankind: Contexts and Texts of the Controversy about Women in England, 1540–1640.* Urbana: University of Illinois Press, 1985.

Heninger, S. K., Jr. *Sidney and Spenser: The Poet as Maker.* University Park: Penn State University Press, 1989.

———. "Sidney, Spenser, and Poetic Form." *Studies in Philology* 88 (1991): 140–52.

Herman, Peter C. *Squitter-wits and Muse-haters: Sidney, Spenser, Milton, and Renaissance Antipoetic Sentiment.* Detroit: Wayne State University Press, 1996.

Hibbard, G. R. *Thomas Nashe: A Critical Introduction.* London: Routledge and Kegan Paul, 1962.

Hodges, Devon L. *Renaissance Fictions of Anatomy.* Amherst: University of Massachusetts Press, 1985.

Holland, Peter. "Shakespeare Performances in England, 1992." *Shakespeare Survey.* Vol. 46. Ed. Stanley Wells. Cambridge: Cambridge University Press, 1993.

Hollander, Robert. *Boccaccio's Two Venuses.* New York: Columbia University Press, 1977.

Howard, Jean. "Sex and Social Conflict: The Erotics of *The Roaring Girl.*" Zimmerman, ed., *Erotic Politics.*

Howell, Roger. *Sir Philip Sidney: The Shepherd Knight.* Boston: Little, Brown, 1968.

Hull, Elizabeth M. "'All My Deed But Copying Is': The Erotics of Identity in *Astrophil and Stella.*" *Texas Studies in Literature and Language* 38 (1996): 175–90.

Hull, Suzanne. *Chaste, Silent and Obedient: English Books for Women, 1475–1640.* San Marino, Calif.: The Huntington Library, 1982.

Hulse, Clark. "Stella's Wit: Penelope Rich as Reader of Sidney's Sonnets." Ferguson et al., eds., *Rewriting the Renaissance.*

Irigaray, Luce. *This Sex Which is Not One.* Trans. Catherine Porter, with Carolyn Burke. Ithaca: Cornell University Press, 1985.

Jackson, Rosemary. *Fantasy: The Literature of Subversion.* London: Methuen, 1981.

Jacquart, Jean. *François Ier.* Paris: Fayard, 1981.

Jardine, Lisa. *Still Harping on Daughters: Women and Drama in the Age of Shakespeare.* New York: Columbia University Press, 1989.

Javitch, Daniel. "*Il Cortegiano* and the Constraints of Despotism." Hanning et al., eds., *Castiglione.*

———. "The Impure Motives of Elizabethan Poetry." *Genre* 15 (1982): 225–38.

———. *Poetry and Courtliness in Renaissance England.* Princeton: Princeton University Press, 1978.

———. *Proclaiming a Classic: The Canonization of "Orlando Furioso."* Princeton: Princeton University Press, 1991.

John, Lisle Cecil. *The Elizabethan Sonnet Sequences: Studies in Conventional Conceits.* New York: Columbia University Press, 1938.

Jonard, Norbert. "Le *Decameron* et 'La Légende de la Bourgeoisie.'" *Studi sul Boccaccio* 18 (1989): 347–68.

Jones, Ann Rosalind. "City Women and their Audiences: Louise Labé and Veronica Franco." Ferguson, et al., eds., *Rewriting the Renaissance.*

———. *The Currency of Eros: Women's Love Lyric in Europe, 1540–1620.* Bloomington: Indiana University Press, 1990.

Jones, Ann Rosalind, and Peter Stallybrass. "The Politics of *Astrophil and Stella.*" *Studies in English Literature* 24 (1984): 53–68.

Jordan, Constance. *Renaissance Feminism: Literary Texts and Political Models.* Ithaca: Cornell University Press, 1990.

Kalstone, David. *Sidney's Poetry: Contexts and Interpretations.* Cambridge: Harvard University Press, 1965.

Kay, Dennis, ed. *Sir Philip Sidney: An Anthology of Modern Criticism.* Oxford: Clarendon Press, 1987.

Keating, Clark L. *Etienne Pasquier*. New York: Twayne, 1972.

Kegl, Rosemary. *The Rhetoric of Concealment: Figuring Gender and Class in Renaissance Literature*. Ithaca: Cornell University Press, 1994.

Kelly-Gadol, Joan. "Did Women Have a Renaissance?" *Becoming Visible: Women in European History*. Ed. Renate Bridenthal and Claudia Koonz. Boston: Houghton Mifflin, 1977.

Kelso, Ruth. *Doctrine for the Lady of the Renaissance*. Urbana: University of Illinois Press, 1956.

Kennedy, William J. *Authorizing Petrarch*. Ithaca: Cornell University Press, 1994.

Kerrigan, William. "The Articulation of the Ego in the English Renaissance." *The Literary Freud: Mechanisms of Defense and the Poetic Will*. Ed. Joseph H. Smith. New Haven: Yale University Press, 1980.

———. "Female Friends and Fraternal Enemies in *As You Like It*." Finucci and Schwartz, eds., *Desire in the Renaissance*.

Kerrigan, William, and Gordon Braden. *The Idea of the Renaissance*. Baltimore: Johns Hopkins University Press, 1989.

King, John N. "Patronage and Piety: The Influence of Catherine Parr." Hannay, ed., *Silent but for the Word*.

Kinney, Arthur. *Continental Humanist Poetics: Studies in Erasmus, Castiglione, Marguerite de Navarre, Rabelais, and Cervantes*. Amherst: University of Massachusetts Press, 1989.

Kinney, Clare. "Feigning Female Faining: Spenser, Lodge, Shakespeare and Rosalind," *Modern Philology* 95 (1998): 291–315.

———. "The Masks of Love: Desire and Metamorphosis in Sidney's *New Arcadia*." *Criticism* 33 (1991): 461–90.

Kittay, Jeffrey, and Wlad Godzich. *The Emergence of Prose: An Essay in Prosaics*. Minneapolis: The University of Minnesota Press, 1987.

Knecht, R. J. "The Court of Francis I." *European Studies Review* 8 (1978): 1–22.

———. *Renaissance Warrior and Patron: The Reign of Francis I*. Cambridge: Cambridge University Press, 1994.

Ko, Yu-Jin. "Straining Sexual Identity: Cheek by Jowl's All-Male *As You Like It*." *Shakespeare Bulletin* 13 (1995): 16–17.

Kofman, Sarah. *The Enigma of Woman: Woman in Freud's Writings*. Trans. Catherine Porter. Ithaca: Cornell University Press, 1985.

Korda, Natasha. "Mistaken Identities: Castiglio(ne)'s Practical Joke." Finucci and Schwartz, eds., *Desire in the Renaissance*.

Kott, Jan. "The Gender of Rosalind." *New Theatre Quarterly* 7 (1991): 113–25.

Krieger, Murray. "Presentation and Representation in the Renaissance Lyric: The Net of Words and the Escape of the Gods." *Mimesis: From Mirror to Method, Augustine to Descartes*. Ed. John D. Lyons and Stephen G. Nichols, Jr. Hanover: University Press of New England, 1982.

Kuin, Roger. "Sir Philip Sidney: The Courtier and the Text." *English Literary Renaissance* 19 (1989): 249–71.

Lacan, Jacques. "Aggressivity in Psychoanalysis." In *Écrits*.

Lacan, Jacques. *Écrits: A Selection*. Trans. Alan Sheridan. New York: W. W. Norton, 1977.

———. "The Function and Field of Speech and Language in Psychoanalysis, in *Écrits*.

————. "God and the *Jouissance* of The Woman: A Love Letter." Mitchell and Rose, eds., *Feminine Sexuality*.

Lamb, Mary Ellen. "The Cooke Sisters: Attitudes toward Learned Women in the Renaissance." Hannay, ed., *Silent but for the Word*.

————. "The Countess of Pembroke's Patronage." *English Literary Renaissance* 12 (1982): 162–79.

————. *Gender and Authorship in the Sidney Circle*. Madison: University of Wisconsin Press, 1990.

Lanham, Richard. "*Astrophil and Stella:* Pure and Impure Persuasion." *English Literary Renaissance* 2 (1972): 100–15.

————. *The Motives of Eloquence: Literary Rhetoric in the Renaissance*. New Haven: Yale University Press, 1976.

Laqueur, Thomas. *Making Sex: Body and Gender from the Greeks to Freud*. Cambridge: Harvard University Press, 1990.

Lenz, Carolyn Ruth Swift, Gayle Greene, and Carol Thomas Neely, eds. *The Woman's Part: Feminist Criticism of Shakespeare*. Urbana: University of Illinois Press, 1983.

Levao, Ronald. *Renaissance Minds and Their Fictions: Cusanus, Sidney, Shakespeare*. Berkeley: University of California Press, 1985.

Lewis, C. S. *English Literature in the Sixteenth-Century, Excluding Drama*. London: Oxford University Press, 1954.

Lévi-Strauss, Claude. *The Elementary Structures of Kinship*. Trans. James Harle Bell, John Richard von Strumer. Ed. Rodney Needham. Boston: Beacon Press, 1969.

Low, Anthony. *The Reinvention of Love: Poetry, Politics and Culture from Sidney to Milton*. Cambridge: Cambridge University Press, 1993.

Lucas, Caroline. *Writing for Women: The Example of Woman as Reader in Elizabethan Romance*. Milton Keynes, Eng.: Open University Press, 1989.

Maclean, Ian. *The Renaissance Notion of Woman: A Study in the Fortunes of Scholasticism and Medical Science in European Intellectual Life*. Cambridge: Cambridge University Press, 1980.

Magnusson, Lynne A. "'His Pen with My Hande': Jane Anger's Revisionary Rhetoric." *English Studies in Canada* 17 (1991): 301–20.

————. "Nicholas Breton Reads Jane Anger." *Renaissance Studies* 7 (1993): 291–300.

Marchesini, Manuela. "Le Ragioni di Alatiel (*Decameron* II.7)." *Studi sul Boccaccio* 22 (1994): 257–76.

Marcus, Leah S. *Puzzling Shakespeare: Local Reading and Its Discontents*. Berkeley: University of California Press, 1988.

Marcus, Millicent Joy. *An Allegory of Form: Literary Self-Consciousness in the "Decameron."* Vol. 18 of *Stanford French and Italian Studies*. Saratoga, Calif.: Anma Libri, 1979.

Margolies, David. *Novel and Society in Elizabethan England*. Totowa, N.J.: Barnes and Noble, 1985.

Marotti, Arthur F. *Manuscript, Print, and the English Renaissance Lyric*. Ithaca: Cornell University Press, 1995.

————. "The Transmission of Lyric Poetry and the Institutionalizing of Literature in the English Renaissance." *Contending Kingdoms: Historical, Psychological, and Feminist*

Approaches to the Literature of Sixteenth-Century England and France. Ed. Marie-Rose Logan and Peter L. Rudnytsky. Detroit: Wayne State University Press, 1991.

Maus, Katharine Eisaman. "A Womb of His Own: Male Renaissance Poets in the Female Body." James Turner, ed., *Sexuality and Gender in Early Modern Europe.*

Mazzoni, Giacopo. *On the Defense of the Comedy of Dante, Introduction and Summary.* Trans. Robert L. Montgomery. Tallahassee: University Presses of Florida, 1983.

Mazzotta, Giuseppe. *The World at Play in Boccaccio's "Decameron."* Princeton: Princeton University Press, 1986.

McCoy, Richard. *Sir Philip Sidney: Rebellion in Arcadia.* New Brunswick: Rutgers University Press, 1979.

McKerrow, Ronald B., ed. *Works of Thomas Nashe.* London: Sidgwick and Jackson, 1910.

McLeod, Glenda. *Virtue and Venom: Catalogs of Women from Antiquity to the Renaissance.* Ann Arbor: University of Michigan Press, 1991.

McLucas, John C. "Amazon, Sorceress, and Queen: Women and War in the Aristocratic Literature of Sixteenth-Century Italy." *The Italianist* 8 (1988): 33–55.

Miller, Jacqueline T. "'Love Doth Hold my Hand': Writing and Wooing in the Sonnets of Sidney and Spenser." *English Literary History* 46 (1979): 541–58.

———. *Poetic License: Authority and Authorship in Medieval and Renaissance Contexts.* New York: Oxford University Press, 1986.

Miller, Paul Allen. "Sidney, Petrarch, and Ovid, or Imitation as Subversion." *English Literary History* 58 (1991): 499–522.

Mills, C. Wright. *Power, Politics and People.* Ed. Irving Louis Horowitz. New York: Oxford University Press, 1963.

Minogue, Sally. "A Woman's Touch: Astrophil, Stella and 'Queen Vertue's Court.'" *English Literary History* 63 (1996): 555–70.

Mitchell, Juliet and Jacqueline Rose, ed. *Feminine Sexuality: Jacques Lacan and the École Freudienne.* New York: W. W. Norton, 1982.

Montgomery, Robert L. "Astrophil's Stella and Stella's Astrophil." Waller and Moore, eds., *Sir Philip Sidney.*

———. *The Reader's Eye: Studies in Didactic Literary Theory from Dante to Tasso.* Berkeley: University of California Press, 1979.

Montrose, Louis Adrian. "Celebration and Insinuation: Sir Philip Sidney and the Motives of Elizabethan Courtship." *Renaissance Drama* n.s. 8 (1977): 3–35.

———. "*A Midsummer Night's Dream* and the Shaping Fantasies of Elizabethan Culture: Gender, Power, Form." Ferguson et al., eds., *Rewriting the Renaissance.*

———. "Of Gentlemen and Shepherds: The Politics of Elizabethan Pastoral Form." *English Literary History* 50 (1983): 415–59.

———. "The Purpose of Playing: Reflections on a Shakespearean Anthropology." *Helios* 7 (1980): 51–74.

More, Edward. *A Lytle and Bryefe Treatyse Called The Defence of Women, and Especially of Englyshe Women, Made Agaynst The Schole Howse of Women. Selected Pieces of Early Popular Poetry.*

Mueller, Janel. "Lesbian Erotics: The Utopian Trope of Donne's 'Sappho to Philaenis.'" *Homosexuality in Renaissance and Enlightenment England: Literary Representations in Historical Context.* Ed. Claude J. Summers. New York: Harrington Park Press, 1992.

Mulvey, Laura. *Visual and Other Pleasures.* Bloomington: Indiana University Press, 1989.

Nashe, Thomas. *The Anatomie of Absurditie.* Vol. 1 of *Works of Thomas Nashe.* Ed. R. B. McKerrow. London: Sidgwick and Jackson, 1910.

Nelson, William. "From 'Listen Lordings' to 'Dear Reader.'" *University of Toronto Quarterly* 46 (1976–77): 110–24.

Nohrnberg, James. *The Analogy of 'The Faerie Queene.'* Princeton: Princeton University Press, 1976.

Ong, Walter. *Orality and Literacy: The Technologizing of the Word.* London: Methuen, 1982.

Orgel, Stephen. "Nobody's Perfect: Or Why Did the English Stage Take Boys for Women?" *South Atlantic Quarterly* 88 (1989): 7–29.

Osborn, James M. *Young Philip Sidney: 1572–1577.* New Haven: Yale University Press, 1972.

Park, Clara Clairborne. "As We Like It: How a Girl Can be Smart and Still Popular." Lenz, et al., eds., *The Woman's Part.*

Parker, Patricia. *Literary Fat Ladies: Rhetoric, Gender, Property.* London: Methuen, 1987.

Pasquier, Estienne. *Le Monophile.* Paris, 1555.

Perli, Antonello. "Le Jeu de la Société dans le *Courtisan* de Baldassar Castiglione" *Littératures* 34 (1996): 23–31.

Peterson, Douglas. *The English Lyric from Wyatt to Donne: A History of the Plain and Eloquent Styles.* Princeton: Princeton University Press, 1967.

Petrarch, Francesco. *Petrarch's Lyric Poems: The "Rime Sparse" and Other Lyrics.* Ed. and Trans. Robert M. Durling. Cambridge: Harvard University Press, 1976.

Plato. *Sophist.* Trans. F. M. Cornford. Hamilton and Cairns, eds., *The Collected Dialogues of Plato.*

———. *The Symposium.* Trans. Michael Joyce. Hamilton and Cairns, eds., *The Collected Dialogues of Plato.*

Poggioli, Renato. *The Oaten Flute: Essays on Pastoral Poetry and the Pastoral Ideal.* Cambridge: Harvard University Press, 1975.

Potter, Joy Hambuechen. "Woman in the *Decameron.*" *Studies in the Italian Renaissance: Essays in Memory of Arnolfo B. Ferruolo.* Ed. Gian Paolo Biasin, Albert N. Mancini, and Nicolas J. Perella. Naples: Società Editrice Napoletana, 1985.

Prendergast, Maria Teresa Micaela. "Engendering *Pericles.*" *Literature and Psychology* 32 (1996): 53–75.

———. "Philoclea Parsed: Prose, Verse, and Femininity in Sidney's *Old Arcadia.*" Relihan, ed., *Framing Elizabethan Fictions.*

———. "Ruptured Closure: Sir Philip Sidney and the Poetics of Contradiction." Ph.D. diss. University of Virginia, 1990.

———. "The Unauthorized Orpheus of *Astrophil and Stella.*" *Studies in English Literature, 1500–1900* 35 (1995): 19–34.

The Proude Wyve's Pater Noster. Selected Pieces of Early Popular Poetry.

Puttenham, George. *The Arte of English Poesie.* Ed. Gladys Doidge Willcock and Alice Walker. Cambridge: Cambridge University Press, 1936.

Pye, Christopher. *The Regal Phantasm: Shakespeare and the Politics of Spectacle.* London: Routledge, 1990.

Quilligan, Maureen. "Sidney and His Queen." *The Historical Renaissance: New Essays in Tudor and Stuart Literature and Culture.* Ed. Heather Dubrow and Richard Strier. Chicago: University of Chicago Press, 1988.

Quint, David. *Origin and Originality in Renaissance Literature: Versions of the Source.* New Haven: Yale University Press, 1983.

Quitslund, Jon A. "Spenser and the Patronesses of the *Fowre Hymnes:* 'Ornaments of All True Love and Beautie.'" Hannay, ed., *Silent but for the Word.*

Rabkin, Eric S. *The Fantastic in Literature.* Princeton: Princeton University Press, 1976.

Rackin, Phyllis. "Androgyny, Mimesis, and the Marriage of the Boy Heroine on the English Renaissance Stage." *PMLA* 102 (1987): 29–41.

Rebhorn, Wayne A. *Courtly Performances: Masking and Festivity in Castiglione's "Book of the Courtier."* Detroit: Wayne State University Press, 1978.

Rees, Joan. *Sir Philip Sidney and Arcadia.* Rutherford: Fairleigh Dickinson Press, 1991.

Relihan, Constance C. *Fashioning Authority: The Development of Elizabethan Novelistic Discourse.* Kent, Ohio: Kent State University Press, 1994.

————, ed. *Framing Elizabethan Fictions: Contemporary Approaches to Early Modern Narrative Prose.* Kent, Ohio: Kent State University Press, 1996.

Ringler, William A., Jr. Introduction to *The Poems of Sir Philip Sidney.* Oxford: Clarendon Press, 1962.

Roberts, Katherine J. *Fair Ladies: Sir Philip Sidney's Female Characters.* New York: Peter Lang, 1993.

Robertson, Jean., ed. *The Countess of Pembroke's Arcadia (The Old Arcadia).* Oxford: Clarendon Press, 1973.

Rose, Jacqueline. Introduction (2) to *Feminine Sexuality: Jacques Lacan and the École Freudienne.* Ed. Mitchell and Rose.

Rose, Mary Beth. *The Expense of Spirit: Love and Sexuality in English Renaissance Drama.* Ithaca: Cornell University Press, 1988.

Rossky, William. "Imagination in the English Renaissance: Psychology and Poetic." *Studies in the Renaissance* 5 (1958): 49–73.

Rubin, Gayle. "The Traffic in Women: Notes on the 'Political Economy' of Sex." *Toward an Anthropology of Women.* Ed. Rayna R. Reiter. New York: Monthly Review Press, 1975.

Rudenstine, Neil L. *Sidney's Poetic Development.* Cambridge: Harvard University Press, 1967.

Rutter, Carol. *Clamorous Voices: Shakespeare's Women Today.* Ed. Faith Evans. New York: Routledge, 1989.

Saunders, J. W. "The Stigma of Print: A Note on the Social Bases of Tudor Poetry." *Essays in Criticism* 9 (April 1951): 139–64.

Scaglione, Aldo D. *Nature and Love in the Late Middle Ages: An Essay on the Cultural Context of the "Decameron."* Berkeley: University of California Press, 1963.

Schalk, Ellery. "The Court as 'Civilizer' of the Nobility: Noble Attitudes and the Court in France in the Late Sixteenth and Early Seventeenth Centuries." Asch and Birke, eds., *Princes, Patronage, and the Nobility.*

Schleiner, Louise. "Ladies and Gentlemen in Two Genres of Elizabethan Fiction." *Studies in English Literature 1500–1900* 29 (1989): 1–20.

The Schoolhouse of Women. Henderson and McManus, eds., *Half Humankind.*

Sedgwick, Eve Kosofsky. *Between Men: English Literature and Male Homosocial Desire.* New York: Columbia University Press, 1985.

Segal, Charles. *Orpheus: The Myth of the Poet.* Baltimore: Johns Hopkins University Press, 1989.

Selected Pieces of Early Popular Poetry Republished Principally from Early Printed Copies. Vol. 2. London, 1817.

Sewell, Elizabeth. *The Orphic Voice: Poetry and Natural History.* New York: Harper and Row, 1971.

Shakespeare, William. *As You Like It.* Ed. Anne Barton. Evans, ed., *The Riverside Shakespeare.*

———. *Hamlet Prince of Denmark.* Ed. Frank Kermode. Evans, ed., *The Riverside Shakespeare.*

———. *The Merchant of Venice.* Ed. Anne Barton. Evans, ed., *The Riverside Shakespeare.*

———. *A Midsummer Night's Dream.* Ed. Anne Barton. Evans, ed., *The Riverside Shakespeare.*

Shapiro, Michael. *Gender in Play on the Shakespearean Stage: Boy Heroines and Female Pages.* Ann Arbor: University of Michigan Press, 1996.

Sherberg, Michael. "The Patriarch's Pleasure and the Frametale Crisis: *Decameron* IV–V." *Romance Quarterly* 38 (1991): 227–38.

Sidney, Sir Philip. *Astrophil and Stella. Sir Philip Sidney: Selected Poems.* Ed. Katherine Duncan-Jones. 1973. Reprint. Oxford: Oxford University Press, 1979.

———. *Astrophil and Stella. The Poems of Sir Philip Sidney.* Ed. William A. Ringler, Jr. Oxford: Clarendon Press, 1962.

———. *The Countess of Pembroke's Arcadia (The Old Arcadia).* Ed. Jean Robertson. Oxford: Clarendon Press, 1973.

———. *A Defence of Poetry.* Ed. J. A. Van Dorsten. Oxford: Oxford University Press, 1966.

Sinfield, Alan. "Astrophil's Self-Deception." *Essays in Criticism* 28 (1978): 1–18.

———. *Faultlines: Cultural Materialism and the Politics of Dissident Reading.* Berkeley: University of California Press, 1992.

Sinicropi, Giovanni. "Chastity and Love in the *Decameron.*" *The Olde Daunce: Love, Friendship, Sex, and Marriage in the Medieval World.* Ed. Robert R. Edwards and Stephen Spector. Albany: State University of New York Press, 1991.

Skura, Meredith. *The Literary Use of the Psychoanalytic Process.* New Haven: Yale University Press, 1981.

Smarr, Janet Levarie. "Ovid and Boccaccio: A Note on Self-Defense." *Mediaevalia* 13 (1987): 247–55.

Smith, Bruce R. *Homosexual Desire in Shakespeare's England: A Cultural Poetics.* Chicago: University of Chicago Press, 1991.

———. "Making a Difference: Male/Male 'Desire' in Tragedy, Comedy, and Tragi-Comedy." Zimmerman, ed., *Erotic Politics.*

Smith, G. Gregory. Introduction. *Elizabethan Critical Essays.* Ed. G. Gregory Smith. Oxford: Oxford University Press, 1904.

Smith, Hallett. *Elizabethan Poetry.* Cambridge: Harvard University Press, 1952.

Smith, Pauline M. *The Anti-Courtier Trend in Sixteenth Century French Literature.* Geneva: Librarie Droz, 1966.

Snyder, Jon R. *Writing the Scene of Speaking: Theories of Dialogue in the Late Italian Renaissance.* Stanford: Stanford University Press, 1989.

Soule, Lesley Anne. "Subverting Rosalind: Cocky Ros in the Forest of Arden." *New Theater Quarterly* 7 (1991): 126–36.

Spenser, Edmund. *Amoretti. The Yale Edition of the Shorter Poems of Edmund Spenser.* Ed. William A. Oram, Einer Bjorvand, Ronald Bond, Thomas H. Cain, Alexander Dunlop, and Richard Schell. New Haven: Yale University Press, 1989.

Spufford, Margaret. *Small Books and Pleasant Histories: Popular Fiction and its Readership in Seventeenth-Century England.* Athens: University of Georgia Press, 1981.

Stallybrass, Peter. "Dismemberments and Re-memberments: Rewriting the *Decameron,* 4.1, in the English Renaissance." *Studi sul Boccaccio* 20 (1991–92): 299–324.

———. "Patriarchal Territories: The Body Enclosed." Ferguson et al., eds. *Rewriting the Renaissance.*

———. "Transvestism and the 'Body Beneath,' Speculating on the Boy Actor." Zimmerman, ed., *Erotic Politics.*

Staub, Susan C. "The Lady Frances Did Watch: Gascoigne's Voyeuristic Narrative." Relihan, ed., *Framing Elizabethan Fictions.*

Stone, Lawrence. *The Family, Sex and Marriage in England, 1500–1800.* New York: Harper and Row, 1977.

Strong, Roy. *The Cult of Elizabeth: Elizabethan Portraiture and Pageantry.* London: Thames and Hudson, 1977.

Stubbs, Philip. *The Anatomy of Abuses.* New York: Johnson Reprint Company Limited, 1972.

Stump, Donald. "Sidney's Astrophil, Vanishing." *Renaissance Papers* (1988): 1–13.

Suzuki, Mihoko. "Gender, Power, and the Female Reader: Boccaccio's *Decameron* and Marguerite de Navarre's *Heptameron.*" *Comparative Literature Studies* 30 (1993): 231–52.

Sweany, Suzanne M.. *Estienne Pasquier et Nationalisme Littéraire.* Paris: Champion-Slatkine, 1985.

Thickett, Dorothy. *Estienne Pasquier: The Versatile Barrister of Sixteenth Century France.* London: Regency Press, 1985.

Tiffany, Grace. "'That Reason Wonder May Diminish': *As You Like It,* Androgyny, and the Theater Wars." *The Huntington Library Quarterly* 57 (1994): 213–40.

Traub, Valerie. *Desire and Anxiety: Circulations of Sexuality in Shakespearean Drama.* London: Routledge, 1992.

Tristram, Hildegard, L. C. "Aggregating Versus Integrating Narrative: Original Prose in England from the Seventh to the Fifteenth-Century." *Mündlichkeit und Schriftlichkeit im Englischen Mittelalter.* Ed. Willi Erzgräber and Sabine Volk. Tübingen: Gunter Narr Verlag, 1988.

Turner, James Grantham, ed. *Sexuality and Gender in Early Modern Europe: Institutions, Texts, Images.* Cambridge: Cambridge University Press, 1993.

Turner, Victor. *The Forest of Symbols: Aspects of Ndembu Ritual.* Ithaca: Cornell University Press, 1967.

———. *From Ritual to Theatre: The Human Seriousness of Play.* New York: Performing Arts Journal Publications, 1982.

Tyler, Margaret. "The Mirror of Princely Deeds and Knighthood." *Renaissance Women: A Sourcebook Construction of Femininity in England.* Ed. Kate Aughterson. London: Routledge, 1995.

Vickers, Nancy J. "Diana Described: Scattered Woman and Scattered Rhyme." Abel, ed., *Writing and Sexual Difference.*

———. "The Mistress in the Masterpiece." *The Poetics of Gender.* Ed. Carolyn G. Heilbrun. New York: Columbia University Press, 1986.

Waddington, Raymond B. "The Bisexual Portrait of Francis I: Fontainbleau, Castiglione, and the Tone of Courtly Mythology." *Playing with Gender: A Renaissance Pursuit.* Ed. Jean R. Brink, Maryanne C. Horowitz, and Allison P. Coudert. Urbana: University of Illinois Press, 1991.

———. "Moralizing the Spectacle: Dramatic Emblems in *As You Like It.*" *Shakespeare Quarterly* 33 (1982): 155–63.

Wall, Wendy. *The Imprint of Gender: Authorship and Publication in the English Renaissance.* Ithaca: Cornell University Press, 1994.

Waller, Gary. "The Rewriting of Petrarch: Sidney and the Languages of Sixteenth-Century Poetry." Waller and Moore, eds., *Sir Philip Sidney.*

———. *The Sidney Family Romance: Mary Wroth, William Herbert, and the Early Modern Construction of Gender.* Detroit: Wayne State University Press, 1993.

Waller, Gary F., and Michael D. Moore., eds. *Sir Philip Sidney and the Interpretation of Renaissance Culture: The Poet in his Time and in Ours.* London: Croon Helm, 1984.

Waller, Marguerite R. *Petrarch's Poetics and Literary History.* Amherst: University of Massachusetts Press, 1980.

Warkentin, Germaine. "Sidney and the Supple Muse: Compositional Procedures in Some Sonnets of *Astrophil and Stella.*" Kay, ed., *Sir Philip Sidney.*

Watt, Tessa. *Cheap Print and Popular Piety, 1550–1640.* Cambridge: Cambridge University Press, 1991.

Weimann, Robert. *Shakespeare and the Popular Tradition in the Theater: Studies in the Social Dimension of Dramatic Form and Function.* Ed. Robert Schwartz. Baltimore: Johns Hopkins University Press, 1978.

Weinberg, Bernard. *A History of Literary Criticism in the Italian Renaissance.* Chicago: University of Chicago Press, 1961.

Weiner, Andrew D. *Sir Philip Sidney and the Poetics of Protestantism: A Study of Contexts.* Minneapolis: University of Minnesota Press, 1978.

Whigham, Frank. *Ambition and Privilege: The Social Tropes of Elizabethan Courtesy Theory.* Berkeley: University of California Press, 1984.

———. "Interpretation at Court: Courtesy and the Performer-Audience Dialectic." *New Literary History* 14 (1983): 623–39.

Wind, Edgar. *Pagan Mysteries in the Renaissance.* New York: W. W. Norton, 1968.

Wofford, Susanne L. "The Social Aesthetics of Rape: Closural Violence in Boccaccio and Botticelli." *Creative Imitation: New Essays on Renaissance Literature in Honor of Thomas M. Greene*. Ed. David Quint, Margaret W. Ferguson, G. W. Pigman III, and Wayne A. Rebhorn. Binghamton: Medieval and Renaissance Texts and Studies, 1992.

———. "'To You I Give Myself, for I am Yours': Erotic Performance and Theatrical Performatives in *As You Like It. Shakespeare Reread: The Texts in New Contexts*. Ed. Russ McDonald. Ithaca: Cornell University Press, 1994.

Woodbridge, Linda. *Women and the English Renaissance: Literature and the Nature of Womankind, 1540–1620*. Urbana: University of Illinois Press, 1984.

Woodhouse, J. R. *Baldesar Castiglione: A Reassessment of "The Courtier."* Edinburgh: Edinburgh University Press, 1978.

Wright, Louis B. "The Reading of English Renaissance Women." *Studies in Philology* 28 (1931): 149–56.

Yavneh, Naomi. "The Ambiguity of Beauty in Tasso and Petrarch." Turner, ed., *Sexuality and Gender in Early Modern Europe*.

Zimmerman, Susan, ed. *Erotic Politics: Desire on the Renaissance Stage*. New York: Routledge, 1992.

Index

Names of characters are followed by the title of the work in parantheses.